TEN THOUSAND PRAYERS

TEN THOUSAND PRAYERS
BY A. NASSER

(Based on a True Story)

ISBN 978-0-9888160-2- 2

COVER DESIGN BY © BOOK WRITERS CLOUD

WWW.TENTHOUSANDPRAYERS.COM
ADMIN@TENTHOUSANDPRAYERS.COM
@TENTHOUSANDPRAY

PUBLISHED BY
BOOK WRITERS CLOUD LLC.
SAN FRANCISCO, CALIFORNIA USA

ADMIN@BOOKWRITERSCLOUD.COM
WWW.BOOKWRITERSCLOUD.COM
WWW.BOOKSTREAMS.COM

To my brave mother Momena and her friends Anayta, Omayra, Saleha, Barawar, and Aqila who, sixty years ago, courageously threw off their Burqa for Afghan women's freedom.

A. Nasser

AUTHOR'S NOTE

This is the tale of a young boy who was born in Kabul, Afghanistan.

It is a true story in that it is based on fact and actual events in the boy's life.

To bring these words to you, I have tried to recreate events, locations, and conversations from the boy's memory. In order to maintain the anonymity of some of the characters in this novel, I have, where appropriate, altered the names of individuals and places. Indeed, I may have changed some identifying characteristics and details such as physical properties, occupations and places of residence.

Some of the names, characters, businesses, place, events and incidents are either the products of the author's imagination or used in a fictitious manner. Any resemblance to real people persons, living or dead, or actual events, is purely coincidental.

Although the author and publisher have made every effort to ensure that the information in this book was correct at the time of going to press, the author and publisher do not assume and hereby disclaim any liability to any party for any loss, damage, or disruption caused by errors or omissions, whether such errors or omissions result from negligence, accident, or any other cause.

A young boy wrote this book when he became a man.

The book you are about to read is based on a true story.

It is my story.

The story of A. Nasser.

ACKNOWLEDGEMENT

The caravan of life passes in a chain of individuals and personalities. No one walks alone on that journey. Whether we meet the ones in the forefront, in the middle, or at the end of the caravan, each one of those individuals leaves an effect in the transformation of our own personality, character, thoughts, and work. Each page of this book says "thanks" to the thousands that in one way or the other have been the reason for each word in my book, and have provided me the thoughts, supports, and encouragement to write and publish this book.

This book would not have been possible without the support of my parents throughout my life. Their way of life is the reason for what I have learned to be where I am.

I would like to gratefully acknowledge the enthusiastic support and efforts of Nanda Olney who made my words, memories, and thoughts, come alive throughout this book. Without her my story would have been an untold story similar to hundreds of thousands of other young boys whose lives were disrupted by war and never got a chance to tell their stories.

Much of what I have learned over the years came as the result of being friends with extra ordinary people such as Basir Yasini and Farhad Ahad who left the comfort of their homes and loved ones in the US and sacrificed their lives for their proud people & country. I thank their families for giving me the opportunity to tell their tragic stories.

My thanks and appreciations also go to Shemane Nugent who believed in me the first time she met me by taking the efforts and risk to write the screenplay of my life story and encouraged me to follow my dreams.

I would like to express my gratitude towards my sisters Flora, Friba, Maryam, Nazima, and my brother Massie for allowing me to tell their stories. They stood up beside me at all times without ever asking me or doubting my intention.

Also, I would like to take this opportunity to thank Alan K. Lipton and Paul Anthony for their proofreading efforts and Ashourina Sada for her video trailer production. I appreciate their valuable advice and guidance.

I take immense pleasure in thanking Zalmai Basharat, Farid Nasrati, Daoud Faqiri, Farid Lutfi, Najib Faqiri, Saboor Sameem, Ahmad Shah Shalizi, Fawad Auzarang, and many other friends who helped me with their arguments, debates, and years' long discussions to develop and conclude the book.

I am highly indebted to those writers, journalists, producers, celebrities and film makers, who never gave up and kept the news on Afghanistan - especially the news on the Afghan women - in the forefront of world news and never let the war in Afghanistan become a forgotten war. I thank those who sincerely cared about a nation that has not seen peace in ages.

I would like to express my gratitude towards my wife Zabina and my sons Omar, Omid, and Sahel for their patience and encouragement, which helped me with the completion of this book. Ten Thousand Prayers would have not materialized without their love.

"A bone to the dog is not charity. Charity is the bone shared with the dog, when you are just as hungry as the dog."
-Jack London

"One who does what the Friend wants done will never need a friend.

There's a bankruptcy that's pure gain. The moon stays bright when it doesn't avoid the night.

A rose's rarest essence lives in the thorn."
-Rumi

1

~ ~ ~

KABULI ASSEEL

Kabul, Afghanistan 2010

I was on a plane to Kabul again, wondering how many times we can end and begin again in the same spot. I closed my eyes on the descent so I would not have to see the way the city looked on the approach. The stewardess had kept my drink full and the plane shuddered just in time for the ice to slip in the cup and the contents to run down over my chin and my shirt. I let out an embarrassed laugh, almost appreciating the distraction. I never looked at Kabul below me when I flew in anymore.

Upon landing, the first I saw of my homeland was through the window in the airport. I had enough time to steel myself for the arrival while we taxied into the terminal, carefully avoiding the memories of my last visit. We had a strange relationship, Kabul and I. I felt that I never touched her soil without feeling either hope or despair in excess.

The Kabul International Airport was a building of washed out blue and fading white. The walkways were crowded. Outside, the morning was smoggy and brown, as if a dust cloud had just blown past and the city was left, choking in the aftermath. In the vestibule of the airport I waited for my luggage. Looking around me at the other passengers keeping mostly to themselves, I saw an old man approaching. Unlike the others, he looked like he knew where he was going. I thought for a moment he might know me since he was grinning, nearly toothless. I wondered if he might have been a neighbor, the uncle of a friend maybe that I had known in my youth. Around us the noise of the many passengers was like the static of a bad connection.

Boarding and departure announcements were made over the speakers but the people went about their business, not really hearing or caring. The old man stood for a time beside me before I greeted him.

"Salaam, friend."

"Ah, my son," he said, obviously pleased. "You were very like one I knew…before."

He waved his hand: a practiced gesture that dismissed everything that had gone on before; the tumultuous decades comprising his past.

"But I know you cannot be him. Where are you from?"

"My father's family was from Shah Rara, my mother's from Shor Bazaar…I am Kabuli Asseel." I added as an afterthought; strangely, because I had not said those words in years.

"Shor Bazaar?" He whispered. "I too am from Shor Bazaar." His voice caught, "She is not the same. She was beautiful; generous, loyal. I had so many friends there…"

His easy talk loosened my mind and memory. I dropped my guard and told him about the jewelry store at *Kotche Ali Reza Khan* that my grandfather owned, about my mother's father and her mother. About my mother as a young girl, the first to throw off her *burqa*, to ride a bicycle through town, to study in secret. All the while he listened with a smile on his face and tears watering at the corners of his eyes, lacking the strength to fall.

"I feel so sorry for her, the innocent girl,"

I did not know if he was speaking of my mother, or of the city he loved. The old man leaned against the wall behind us, giving it all of his weight. I believed his health might be failing him, but then he spoke.

"My father, he used to play the *rebab.*"

The old man's voice was a thin reed with air whistling through it. "The music of it spread out and into the night and called to lovers everywhere. I was a young boy working the dough into the rough boards laid on the ground in the *naan* shop. I used to love the sounds of that music more than anything. More than the eyes of a beautiful girl. More than the feel of running. I was a good runner then. But it was the music that spoke to my heart. I loved the music and I loved the bazaar. The sounds of the people walking by and the vendors shouting, selling their wares."

The old man turned to me and only then did I see the glaze over his eyes. The old man was nearly blind.

He grinned again, "I only wish God made me blind sooner. Do you know what I have seen? I have seen horror. Yet I have seen no different than any other Kabuli has seen. I grew up to work at the zoo. I was there when it began, in 1967. I learned so much about the animals in that time. They were like people, only tamer. During the civil war, I saw them slaughtering the animals at the zoo. To eat them! Can you imagine? I am older than you, my son, but I do not remember a time that my life has not been touched by war. It is unjust to take away a man's sight and leave him with his hearing. I hear the gunshots. I hear screams and explosions and then I sleep and dream I hear the music of the *rebab*. But I know it is a dream because I see my father. Waking is the only nightmare."

It moved me; the spontaneous bursting of memory, the longing for a different time regardless of whether that time was better or not. Our baggage ran in circles repeatedly and we did not rush to claim it.

"I'm not sure I am ready to step outside. I don't know what waits for me," I said.

The old man nodded as if he understood.

The air conditioner in the cab blew loudly but I felt no coolness coming from it. I doubted it did anything but kick up dust. The stereo, too, blasted the stale voices of talk radio. The home that used to be mine rose up in front of me as the cab turned a corner and we were in Micro Rayan.

14

"Stop here," I said with a hand on the driver's shoulder. His eyes met mine in the rearview mirror.

The road ahead was clogged with vehicles and children bobbed and weaved through the knot of traffic to tap on windows and display the goods they had for sale. There was a general chaos of voices and honking horns.

"Where are you from?" the driver asked.

I laughed to ward off his suspicion, "From behind those walls," I gesture at the building ahead of us, at the apartment I spent the first years of my childhood in. I clapped him on the shoulder again. He took my money, counted it swiftly while I was still gathering my bag. A nod as I departed was the only gesture of brotherhood.

Out of the cab and on my own, I decided to walk the rest of the way on foot. I saw the building ahead, the apartment complex built by the Russians, where we lived. Father, mother, my sisters and me. There was the field next to the complex where we played soccer when I was a young boy. I could see myself running there with Baraymal Dost, yelling at our neighbor's dog to stop chasing the only ball we had.

At school back in that time, there was an old man who guarded the gate. He prayed at the same mosque as my uncle, so he knew me. Well into the school year, I grew tired of waiting in line at the school kiosk to buy a snack with the other kids. The line was always long and sometimes I would not reach the front before the bell rang. I approached the old man and we reached a deal. From then on, he turned his back while I slipped through the gate and ran to the nearby stores. The first time I escaped I bought only enough *poury nakhod* for myself, my entire savings worth. But when my classmates saw what I had done, they offered me their money to buy the treats I had. That first time I sold them to my friends for a profit. I learned from this and the next time I made even more. When I made enough money vending to the kids at school, I bought the soccer ball. It was the first toy I owned that was not given to me second-hand by a generous neighbor.

Dust kicked up from the empty field next to the apartment building as I stood there reminiscing. A scrawny dog ran across the lot, slinking through a hole in the fence. In the way that happens when you were thinking of the past and the present intervenes, I thought for a moment that this was the same dog from my childhood. Then the addition of years reminded me it could not be so.

When I turned down the next alley on the path I used to take home, the noise of the road faded behind me. Here the only sound was that of the birds. Laundry hung on clotheslines from the high windows over my head and flapped gently in the breeze. The sky was blue and the birds… the birds reminded me of who I once was, though I was no longer that boy and might not recognize him if he passed me on my walk. The roses were in bloom and the grass in the fenced in yard was as ripe and green as the memory of youth. I might have stepped back in time. I spotted Swifts and Starlings and Oriental Skylarks, diving in and out of the branches of the overhanging trees and hopping around in the shady grass, pecking for bugs. I stood there for a long time, taking in the familiar sights and sounds. I shaded my eyes and looked up, the sun glowing behind the sheets that flew in the breeze. There on the clothesline above me was a small black bird, bobbing on the line. I squinted to try and see it clearly but the sun intervened and I had to blink the sun-blindness from my eyes. As I looked back the bird flew off and I followed its path to the window ledge. It was too high up to tell for sure but I would have bet on its being a Black Drongo by the curl at the end of the tail-feathers. It flew and landed for a moment at my feet and took off again and then I was sure. But it had been many years and many places since I last saw that bird.

In Kabul of recent years, I often found myself transported by memory to other places and times in my past. There was history running through my veins. I recalled myself to the present. Instead of bleaching the color out of the afternoon, the sun seemed to have poured warm color into everything. Women walked by me, their *burqas* bright under the sun. Blue and green, yellow and red. I picked the window out of the dozens that lined the wall. The one my mother used to lean out of to call me, or to pinch the dry clothes from the line. The building was four floors and typical of the Russian-built apartment complexes installed in the 1950's; another gesture of good will that ultimately seemed self-serving. Sometimes you do not know your friends from enemies.

I could not ignore the fact that I came to sell the home of my childhood. It was maybe the last good thing that remained of what used to be mine in that city. The following day I would be meeting with the realtor to go over the details and to see the apartment for the first and last time in years. That day, I had only to tear myself away from the ghost of the past. I walked away although the smell of roses clogged my senses. I returned to the street and to the chaos and noise of the known world. There were so many instances of this in Kabul: of stepping back and forth through time. One hardly felt they had a right to belong to anything there.

Imagine this. Imagine you are walking down a crowded street in Micro Rayan, where the noise of pedestrians and the voices from cab radios creates a layer of interference almost as thick as the smog that settles over the city. Imagine you take a detour down an alley that you suddenly remember, feeling again like a child in your old haunts, remembering the contours of the path where your feet once pounded on the dry dirt and your heart pounded to match. It is dusk now and the black cloud leaks across the sky. A girl in a *burqa* passes by, lifts her eyes in a way that young girls are trained not to. You think perhaps you know her, but her eyes are those of a stranger and they are haunted. Imagine she whispers to you,

"Do not go that way."

You watch her pass you by until she is a shadow disappearing around the corner of the wall; stand in the middle of the alley, torn. You walk on despite her warning.

Imagine there is a man at the end of the alley with a hole in his chest. A woman crying over him. There are shouts from the other end of the street, groups of men arguing, another girl running to summon the police, who walk slowly in the direction of the dying man and who will wait to settle the evidence of his death in the favor of the highest bidder. And then imagine she stays with you; the girl in the alley with the haunted eyes. The hole in the man's chest becomes the hole in yours. The crying woman... She too stays. Imagine you are one with all of humanity. You bear the mark of every person you have met and forgotten, met and remembered. What would you do?

You would go on living. We all do.

*

2

~ ~ ~

KNOWLEDGE & CREATIVITY

After returning home to northern California from the sale of the apartment my parents owned for over thirty years, I was grateful for the comfort of my wife and sons. For the past few years we had made Northern California our home. It was there that I brought my wife when we first married. We left for five years to try our hand in Las Vegas while our boys were young. Life we had found to be unpredictable but always bountiful. Yet it still had a way of intervening with our best laid plans.

While we lived in Las Vegas, on September 17, 2008 with two months until the presidential election, I took my older boys to see Barack Obama speak at the Las Vegas Springs Preserve. I woke before dawn as habit taught me to do. The peace of early morning was invading the house. I listened to my wife's quiet breath whisper the tune of her dreams beside me. It was hot in the morning. It was hot all through the night in the desert in the late summer and the heat did not abate. But the early darkness had a cooling effect of its own. I turned the light on in the kitchen. I had not been comfortable in the dark for a long time.

When we left in the morning, Omar and Omid had their hair combed slick and they were buttoned up into their shirts. I smiled with pride as I looked at them. Little Sahel was crying and trying to wiggle out of Zeba's arms to come with us. She laughed, cooing at our youngest son and waving to us as we drove away. Omid played his video game in the back seat, but Omar sat up front with me, asking me questions about the man that might be President.

"I worked for his campaign," I said and Omar wanted to know what a campaign was.

I explained the election process to him and tried to define for him the pride I felt at writing the campaign blogs on Afghanistan.

In the way that children jump from one subject to the next, Omar moved to the next topic.

"When will I go to Afghanistan?"

"I don't know if you will ever go. None of our family is there anymore. Kabul is not the same anymore as it was when I was a boy. It isn't safe and there is a lot of fighting among the people there. We have to rely on leaders, like the president, to help Afghanistan grow into what it once was."

Omar was quiet after the conversation and I wasn't sure what he took from my comments. He often heard Zeba and me speaking about Afghanistan and the tumultuous situation there. The last time I was in Kabul, it was just after 9/11 and I thought at the time that I could make a difference there. Then tragedy and circumstance intervened and my efforts were not rewarded. I had not thought about returning for a long time. Since I learned more about Mr. Obama, I began to think again about the possibility of returning to my homeland and bringing something good to my native country.

The boys and I arrived early and walked for many blocks, to where a crowd was already gathered. The excitement stirred the air but still the day was so hot it stuck to me like American bread to the back of my teeth. The atmosphere of a crowd is an interesting thing. The energy, the potential of a crowd is like a small piece of society, magnified a hundred times. In that particular group I felt proud. I felt the pride of myself and my sons. I felt the pride of my ancestors, but I was saddened too. I was saddened that such pride should come at such a cost, and be so hard-won for most.

Omid tugged at my shirt to tell me how hot he was.

"Yes, yes. I know," I said, "But listen - Listen to his words and you will forget the heat."

When Mr. Obama took the stage and began to speak, perhaps it was only I who forgot; only I who was carried away on the tide of his speech, the confidence in his voice.

"Our friends have fought and bled and died alongside us in Afghanistan. Now, we must come together to end this war successfully," Obama said and I got chills up and down my back. My sons were quiet until the crowd echoed approval and Omar and Omid visibly relaxed.

"Can we go now?" Omid asked when it was over.

I laughed. "Yes, now we can go."

On the way home, we did not speak more of politics and ideas, but at night, Omar asked me, "Do you think he will win?"

"I think he will. I believed in him when others did not. Because he understood things as others did not. His eyes were open."

At night Zeba and I sat on the porch under the stars. It was warm and she drank iced tea. I had a glass of wine and I swirled it absentmindedly. The yellow lights of the city spread over the valley below. The neon strip of downtown Las Vegas had been a beacon of hope in my past. I realized in that moment, looking out at the shining distance that I no longer felt so certain that I belonged there.

"What will we do now?" Zeba asked, as if reading my mind.

The recent economic depression hit the country hard, but had been most devastating in Las Vegas. The real estate industry was crumbling and I had been looking at different possibilities for our future.

"I've been thinking a lot about the business. It might be different this time. There have been changes and I hope that if Obama becomes president there will be more. Maybe Kabul is ready now."

"Are *you* ready?"

I told her, in ways too difficult for most to understand, that I was torn by the need to return to Kabul and the good sense to stay away.

"You will go then?" she said with a smile. I saw that she understood perfectly.

"I will wait until I find a company to work with that will provide affordable satellite coverage to Afghanistan. Then I will probably go. It has been several years since the last time, but I can't seem to let the idea go."

She reached out and put her hand on mine. We spent hours on the balcony, staring into the distance and thinking of where we might take ourselves next. In the past year I attended the National Association of Broadcasters convention in Las Vegas. For that amount of time I had also been building the foundations of a company that might do my part to provide infrastructure to Afghanistan in the form of distance-learning and telemedicine. Without a satellite provider, the business would struggle to take off. It was the second time I would try to launch the same business model in seven years. The time had come again to commit myself one way or the other; to move on with the next phase of life or to stay and falter in this one.

After that we decided to move back to the Bay Area. Northern California was familiar and felt like an old friend greeting me. The house we moved to was more modest than the last but also more comfortable. It was older than our house in Las Vegas by many decades and had a feel about it of having lived a full life. I had often thought that the walls and floors of a place bear the imprint of memory. Perhaps I was more comfortable in haunted places than in the vastly modern. It was less than Zeba had been used too lately, but she handled it gracefully. She, too, had not always lived in luxury. She grew up in Kabul, the same as I did. The kitchen in our new home was smaller than the kitchen she loved in our Las Vegas house. In spite of this, Zeba laughed and made do. She hung the pots from hooks on the wall above the stove to save space in the cupboards.

In January of the New Year, President Barack Hussein Obama was inaugurated President of the United States of America. I had renewed faith in the possibility that men could be made to see the ineffectiveness of current attempts to rebuild the infrastructure of Afghanistan. I followed the status of Afghanistan through all the years since my escape. Her trials and tribulations. The tears of blood she cried and I understood that creativity was dead and buried among the long list of casualties in Kabul. There were no original ideas. Only by bringing knowledge to Afghanistan would her people begin to think for themselves, to fashion a life out of the ashes and to spark new ideas that would ignite the fire of progress.

Years of improvised living taught me that the best way for me to accomplish anything was to do what I *ought* to do in the context of what I know *how* to do. I know telecommunications. I know that information has existed throughout human history. Revolutions in human thought were evidenced in the development of libraries, in philosophy, in the way we relay stories through the ages. Internet and video were the evolved process for relating information. If I could bring affordable broadband internet access to the provinces of Afghanistan, and to the very heart of Kabul, I could bring telemedicine and distance-education to the people. It was the best I could think to do.

I had been told often over the past years that there was no affordable broadband satellite that would support my efforts to build infrastructure for health-care and education systems in my homeland. One afternoon in May I received a call that changed everything. A new satellite was being launched by one of the companies I followed since the convention in Las Vegas. The satellite would cover all of Central Asia, including the areas of Afghanistan that I wanted to bring cost-effective Internet access to.

When I got the call, goose bumps rose along my arms. I walked into the room where Zeba was putting away our laundry and I watched her. She did not realize I was there and I was happy to watch her.

She turned and saw me, smiling.

"What now?" She teased.

"Now we change the world," I say.

"Ah," she said, "That was what our sons were for. I was too busy with the laundry."

"We are ready to take the business to Kabul."

That evening at dinner, my sons had many questions about Kabul and I was excited about the prospect of getting my business off the ground so I filled the conversation with all of the endless possibilities that I saw for change there. Zeba was quiet, listening to me speak. When we were alone later that night, she said, "I worry about you going there. It wasn't safe."

"No. It wasn't safe but I know how to avoid trouble. If I were meant to die in Kabul I would had done it long ago. It will never be safe there unless we do something to help when we can."

"That's what Farhad said."

I bowed my head, "And he was right to say it. He was right to try to do what he could. He's a hero and an example to us all."

"Weren't you afraid that they will take until there was nothing left to give?"

"I can't believe that. Not because I don't believe that was the desperate state of things in Afghanistan, but because I want so much for it to not be so. I want our sons to visit our homeland someday without shame or fear. I want to give them what we did not have."

*

3

~ ~ ~

WARLORDS & CORRUPTION

Kabul, Afghanistan 2010

It was the first time I returned to Afghanistan for business since 2002. I was travelling there to begin laying the groundwork for my business by setting up an office and hiring employees. At that time, a young man named Osman sought me out. He was one of the many unemployed young men of Kabul who heard about an opportunity and contacted me to pursue it. So many of the young men in Kabul were caught up in the corruption that bled the city; leeches on the belly of the beast. I could not say which was worse: the beast itself or those that fed on it. I knew I had to be careful in my choice of employees as they would largely run the Kabul office while I worked remotely from the U.S.

Osman was reserved but polite. I watched his eyes but he was hesitant to meet mine. I read this as the usual lack of confidence and experience. He was diligent about going to school. His mother, he said, made sure he was educated. I felt the common bond of this between us. Before the day was over, I hired him and three others who walk through my door. It was just the beginning. By the end of the week I employed 13 young people, including several young women. Zarghona and Freshta were the two girls that I assigned to run the office. The irony did not escape me that those who I perceived as the most loyal and trustworthy members of Afghan society were also those that likely suffered the most from oppression during the decades of war that plagued the city.

The offices were set up on the second floor of the five-story Kabul International Hotel. The fourth floor was where we had our rooms. I brought with me an associate from Germany named Fawad. He was a Technical Sales Executive who agreed to partner with me in the business. The atmosphere of the hotel was rich. It was like the airport only everyone was not bored and lifeless as they appeared in transit. At the hotel, there were people from all over the world, talking and gathering and flooding in and out of the doors. Fawad, who has never been to Afghanistan before, was amazed by the color and variety of the landscape and the people. He, like many, had been taught one thing by the media but found another to be true. He was very quiet on the first day, but over dinner that night, he ate slowly to savor each individual taste of his *kofta challow*. The food, to my taste, had lost its authentic appeal but I did not tell him this. I imagined to him it was a new world and in a moment he confessed this.

"This, all this, makes me feel kind of small," Fawad said, "It's humbling. I've spent my life believing what I was told. I didn't try to look for the truth."

"You expected something different?"

"I didn't expect anything at all. I'm ashamed to say it."

We met with many potential investors throughout the week, many of them high government officials. I spent much of the time explaining to Fawad how everyone was connected at that level and how some of those connections could be dangerous. At the end of the week we met with the wholesalers who we partnered with to distribute our satellite Internet service. During the meeting, I read some numbers to them that showed the business was getting off to a profitable start. The executives on the other side of the table exchanged glances.

Baktaj was the owner of the resale company and while he usually wasn't present at the meetings, he was there that day. We had exchanged business e-mails while I was in the states and negotiated an agreement to work together. He was a well-dressed man of middle-age with a trim beard that was graying. His eyes, I couldn't help noticing, were different colors. The watch he wore was expensive and he continued to adjust it on his wrist. He remained quiet as I spoke. I outlined briefly how I thought we might best proceed with our professional relationship. Only at the conclusion of the meeting did Baktaj speak.

When he did so, I could not find the words to answer.

"I will have my fifty percent of the company shares," he said, "I will not be just a wholesale partner."

I was at a loss. Not only were these not the terms we agreed to, but he was foolish to expect that I would give away fifty percent of a company that would be worth tens of millions of dollars in a few years. I told him I could produce the documents that proved our business relationship only consisted of a five percent profit share, but he waved me off.

"There were no such documents."

Fawad tried to speak up, but it was of little use.

Baktaj requested then that the two of us be left alone and his men escorted Fawad from the room.

I faced Baktaj across the table.

"You do not know what you are dealing with," he said.

"I was dealing in good faith. I thought your business was operated under the same premise."

"You were in over your head, Abdul. I have been doing business in this city for years. We do not have room for outsiders to come in, make money off of us and take it away to the U.S. You will turn over half of your company, or we will take it by force."

It was then I understand what he already knew. I did not have the backing of power that he had. To function on ethics alone in this setting would be nearly impossible.

"I would like time to gather my documents and to meet with you again at the end of the week to discuss this further," I said and he watched me.

His stare was incongruous. He knew this, too. It was like the balance of power in that room, and his stance was one of intimidation. I had nothing left to offer him, and only time to offer myself. He nodded in agreement and said nothing more. As we were leaving, he put a hand on my shoulder and the grip was firm and unyielding.

He leaned in slightly, "You will meet with me again. You may bring your papers," he smiled, "But you would be wise to also bring the money."

As we drove away toward our hotel, my hands on the steering wheel were tightly gripped. A car followed us through the streets. It was not the car that they drove away in with Baktaj, but another and this I figured was the muscle behind the threat.

They followed us through the din of the city and Fawad knew something was wrong though I would not speak of the situation yet other than to tell him that a threat was made. We parked at the hotel and the car that followed us waited by the entrance. I did not want to get out of the car, but eventually we did not have a choice other than to stay there indefinitely.

We exited the vehicle and moved toward the hotel as soon as a crowd approached, trying to blend in. The car waited until we were inside before it left. I would have done nothing to question their intentions. I only took the opportunity, once inside our rooms, to explain to Fawad what happened when Baktaj and I were alone.

Fawad knew, even less than I did, what Baktaj's demand meant to us. I had no resources to fight back with. It was not like doing business in the U.S. and other countries where government regulates ethics and there was a legal process that supports recourse against unfair business practices. In

Afghanistan, the government was run on the bribes of warlords, by politicians who had lost any global awareness they once possessed in a futile attempt to persist. To those who had lost the ability to believe in anything other than what they were told, this was survival.

We were unable to sleep. We did not go near the window and every sound of footsteps in the hallway caused us to hold our breaths. Fawad thought we were safe because we were in a hotel. He did not understand until I told him, that even the police in that city were well-fed on the money of warlords.

I did not take the following days to gather my documents as I told Baktaj, but spent the hours making calls to people I had no choice but to trust. I was put in contact finally with a Senator who lives in Green Zone, in the Wazir Akbar Khan District. Fawad and I had to leave the hotel to meet with him and to secure different lodgings if we were to feel safe through another night.

Senator Rasheed agreed to meet with me in his offices in a new building in the government district. He had thick hair that he combed over to the side and wore glasses. He was older than myself by a few years at least and greeted me cordially, gesturing for me to have a seat. His office was wide with blue carpeting and white walls. News clippings and photo memorabilia were framed along the walls. Along the far wall was a green couch with flower embroidered pillows. Pictures stood on his desk as well, but seated as I was behind them, I could not see the contents of their frames. I faced the window instead and outside the sky was gray and it began to rain. The Senator leaned back in his chair as I explain to him the situation with Baktaj. He narrowed his eyes and nodded in response.

"After I called you this morning, I contacted an acquaintance named Qassem, who has a long list of contacts from which he believes he can find an investor quickly. With the investment money I can pay off Baktaj. I do not want to do it, but I also don't have the political backing that Baktaj has," I conclude.

"I do not know Baktaj and cannot say what he might do. I know it was not what you want to hear now, even though you come to me seeking help, but I think I can offer you a solution. I can tell you only two things. I can tell you that I do know of Qassem and I do not trust him. He has been involved in business here for a long time and has consistently failed. He suffers from a bad reputation. I do not doubt that he has many contacts, but I cannot say that those contacts will serve you well in remaining an honest man. I see you mean well. I can offer you one other option," the Senator said, and took his glasses off momentarily to pinch the bridge of his nose. He wore a large gold ring on his middle finger. It reminded me of one my grandfather wore that I had forgotten until that moment.

"You have found out the hard way that you need political backing to operate your business with any success in Kabul. You had created a business that was generating a large amount of profit. Your competitors had become angry. Those you trusted had picked up the scent and become greedy. I can offer you my own political backing. This, of course, means that you would have to take me in as a partner in your business."

He looked at me, knowing I was sure, the irony with which this offer came.

"A lame crab walks straight," he laughed, quoting an ancient Afghan proverb.

Without giving him an answer, I told Senator Rasheed I needed to speak to my associate and I left his building, anxious for some time to think over his offer.

Based on my initial call for help, within days Qassem had an investor lined up who was willing to put millions of dollars into our business. I understand that if it seems too good to be true it probably was, but I could not afford delay. I accepted Qassem's offer of assistance in return for some company's shares and we moved forward to secure the investment. By the end of the week I offered Baktaj a payment significant enough to discourage his continued threats.

Fawad and I secured new lodgings in a guest house in Charahi Haji Yaqoob. The guest house was managed by two Americans who had been abroad for over 25 years. There were thirteen British and American security guards on the property. One of the owners, who introduced himself as Peter, came to greet us at the gate after the guards checked us in. He was wearing a loose linen suit and his skin was deeply tanned. His hair was white but sparse and he extended his hand, speaking fluent Dari.

"Welcome to my home, brothers. I respect your need for safety and I was happy to offer you a place to work from as well. Let me show you around."

Peter showed us through the premises, speaking volumes as he did so, clearly embracing the cultural hospitality that was fading from the country and her people. He led us out onto a veranda from which spread a wide green lawn with shaded tables and chairs. The back wall was lined with fig trees and Peter led us to a table in their shade. He took a moment to carefully select a handful of ripe figs from the trees and laid them on the table for us to share. Moments later, a staff member walked onto the lawn with a tray of kebabs and rice, served cold—as the woman explained—to soothe our bodies from the heat.

Peter told us of his adventures in a variety of areas across the globe and it was pleasant to listen to his stories and to enjoy the comforts of the place. It was only when we went to work later, setting up the computers while darkness fell over the city, that I heard the distant sound of gunshots. The presence of security increased in the hallways of the house at dark and I was once again living in fear in the land that gave birth to me.

The next morning we did not see Peter. I found a newspaper and carried it out onto the lawn where we sat the day before. The same woman brought me a tray with steaming black tea, sugar and *naan*. I spread the newspaper out on the table and the headlines chilled my blood.

Kabul's Intercontinental Hotel Attacked by Gunmen
...power was cut to the hotel and gunmen laid siege to the popular international hotel in a standoff that lasted more than four hours. Several suicide bombers were also involved in the attack and Taliban spokesman Zabiullah Mujahid said the group was responsible. Nineteen civilians died at the hands of the armed insurgents. Those responsible for the attack were killed on the roof of the hotel when NATO helicopters returned fire...

I left my tea cooling on the table and went to the room that Fawad was staying in. I found him sitting in a chair and watching CNN on the small television in the corner. He looked up when I entered and I could see that he had heard the news and was stunned. He was quiet throughout the morning and after lunch he told me that he would not stay.

"What do you mean? It was safe here at least."

"I mean I can't stay here and help you with the business. Not when only days ago we were in *that* hotel, in the same spot where the Taliban stormed in and took control with their weapons last night. There is no rational thought here. No order to the chaos. I will not stay."

I told him I respected his wishes. He asked me what I would do and I told him that I would do what I must. I called my wife that evening as Fawad prepared for his departure. I knew she would not have seen the news because she never liked to watch it when I was away. But I revealed to her the situation. She was concerned that I would be alone now, without a partner to talk things through with.

"You were always my best partner. I will just had to call you now," I teased.

"Abe..." she began, but she didn't continue with the admonitions that were likely at the forefront of her mind.

In the space of her silence, I heard my sons in the background and it brought tears to my eyes.

"Your other business associates here would like to speak with you," she said and put Omar and Omid on the phone.

When the conversation ended it was much too late to think, but I lay awake anyway staring out the window at the stars that were blinking through openings in the cloud cover. The night was silent and for the first time in months I allowed myself to be afraid that I might fail.

When Fawad had left, Peter joined me for nearly every meal. He had worked all his life in finance and was interested in my business and the context of corruption that I was trying to operate within. I left the safety of the guest house only when I had to, to meet individually with more potential investors. Often we would meet in the park that was near Amani High School where I attended school. The park was famous for its restaurants, ice cream shops, cinema and other leisure activities.

I met with a potential investor one afternoon at the old *Hotal-e Dad Khodai Charikari* where I had gone as a teenager for the best Kebabs in town. I stopped in at the Comdish restaurant next door and asked about the owner I had known as a boy. I learned that he had left the country a long time ago. It was obvious the new owner had tried to keep the atmosphere the same but without much success. Only those who had visited before would notice the difference. The Comdish restaurant was built around a tree that had now been cut down. Only the stump and some roots still remained inside the restaurant suggested what it had once been. When the civil war broke out in Kabul, the restaurants had been emptied and it was a long time before people returned to claim them. Over the years the trees in the park had all died off. Millions of dollars had been poured into the country to try to restore the trees and other natural beauties of the place, only to disappear into the deep pockets of warlords and other corrupt officials who had no interest in repairing the damage that had been done. Many of the restaurants and shops that once existed had been replaced with NATO, UN and other government offices. Now the area was one of the safest in Kabul, the crowds had increased ten-fold but no one smiled; ownership of the properties in the park changed faster than dice on a Vegas table. The park had the atmosphere now of a train station or an airport where everyone was just passing through. It had not always been that way.

One of the meetings I had at the park was with Haji Khalil Ferozi, the CEO of Kabul Bank. When Peter and I were sitting over drinks one evening, I told him that Ferozi had offered a rather large investment.

"What will you do?" Peter asked.

"I will hope that he chooses not to go through with it."

The truth of the matter was that during the meeting with Ferozi I downplayed the opportunity that the company offered. In making it sound less desirable, I hoped he would become discouraged and look to other opportunities to invest.

"He's going to end up in jail soon anyway. You could walk away with the money. They would never be able to recover it."

"I had learned nothing if I had not learned that money always leaves a scent. The hounds will follow."

On another morning, I was travelling to a meeting with my staff in the main business office we had since set up in Sher Poor near the German and U.S. embassies. In the cab, I realized that I had left my laptop in my room at the guest house. I told the cab driver to turn around and I retrieved my computer. When I at last arrived at the offices, they were empty. The man who operated the business next door rushed out to me.

"They took them, only moments ago. The police came and arrested all of them. You must go, too. The officers came in and asked me if I was hiding anyone else."

After this news, I caught the first flight I could find to Dubai where I spent the rest of the week making phone calls to the police and everyone I could who has a connection with the business. The employees were released after two days and at that time I was able to speak with Zarghona.

"They told us this was just a warning," she said. Her voice was tired and no stronger than a whisper.

"They said they only wanted you, and that if we don't start cooperating and giving them the information they want, next time they arrest us it will not be so easy."

"What did they ask for?"

"They wanted to know where you were staying."

"Did anyone tell them?"

She paused for a long moment, "Osman did."

For two additional weeks, I worked remotely from Dubai while telling everyone I spoke to that I was still in Kabul. Not long after, the threats started coming in to my personal cell phone. The voice at the end of the line told me to give up my location or my employees would be arrested again. I acted quickly with Zarghona and between her and Freshta and a few other trusted employees, the offices were relocated to an undisclosed location. I decided to keep only four employees there, including Zarghona and Freshta, to operate the heart of the business. I could not ignore the fact that beside my wife and sons, and my mother, the only other person I had given my personal mobile phone number to was Qassem.

I could not imagine the web of connections that brought about this latest threat to my company. In less than a year, we had become the fastest growing satellite internet provider in Afghanistan. In less than a year I had effectively been precluded from ever returning to Kabul. After all those long months of being unable to stay away, I knew I could not return. She might have been my home once, but she was no more.

Once things were stabilized and I had let all but the most essential of employees go, I returned home to the Bay Area. I had been spending more time than usual thinking about the last time my business faltered. I thought about the friendships I had treasured with those who I could no longer count among my closest allies. In the comfort of my home I decided to write a letter to an old friend. The contents of the letter had been at the back of my mind for a long time. From another room there came the laughter of my sons. The letter began this way:

I have come to the fact after so many years, that I have a story to tell. It was important to me because it was mine. It was important to you because it is yours also....

From somewhere else, the movement of my wife intruded on my thoughts. Through my mind a hot wind blew through the doorless room of a mud house as past and present overlapped. Another man leaned over a drafting table, writing precise black lines on a white background. A black and white photograph fluttered and I wrote: *the tally of the small tragedies of life adds up to this: the human spirit will seem to bend endlessly until the spine of the world breaks. Our Robert Frost talks of yellow woods. For me, the roads diverged somewhere else entirely. But what can I tell you, old friend, that you do not already know? You, who had been there yourself, had struggled in both the same and different ways. I offer my apologies. I offer forgiveness too.*

*

4

~ ~ ~

THE FACE FROM THE PAST

San Francisco, California 2011

Business in Kabul continued to be operated remotely by myself and held in place by Zarghona and Freshta who proved more than capable. I had many opportunities to value their trustworthiness and I spoke of this often to Zeba.

The call came late in the evening when it was still morning in Kabul. We had just finished dinner and Zeba was in the kitchen. My older sons were doing homework. The youngest, Sahel, was drawing pictures from his favorite cartoon. We had made improvements on the house and Zeba had grown to love it. She took pride in our home as she did in raising our sons and in everything she set her mind to doing. She was proud of the way we live with what we were given and I couldn't help but feel the same.

The phone rang and Zeba brought it to me. I heard her speaking to Zarghona and her hand approached her mouth in a gesture of surprise as she walked toward me. She stayed close to hear that everything was okay. She felt close to not just Zarghona and Freshta, but to all of the girls who worked for me in Kabul. She thought any one of them might have been her if things had been different. When I got on the phone, Zarghona's voice was steady, only lower in tone than usual.

"They found us, Abdul. They took all of the computers yesterday," she said, "The whole network."

"Who was it?"

"I do not know for certain. It was Osman and I did not see the other man. He was covered."

"Did they threaten you?"

"They shouted at us. They waved a gun around and then Osman; he came to me especially and put the gun under my chin. He said 'I watch you still. I won't forget you.' And they *had* been watching. They knew the money wasn't here. They didn't even look for it. They took the computers and nothing else."

"Will you tell the police everything? Will you make sure they call me? I will do what I can to help."

She was silent for a few moments, the phone connection trembled with static, "I was not afraid," she said, her voice firm but far away, "They will do nothing to me. But if you come - you won't come will you? But if you do, come quietly. They ask about you all the time."

I returned.

I returned even when I said I would not. The safety of the people who trusted me was worth the risk. The survival of all that I had worked for and believed in - all that my old friend Basir had worked for and believed in, too - was worth it.

I arrived at the end of November. The city that gave birth to me stifled a ruthless cough of winter. The streets of Kabul, again.

My breath on the air was the only delicate, fragile evidence of life. Around me the concrete walls of the buildings that housed men of importance were thick as stacks of discarded books. These fortresses stood in every corner and lined the main streets of Kabul at intervals of several hundred feet; stark, gray giants lurking. While the walls were of recent construction, they showed the signs of war. Concrete facades were pockmarked with bullet-holes. The knowledge that built the walls was a separate thing from the power that lay within. The frost that clung to the edges of the valley rose upwards over the mud houses on the hillside causing them to shimmer in the sunlight with a beauty they did not ordinarily possess. I had never been able to stand still in Kabul. It was a luxury I never possessed there, so I walked north along the street. I did not hail the cabs that leaked by in the crush of traffic. It was faster to walk.

Zarghona and Freshta met with me in a *hotal* on the outskirts of the city. The restaurant was dark and we arrived separately, meeting at a table near the back. I arrived first and when they each stepped through the door I felt relief over the confirmation of their safety. Zarghona smiled, always the optimistic one. Freshta kept her head down, and quietly nodded along to Zarghona's version of events. I revealed to them what I had learned in the past few months of what was happening in our other offices. I had been tracking the bank accounts remotely and I had discovered a paper trail that covered hundreds of thousands of missing dollars. I had learned that loyal employees had been fired without my knowledge. And most recently, I learned that Zarghona and Freshta were not safe. I went to Kabul to release them from their obligations as my employees.

"I will not be able to meet with the police while I was here," I said, and they both nodded and stirred their *kabuli palaw* with their forks.

Freshta wore glasses and reminded me of Zeba when I met her. She was timid and shy, but too young to know that she was brave beyond words.

"How was Zeba?" Zarghona asked, almost reading my thoughts.

"She was well. Sahel will not let her out of his sight."

On that trip, I was only in Kabul for the day. I meant only to tell the girls in person what they needed to do to remain safe and what to tell the war lords who would eventually question them as to my whereabouts. I was walking the long road back to the airport after our lunch, when three men approached me. I was expecting this, but still it made my heart thunder in my chest. Two of them I recognized the third I did not.

I had become good at reading body language, at defusing and deflecting stressful situations. It was because of these perceptions that I quickly judged the third man to be the most dangerous. Though he was smaller than the other two, he was also more intelligent and his eyes shifted in a way that told me his intentions were not good.

"Osman," I said, "I assume you had heard the bad news?"

"I had," he said, "I expected we might run into you. It seems our luck has not betrayed us."

"Speaking of betrayal," I lied, "I came to meet with Zarghona and she did not show up. I was afraid I may have left my company in the wrong hands."

"I'm certain you did. Were you leaving so soon?" Osman asked, gesturing to my travel bag.

"Only just arriving, I'm afraid. I'm heading to the hotel now."

Jamshaid, the second man I recognized, dug the grime from his fingernails as we talked. The third man remained rigid, hands in the pockets of his *wazkat*. I wondered if he had a weapon there.

"We should meet again," Osman said, "But I imagine you will try to rush off again without remembering your old friends. You keep doing that and I don't think I like it. How long will you be in Kabul this time?"

"I cannot stay more than a week."

"No, of course not. I know where to find you, now. Don't think of leaving so soon this time."

Osman looked around him at the crowded streets, then gestured to the other two and they walked away, leaving me there. Unlike others, they had chosen not to enact their crimes under the eyes of so many. Around me the vendors shouted and bargained, the taxis honked and I was just a man on a road, pushed past and ignored; spared again. But as I tried to slow my pace in my hurry to arrive at the airport and board my plane, it did not go unacknowledged that I was not so very far, at times like this, from the man at the end of the alley with the hole in his chest.

Once I was in the air, I felt safe again. As usual, I chose the flight with the layover in Germany. I took the opportunity, whenever I could, to revisit my other old home. And this time I had a purpose.

It was nearing Christmas and the lights in the square were being lit. There was a bell above the door of the market on the edge of the narrow street that led away from the center of town. Inside, I knew the man who was sitting by the counter. I had seen him there. I walked by twice, to make sure I was not mistaken, but I would have recognized him anywhere. For so many years I had looked for his face in the crowds that swarmed through various cities, only to meet him by chance one afternoon, years ago. Here again, after losing touch once more, I was presented with the familiar image of a boy I had known in my youth; of a man who had both stayed the same and changed in many ways. He sat, waiting, and the scene was so much the same as the last time we met that it prevented me from entering for a moment. The clattering of the bells finally woke him from his silent reverie and he stood to greet another customer. The girl behind the counter—his daughter—did not look up from the magazine she read.

"Good Afternoon," he called but only when he turned did he see the face from the past.

"Good Afternoon, old friend," I said.

The shopkeeper stopped where he stood, unsure and hesitant.

"You got my letter?"

"I did."

"Wali," I said, "I would like to forget the past. I believe I keep meeting you again by chance for a reason. After all these years, it seems you and I are the only ones left." But those gestures of my hands and my heart—I did not know if they were enough to change the future. He bowed his head. The moments slid by.

*

*

"This is love: to fly toward a secret sky,
to cause a hundred veils to fall each moment."
-Rumi

*

5

~ ~ ~

THE WOMAN WITH NO HIJAB

"An illiterate woman is powerless and has to rely on others," my grandmother would say. She was the source of stories about my mother. "I did everything to make sure my daughter goes to school."

My grandmother was not a traditional woman though she appeared to be. When she removed her veils upon entering the house, her face revealed itself as deeply lined but her eyes were large like those of a child. Her fingers were crooked with age. I had four sisters and she would tell these stories to them. I was the middle child, and by the time I came along my mother was both too tired and too grateful at finally having a boy to care if I was coddled. But in spite of the love of my parents and sisters, I was not idle. I could make something out of nothing. It was the way she looked at me—my mother who was always busy at something—she would stop for full moments at a time and watch me with an odd mix of worry and satisfaction on her face.

All the way down the road I could see the riksha that carried our grandma, climbing up the hill to our apartment. The face of my grandmother was dark in the shadow of her *burqa* and the robes wrapped around her, even in the hot summer. She had a frail body, slender and bony and full of sharp edges but she wore so many layers of material that she was like the tawny owl, with layered feathers so thick it made it possible for the bird to swoop down and grasp prey that weighed no less than the owl itself.

My sisters gathered around her and she gave a treat made of raisins and beans, called *Kishmesh Nakhod* to them and then looked around for me, pretending not to see me peeking from around the corner.

"I do not see him. I will have to give his treat to you, Flora," she said to my oldest sister. This would always flush me out, crying "Grandma, Grandma! Here I am!"

I got my treat and a rugged kiss on my head. When my sisters asked her for a story, Grandmother would tell me I could run off to play even though we all knew that I would sit in the next room, stacking goods from the pantry into buildings and villages, but listening all the while.

"There was a girl who was named Momena," Grandmother began, settling into the best chair in the house; the one reserved for guests. "She was born in a different time and when she met with the world for the first time, she did not cry. Her mother was worried at the silence of her daughter. A silence that lasted until the child was nearly three years old, though the mother tried and tried to make her speak. She told Momena stories all day long and filled the house with words and songs. Momena would not speak, but her mother new by the way she watched her that she was listening to every word. The men in the village said the child was mute or deaf or - more quietly and in the privacy of their own homes - dumb as dirt."

Nazima, the youngest of my sisters, squealed with delight at the obscenity but Flora shushed her.

Grandmother continued, "But she was none of these things. Momena's mother did not argue with the villagers, only kept quiet in front of them and whispered to her daughter as they walked from the market. She would say, 'My daughter, choose to hear only the truth and speak only the truth, and you will be as smart as the wind who is gentle and calm and fierce when he needs to be.' Momena listened and said nothing.

"On the very evening of her third birthday, Momena and her mother were cooking dinner in the kitchen when the mother reached for a pot and Momena put out a hand to stop her and said, 'Mother, do not touch that. It has been heated from the fire.' And sure enough, the mother had not seen that the proximity of the pot to the fire had caused it to become scalding hot. But she was more surprised that her daughter had finally spoken than by the fact that she had saved her from a severe burn to her hand. From that day on, Momena spoke as if she had been doing it her entire life, and spoke better than most of the villagers who had whispered to their wives that the little deaf girl was dumb as well."

"Such nonsense," said my mother when she came into the room, but she was smiling.

"How can you say so? You do not remember," said Grandma.

As for my sisters and I, we all believed her stories because we knew the magic that beautiful Momena possessed. She had been spreading it through our house all the years we knew her as our mother.

"I didn't go to school and all my life I had to bend to the will of others. It is lucky for me that I am like the river grass, easy to bend. When I was married I was very young and I spent more years of my life cooking, washing and cleaning and taking care of children because I did not know that I could do anything else. But that life was not for my Momena. When she was six years old, I made her go to school."

The girls held their breath because they knew this part. Grandmother whispered, "I did not tell your grandfather," and my sister's giggled at the secret power our Grandmother wielded. "He did not think girls needed to go to school or to work. He thought a girl did not need to know anything but how to cook and clean and take care of children as I did. But Momena went to school when her father was working at the jewelry store at *Kotche Ali Reza Khan* in the bazaar. As for myself, at least I always had fine jewelry..." she winked.

"The only time Momena missed school was when your Grandfather didn't go to the jewelry store. She could not keep books and pencils because he might find them and she studied in secret. She studied under candlelight in the bathroom on top of the house roof. If she heard her father coming, she would blow out the candle and put it together out the window onto the roof ledge. Some nights before exams she would spend the night with my sister whose husband had died. The rest of the time, she was with me learning the things her father said she ought to know how to do to be a wife and mother. But all the while she whispered her lessons to me, over and over so she could learn them.

She did not see, but sometimes it made tears come to my eyes, just to hear her voice."

By this time, I abandoned the contents of the pantry and sat with my arms wrapped around my knees, as close to the next room as I could be without getting caught listening. It was not until many years later that I understood these stories were told as much for me as for my sisters.

"What was it like, Mama, to go to school in secret?" Flora would ask her later.

My mother, cooking at the kitchen stove, wiped her hands in a towel and said, "Like learning the truth after you have been told a lie."

Such stories filled my childhood. My father had his own stories, not about himself but about his own father, who he often praised. His father was a *Tika Daar*, a real estate developer who had his part in the building of the National Museum of Afghanistan in Kabul.

He only told one story about himself and it was not truly about him. He met my mother when she was eighteen, he said. She was riding her bicycle down the road and her hair was tied back but flying behind her, otherwise free. There were children along the side of the road, shouting and calling her *zane roy lotch*, the woman with no hijab. He followed her that day and many days after and saw that on most days the scene was the same. Sometimes the children would not throw rocks or would not be there, but it did not seem to matter to her either way. She rode by each day with her back straight and her hair loose. He followed her to the Maiwand hospital where she worked as a midwife and after she went into the building he would sit on the bench outside and think about this strange woman. He could not make heads or tails of how he felt for many days. She was bold and unlike any women he had ever met (or not met), and he did not know if this should scare him away or make him love her. He decided that the only way to know for sure was to speak to her. When she came out of the building on the fifth day, he was waiting for her. As if it was not enough to see her black hair shine in the sun, her eyes were beautiful too. But it was not that which made the decision for him. It was decided when he asked her, without warning, why she wore no hijab.

"My beautiful bird," he said. "She told me she threw the hijab off because she felt like she was in a cage."

*

6

~ ~ ~

IMPRESSIONS OF YOUNG LOVE

On an airplane leaving Kabul, Afghanistan, 1980

"Friba," mother said and proceeded to whisper in my sister's ear.

I would have tried to listen, but I was too distracted by observing the other passengers on the plane. Were any of them like us; fleeing and leaving behind family and friends in untold numbers?

I knew from the conversations I had overheard between my father and mother that we were one of only a few who were able to obtain the documents necessary to leave our native country. The rest of the passengers all looked so solemn; closed books.

Friba nudged me, "Do not stare," she said and it made me remember a time not so long ago when the faces of the people I met were open and inviting. I could hardly pinpoint the myriad ways the world had changed since then. My memories leading up to the airplane were a series of beautiful visions; all of them gilded in the hopeful tint of youth.

As a young boy I played mostly with my sisters. They would put on plays with the other girls in our apartment community and I would have to play the boy's role in each production. I did not mind until I was old enough to realize that some of the older girls were taking too much pleasure in dressing me up and then giggling behind their hands at my acting. About that time, my mother felt more comfortable with letting me play with the other boys in the neighborhood. She worked as a midwife with Professor Rahim Nevin, who was the cultural minister at the time, in his medical clinic in Share Naw. Because of her position as a midwife, she knew many of the families in our neighborhood and had delivered a number of their babies. She trusted that there were enough eyes on me that I could not get into much trouble. I almost never did, aside from exacting minor revenge on my sisters for forcing me to take part in their humiliating plays.

Flora and Friba, who were both older than me, had been given rollerblades by my father and were often with their friends, swaying down the roads like new deer. Some of the other boys and me took to following them and waiting for them to fall so we could laugh and watch their cheeks burn with embarrassment. My sister's would go home and tell my mother in the evening what I had done, and I heard their complaints, but my mother did not mention it to me.

One evening, she called me into the kitchen where she was preparing dinner for our family. She handed me a knife and some fresh vegetables and I began to cut them. After long moments of silence she said, "Abdul, I am so proud of how you care for your family. I am proud of the respect you show for your sisters. This will make you a good man, a strong man." She went about cooking dinner and when the vegetables were cut and thrown in a pot, she excused me.

As I grew up, I had many friends at school and in our community. Baraymal Dost lived in the complex across from ours and we became friends when we were put into the same class at school. One afternoon we were sitting in the hallway near the apartment of Khessrau who was in another class at school, but lived in the same block as me. Khessrau's father, Nainawaz, was a musician but we did not know it yet. As we sat there the door to the apartment opened and we stood, prepared to meet Khessrau coming out to play, but the voices that drifted out were those of two men and not of our friend. One of the men exited the apartment and Baraymal gasped.

It took me only a moment to recognize the man as Ahmad Zahir, who has long been known as the Afghan Elvis.

"Salaam," Baraymal and I said together and Zahir's eyes met ours. He gave us a half smile and a nod. His long hair and thick sideburns made me vow not to sit for the next haircut my mother tried to give me. Behind us we heard a laugh and turned to see Khessrau's father standing by the door.

"Khessrau!" he called, "I think your friends are waiting for you."

Moments later Khessrau came out, chewing the last of his lunch and looking as unenthusiastic as ever. His eyes were hooded and they drooped down a little at the corners so that he always appeared to be both bored and tired.

When we were outside, we bombarded him with questions about Ahmad Zahir and learned that Khessrau's father wrote many of Zahir's songs. Khessrau seemed surprised to find that we were so interested in his father's business. After that Khessrau sang to us some of his father's new recordings that had not made it to the radio yet and we were among the first to hear them. I talked so much about Zahir that summer that even my sisters grew tired of hearing his name.

When the heat covered Kabul, we would go to the community swimming pool once a week. Every other Friday was swimming day for the girls. My mother would prepare lunch and tea and I would carry it around the back of our complex to the nearby pool. My sisters were always waiting impatiently. I was often aware of being watched on my approach, the only boy in the pool area and I tried to place each step carefully so as not to slip on the wet pool deck.

"Abdul! You walk so impossibly slow," Friba would say from the pool, causing her friends to giggle.

Flora at least would jump out of the water and take the tray from me, though she said nothing by way of thanks and did not offer me anything to eat. I rushed away, grateful to be free finally to find my own friends.

One day as I was leaving the pool in a hurry, I saw her for the first time. She was standing with a group of older girls, of which my sister Flora was one. My sister saw me looking and made a face. But the beautiful girl with the long hair looked at me and just as quickly looked away. But not before I had seen them; those eyes like deep pools of promise.

I ran the rest of the way back to block 28, where my friends were waiting. We took off in the direction of the city, running down the hills.

Above us, two kites floated in the unseen breeze that did not sink low enough to mingle with the throngs of people that clogged the streets of Kabul. The cinema was filled on the weekends with Russian children, but we waited until the movie started to slip through the doors in search of empty seats. Often there were none and we stood along the back wall and watched the Russian cartoon *Wolf and Rabbit*, laughing with the rest of the children and forgetting who had preference there and why.

Through all of this, I could not get the beauty of the girl by the pool out of my mind. For the rest of the day and the rest of the week I looked for her. For once I was hopping around anxiously rather than agitatedly while my mother prepared the meal for me to take to the pool on the following Friday.

After that, I approached Flora as casually as I could and said, "Why do you not bring your friends here? I miss doing the plays as we used to."

She looked up at me from her homework and then went back to work, uninterested.

"Nice try," she said, "I see right through you, Abdul. You could try not to stare so hard. She's going to tell her mother on you."

I ran away embarrassed, but when I found myself outside I felt at peace. I was comforted by the fact that Flora did not know my true secret. That I had passed the beautiful girl on the road that day as I was returning from my errand to the pool. That I had been running and stopped when I saw her walking toward me. That she had lifted her eyes in my direction. She was shy I knew because she looked away. Then she looked back and there was a tiny smile teasing her lips. It made all the difference in the world to a young boy in want of only the slightest encouragement to fixate on a dream. These were my impressions of young love: breathing so hard it was the only sound I could hear, feeling my heart in my throat, and my entire soul lifting up on the sudden breeze; as high as a kite.

The walk to school laid the whole city out before me. The sun rose over far off hills and covered Kabul in gold. I kicked rocks and tried to see if I could kick one all the way to school. Sometimes I hopped on my left foot, holding my right leg behind me with my left hand, practicing balance and maneuvering for the game of *Khossai* that we sometimes played during breaks at school. That day I realized why I had seen the long-haired girl in our neighborhood all summer long. I was sitting in my seat talking to my friends when I looked up to see her standing in the doorway. We froze, my friends and I and moved our chairs as quickly as if the teacher had just walked in to find us misbehaving. By the luck of the draw, I ended up next to the vacant seat and here she sat for the rest of the school year, intent on her studies while I dreamed of touching her hair.

After school the boys in our neighborhood would gather and the older ones would play soccer on teams while the younger boys like me would stay along the edges of the game, waiting for the ball to be kicked our way; to be noticed; to be invited to play. It rarely happened that I got a chance to play until I managed to put together enough money to buy my first soccer ball, and then suddenly the older boys took notice. The younger boys too, all wanted to be close to me because it meant they had a better chance of getting involved in a game.

The first time I was invited to play, the boys did not pass the ball to me.

Even the neighbor's dog stood on the sidelines watching, and I was mortified. After the game, I took my ball home with me and put it under my bed. I did not bring it out for a week and I ignored the older boys until they finally saw the error of their ways. The next time I was invited to play with them, I got the ball several times and managed to score a goal. The older boys punched me in the arm like I was part of the team and my friends on the sidelines cheered.

After that, I did not want to play with them again. My real friends, I thought, were those on the outside of the game and I knew how it felt to be there.

"We have our own ball," I said to Baraymal at dusk as we were heading home, "We can start our own team."

Baraymal Dost was excited about this and we ran the rest of the way home. He pulled me with him into his family's apartment. His aunt and uncle were there and his mother was carrying food to the table. Baraymal's father sat us down and took off his glasses, nodding as he listened to our idea.

"Let me think about this tonight," he said and Baraymal was nearly bouncing on the sofa beside me, "I want to see you back here tomorrow, Abdul. Baraymal and I will have a plan for your soccer team. Baraymal and I ran out of the apartment with his aunt yelling after us to slow down.

The following day, I walked home from school with Baraymal, planning all the way what the colors would be of our uniforms and who would be the best players for each position. We dreamed of challenging the older boys and of winning; of achieving great fame as soccer players in the way that only children know to bring a dream to life. Baraymal's father was not yet home when we arrived, but we waited on the stairwell by a window where we could see him when he came up the walk to the first floor entrance of our complex.

While we waited, some of the other boys joined us and down the stairs came one of our many Russian neighbors. We all quieted our noisy chatter and stood up a bit straighter, as we knew this man and would have been reprimanded if we forgot our manners. He looked sternly at us, and then from a bag that he carried, he pulled out a Russian chocolate bar, covered in a wrapping that bore the picture of a bear. He handed one to each of us and then looked at us disapprovingly as we all thanked him.

We waited until he had gone back upstairs to run outside and tear into our treats. We sheltered under one of the tall trees along the path that connected each entrance of block 28. We could see from there if any of the other children were approaching so we could hide our treasure. There were five of us, as I recall, sitting around the trunk of a persimmon tree. We were laughing about something, and savoring the almond and sweet sugar flavors of our chocolate bars. Summer laid itself over us like a comfortable blanket; never stifling. The afternoon rang with the sound of the birds in the young trees swooping low and the sound of Baraymal's father's boots on the sidewalk. He nodded at us and Baraymal and I went running, stuffing the candy wrappers in our pockets as we went.

He was very professional. Baraymal and I sat as quiet as statues while his father pulled a sheet of paper out and laid it on the table between us. I felt very grown up all of a sudden and Baraymal, I sensed, was on his best behavior as well. We read the letter his father handed us and understood that it was a letter of introduction, meant to inform our neighbors of our intentions to set up a soccer team for the young boys of our community.

For days after that we knocked on doors, greeted neighbors and collected money. After a week and a half, we had enough to support our team. Baraymal's father patted us each on the shoulder and I was invited to dinner that night.

A week later, there was a knock on our apartment door and Baraymal was on the other side. My mother invited him in and served tea to our guest. Baraymal put a package on the table and told me to open it. He sat there grinning at me, barely able to sit still. I told him to come to my room and we darted off, leaving our tea to cool on the table.

Inside my room, we tore into the package. The uniforms inside were the brightest shades of color I had ever seen. They smelled like laundry did when it came off the line, but the colors were deeper, the folds crisper than anything I had ever seen. The T-shirts were green and the shorts red, and each was numbered in perfect black ink. We stared at them and then we each put a uniform on and walked into the living room, giddy with excitement but trying to act grown up. It was one of the few times in my life I recall feeling too overwhelmed to remember my manners and thank my mother. In the way of memories, it stands out as one of the last brilliant days in my childhood.

The sky began to spit rain in the evenings and the ground became too muddy for soccer. September fell into October and before we knew it the snow cover sank lower on the surrounding mountains and the end of 1979 was almost upon us. I did not understand then about friendship and how fragile it could be. There is a time in youth when you think friendship and loyalty are the very same thing. When you think the eyes of a girl tell the whole story and there will be time and more time still to learn the words. These things we believe in are dreams.

*

*

"Honor the guest, O son. Even though he be an infidel, open the
door."

- Afghan Proverb

*

7

~ ~ ~

THE HOSPITALITY OF THE KING

Before there was one kingdom, there were many. There are times in the history of each land where war is the rule that people live by. It was thus in the Kingdoms of Kabul Shahan. Each territory was sovereign, but also a part of the whole. When the invading armies marched forward to claim the land for themselves, the territories were forced to defend themselves. (I beg you to withhold your judgment. It is only the way of the world. It is how it has been done since time immemorial.) Throughout the history of this region, many empires fought for control because of its strategic placement along the major trade routes of South and Central Asia.

One of the Kingdoms of Kabul Shahan was approached at night by an invading army.

There was a great wall around the kingdom and the people within the wall fought bravely to keep the invaders out. Night after night and day after day, the invaders failed to breach the wall and enter the kingdom. Soon the Arab invaders ran out of food and their soldiers began to feel the effects of the prolonged fighting. The men began to grow weary and many among their number fell from exhaustion and hunger. Both sides stopped fighting during the night and saved their strength to fight during the day.

One night, the people of the kingdom sent food over the wall to the invaders. At first the Arab soldiers were suspicious of the generous offering, but they could not resist indulging in the restorative foods that were provided. They ate the kingdom's food and they were strengthened by it and during the day both sides continued to fight. This happened (day after day and night after night) until the leader of the invading army sent a messenger to the King. The messenger was to ask why the King continued to feed his enemy. He could not understand supporting an enemy in such a way, even if it benefitted his army.

The messenger returned and brought with him the following message, written in the hand of the King:

In our culture and tradition we love our guests and in the spirit of hospitality we give more to our guests than we keep for ourselves. Our past has shown us that you, like every other invader who has sought to breech our defenses, will leave this land sooner or later. We will defeat you as we have defeated many others so we know your stay is temporary and thus you are a guest in our homeland. We fight you during the day to show you a strength that will not succumb to any invader, but we feed you by night to show you our passion for our traditions, and these too make us strong. In every moment, even the most undesirable, we exercise the hospitality our ancestors taught us. History converges on these two points. We have never failed in either.

The leader of the invading army was astonished by the Kings message. He decided to leave the kingdom then and there and to return his army to their own homes. The physical strength of an army is one thing, but the strength of belief is an entirely unmatchable other.

*

8

~ ~ ~

THE RED ARMY INVASION

June - December 1979

It seems to me now that things changed overnight, but it could not have been so. Change had been on the horizon for those who dared to look so far. We were in the midst of a civil war at the time. The People's Democratic Party of Afghanistan had taken power but war had not touched my life in Micro Rayan as of yet.

Then I came home one day to find my mother furiously cleaning out the oven. When I came in she sank back on her knees and I could see that she had been crying.

"Mami, what's wrong?"

She stood and moved to the sink to ring out her towel. I had not ever seen her use such force with anything. She did not look at me.

"My cousin Majid was taken by the government today."

My mother went back onto her knees and disappeared once more up to the shoulders into the act of scrubbing out the oven.

That night at dinner my father said, "Have you spoken to your family?"

"They do not know where he's been taken. They don't know... They just don't know."

It was these disjointed comments that unnerved me more than the lengthy discussions they shared more frequently of late.

Not long after this we heard that Khessrau's father had also been taken.

"If you see Khessrau, tell him that he is welcome here anytime," my father said by way of consoling me.

The moment I heard the news, I ran outside and looked everywhere for Khessrau but could not find him.

Baraymal asked me what I was doing and I told him nothing.

I walked as far as I could to find a place to be alone. In a matter of days, I was playing soccer again just to forget that everything else in the world was unpredictable. I still shouted and laughed with my friends but there were those moments when I remembered that this life was not the same as that other life. It was not the same for Khessrau. It was not the same for Majid or for my mother.

After the disappearance of his father, Khessrau did not play soccer with us again.

In June, Ahmad Zahir was killed in a car crash. Later, the bullets in his body would confirm that Ahmad Zahir was killed under other circumstances for which the car crash was a mere cover-up. Even at the time of his death people whispered of the likelihood that that Zahir was assassinated, but it was not the type of thing spoken aloud in mixed company.

At the time of his death, my family and I were busy packing the contents of the only home I had ever known. My parents had been forced by a lack of substantial income and pressure from Dr. Najib, the head of Afghanistan intelligence agency, to rent our home out to a foreign family; one of thousands that came along with the invading army. My mother wanted to stay in spite of the financial burden, but my father clearly heard the veiled threat in Dr. Najib's suggestions that we leave.

On the day of the funeral, we went downtown where it seemed the entire population of Kabul had gathered for the remembrance of Zahir. From that moment he took on the role of a legend in the minds and hearts of Afghans. It seemed to me, in the way that children associate things, that from that moment the smiles fell permanently from the faces of the Afghan people. But for that moment—no more and no less—I felt closer to my community than I had in many months. I stood there, shoulder to shoulder with my fellow Afghans mourning one man who represented so many that would bleed mercilessly for their country.

The Russian's, when their troops arrived, said they occupied our land by invitation of Prime Minister Amin, who wanted support for the newly installed communist government of Afghanistan. Many of the Afghan people were not ready to relinquish their Muslim tradition.

The Russian's said it was not an invasion. But on December 27, those same men assassinated Hazifullah Amin who had been a pawn it seems, in a nation that was useful in putting a checkmate on the Cold War enemy.

It was early morning in the calm of a frigid December that there was a knock on our door. My mother, carrying a sleepy in her arms, opened the door. She invited my uncle inside. I was in the habit of waking early, but my older sisters were still sleeping in the next room. My uncle was quiet and his face showed signs of worry. He glanced at me and nodded and I saw from the look he gave my mother that he had troubling news. I tried to appear as uninterested as possible so that I would be permitted to listen. As it happened, my father came into the room at that moment and took the coat from my uncle, then led him to a seat at the table while my mother went to prepare tea and I was mostly ignored.

"I have just returned from the city center," he said, "where Russian soldiers and their tanks are securing each major crossing in the city. We have been invaded."

My mother was just returning from the kitchen at that time and met the eyes of her brother-in-law, then my father. Her face was captured suddenly by concern and I could tell by the silence from my father that he was thinking of the right thing to say. I dared not move in case they remembered I was there and sent me out of the room.

I was not allowed to leave the house alone for several days after that while our relatives came and went and drank tea and spoke of the news and I remained close, listening. They each made similar reports, but each offered a new detail and it was these details that captured my mind. They said the soldiers were young men, many as young as 16 years of age. I tried to listen for clues about how they looked, what they wore and carried, and what they did on the streets.

Even as a young boy, I could feel the tension around me.

The muffled voices of grown-ups from another room might as well have been the thunder of an approaching army. It is the excitement of change that captures the imaginations of children. I was no different. I was curious and could not wait to go into the city to see the men they spoke of.

Finally, I was permitted to go with my father into Kabul and for the first time I saw the soldiers walking in pairs down the streets of our familiar city. They wore heavy uniforms with sheepskin hats and thick jackets. They looked very much like the soldiers I had seen in Russian war movies that showed how the Russian's defeated Hitler or how the Bolshevik Revolution was started. They did not make eye contact with the people of Kabul, but walked past them, staring straight ahead. Although it was clear from the set of their shoulders and their confident steps that they were exactly aware of their surroundings.

Once the shock wore off, I understood from the attitudes of my parents and of the other residents of my city that these soldiers were not to be feared. My mother expressed sadness that they should be so young and having to perform such duties as they did in a country that was not their own. Feelings toward their leaders in Moscow were the opposite.

On the surface, things remained the same but with an undercurrent of fear and uncertainty. We still went to school but were told repeatedly by our parents to be careful about discussing the government and its new policies with anyone outside of the family. My mother continued to support the family by acting as midwife for relatives, friends and previous patients, though many of the communist patients she once cared for no longer sought her services.

I had not seen Baraymal since the snow came and went and came again. I did not understand why I could not go across the path to the entrance of his building and up the stairs to the apartment where he lived. I must have asked a dozen times, not understanding why I was forbidden from this small journey when I was still permitted to walk to school.

One night my father had started a fire in the electrical stove and I was sitting by it with my younger sisters, Mariam and Nazima while my mother brushed out Mariam's long hair. It was a treat to have electricity. Power for the city was generated at Soroobi Dam and freedom fighters often set explosions there in an attempt to cripple the city. Other times, the power was shut off by the government to save energy for the Russian, government, and military entities. We usually spent nights under candlelight doing our homework or reading magazines.

On that particular night, Flora and Friba were still doing their homework in the next room and there was a knock at the door. My father folded his newspaper and stood to answer it. I could not see around the wall that divided the room from the entrance to our apartment, but I heard my father's voice and that of another man. He returned and stood in the doorway, leaning against it like he was exhausted and ran a hand through his hair that was beginning to gray.

"It's Dr. Najib's youngest brother Roshan Ahmad Zai," he said to my mother, "Mrs. Kokai Sangar is in need of you."

Mrs. Kokai Sangar was the sister of Dr. Najib and was my mom's patient as they lived in the same apartment block that we lived in. Her youngest brother, Roshan Ahmad Zai was 2 or 3 years older than me, but we did not spend much time together except during the occasional soccer match.

"Tell him to call the doctor. I will be there as soon as I gather my things."

Before the communists took power Kokai was a regular patient; however, my mom had requested to deliver her baby while her private family doctor was present in another room. Mrs. Sangar's family tradition did not allow her to be treated by a male doctor. Their private doctor, Dr. Zahir, was introduced after the communists took over the government. My mom told them even before the baby came that the situation was different and that she did not want to take the risk to treat Kokai alone while her brother, Dr. Najib, was the head of Afghanistan's intelligence service agency called KHAD.

My mother ran the brush through Mariam's hair one last time and stood, handing the brush to Mariam so she could struggle with Nazima's curls. On impulse I stood and ran between my mother and father to the front door to see if Roshan was still there. He was not and the doorway was empty except for my father. I leaned out and saw the back of Roshan as he walked down the hallway, his shoulders hunched as he prepared to walk back outside in the storm.

From behind me my mother put her hands on my shoulders to move me back inside. She wrapped her heaviest wool shawl around her and even though she was needed elsewhere, she put her hand under my chin and I raised my eyes to meet hers.

"There is no right or wrong as long as you act with the intention of helping rather than hurting," she said. I do not know if she said this for my benefit or for hers. She pulled the veil over her face, and when she left I returned to the scene almost as I had left it: my father was reading the news, Flora and Friba were whispering over their homework and Mariam and Nazima had left off with the hair-brush and taken up a pair of dolls. My father looked up at me and I knew that he had not truly been reading because his glasses were still on.

Most of the time in those days, I could not understand the cryptic way my parents were speaking. I could not understand why my aunts and uncles would come over and bring our cousins and then leave us all to play and still look so serious when they left. I did not know why Kokai Sangar had been delivered of a new baby and yet we had not visited the Najib home bringing food and gifts to celebrate. I kept asking my father if we were in danger and he said we were not, but I saw that he was not telling the whole truth.

One morning in January, I woke early and found my father alone in the kitchen. He had taken several bites out of two-day-old *naan* and was pouring tea into a cup. He looked surprised to see me up so early as the sun had not yet broken through the dark. I sat at the table with him and he silently handed me some *naan*.

"Something is worrying you?" he asked.

"Can I still play soccer after the winter is over?"

"Yes."

I was quiet while I picked at the *naan*, not really hungry but thankful for something to keep my eyes and hands busy.

"Is there something more?"

"Friba says we will have to leave. She says we cannot live here anymore."

My father sighed. In the early dawn without his glasses on and with his hair not yet smoothed he looked much younger than I thought him to be.

"Abdul," he said, smoothing his mustache with his fingers, "We do not know what will happen, but in that way it is no different than any other day." My father was a soft-spoken but confident man whose voice was rarely raised in anger. Likewise I had not often heard him sound concerned or unsure about anything before, and so I was more frightened by his words than I let on.

We sat there some time longer and I accepted the tea he offered me, wishing to prolong the moment I got to share with him. I felt, not for the first time in recent months, as a young man rather than a child. I felt my father look at me occasionally and perhaps he understood this, for he began to speak again.

"Do you understand what is happening?"

"Mostly," I shrugged, not wishing to appear ignorant to him.

"You understand then that the government is changing and therefore the way we live must change. Many people do not want to change the way we live."

I nodded in agreement, thinking we were one of this group of people.

"I don't want to change," I offered.

He shook his head, "The way we live must change if there is to be progress. If we are to uphold human rights and have freedom for all people, it is necessary to change. But fighting is not the way to freedom. It is difficult to fight against the government and the mujahideen are taking up arms against the Soviets, to fight against the Communist government. Any time the hand of a nation is forced, the rebels will become desperate. The Russian's call them terrorists; the Muslim countries and the western world call them freedom-fighters. They are not one or the other but they are both of these things. The danger of war is that both sides believe their way is the only way and with this type of thinking there can be no progress. There can only be loss. And those who do not lose from one moment to the next will only grow stronger and become more convinced of their superiority until it becomes impossible to tell anymore where the truth and goodness is in their belief."

"Why am I not allowed to go to Baraymal's house?"

My father looked down at the table, as if he hoped I would not ask this.

"Because his father is becoming a Foreign Minister under the new regime."

"But everything is okay as long as they know we are not against them."

"No. We are not against them, but we are not with them either. A war tries to force everyone to take sides. A fighter must know his enemy if he is to fight. In war there is no balance; there are only extremes. If you do not believe in either, then both sides believe you are the enemy."

When my father left I went back to my room to watch the sunlight fill in the gaps in the sky. The gaps in my understanding were not so easily vanquished. I kept thinking, *But we are right! If we do not join the sides that hurt each other then we are right!* I thought too about what my father said; that there is danger in believing too much in your rightness. And what my mother said about helping more than hurting and I became even more uncertain about what I thought I knew.

With the spring came the thawing of the ground and the children of our neighborhood began to enjoy time spent outdoors once more.

Baraymal and I, while still in the same class, had gotten over the initial uncertainty relating to political changes and once more felt our friendship grow as we planned our soccer team. But it was not the same. I had been told by my mother, my father, my older sisters, aunts, and uncles to never speak of the war or the government among any of the children I played with. It seemed Baraymal was told the same, because it often felt that there was another party to our conversations that neither of us could hear, but that constantly interrupted and left us with nothing to say. I imagine it was the voices of our families and while this made me feel that we had something in common, it was not enough to fill the sudden void in our friendship.

Life became easier when we had soccer again. We held games and tournaments and laughed and shouted, but there was the obvious absence of many of our friends. Even the neighbor's dog no longer ran around us, barking at our heels as we played. Some weeks we would notice another friend was gone. None of us would say anything, trained as we were to ignore the obvious division of lines, but I would go home and ask my parents about Fahim, who lived next door or Jawid in the next building only to have them tell me that my friend's family had left. This always caused them to exchange glances and I was beginning to understand that "leaving" meant more than just moving away. It meant the thing that my parents tried not to say in front of us; it meant *escaping*.

In the evenings my mother moved through the apartment, closing windows and pulling the curtains. Her and my father would put on earphones and listen to BBC radio in Farsi, whose news reports detailed the victories and defeats of various factions fighting in remote areas of our country. We children sat nearby as though we too could hear the reports that were for their ears only. I watched the faces of my parents and waited for them to give us the diluted version of events. With our parents otherwise occupied, Flora and Friba would discuss the friends that they had lost and in whispers they would keep tabs of who had mentioned that they might be leaving. My parents—had they heard that my sisters were having such discussions with friends—would have been angry, but I said nothing. I only listened to them and wished I had a way of knowing who would be gone next.

During the summer, there was more tension in our house and my mother and father were often found in conversation with each other, sometimes looking upset, and sometimes looking tired. Mariam and Nazima clung to my mother more often and

Flora and Friba clung to each other. As usual, I turned to my older sisters who were better able to decipher the conversations between my parents. I was fortunate in that they were more willing than usual to accept me as their confidant being that they too were trying to muddle through the mixed messages they got from nearly everyone.

"Mami just doesn't have the work anymore. All of the old families are moving out and all of the new families are Communists. They already have midwives or doctors that they have used before and nobody asks for mother anymore."

"We can't go on living here, Baba says."

"Where will we go?" I asked.

"They don't know yet. Everyone else is leaving the country," said Friba, "I don't know why we don't escape too and live in some beautiful country where they aren't fighting all the time."

Flora, who had recently turned seventeen, felt herself to be quite worldly and chastised Friba, "You can't think that way, Friba. People get killed when they try to escape. You have to think that it would be better if things only returned to the way they were."

"I don't have to think any which way. Mother and Papa said I can think however I want to."

For weeks I thought about ways to make money to help my parents. A few of my friends and I would still go to the Cinema once in a while and as we passed through the busy streets of Kabul I would walk more slowly, looking at the busy vendors on the side of the road and brainstorming business ideas. I tried to enjoy the movies as I once did, but the movies that seemed so sublime before now seemed to be breathing the communist political agenda down my neck.

On the streets it was impossible to ignore the increase in military presence. Banners were hung to thank the Russians for their international responsibility. Russian and Afghan soldiers carried their guns in plain sight and stood at their posts on the street corners. Russian Humvees moved thunderously down the streets alongside bicyclists and the shrouded women selling hand-woven *burquas* and sundries. Young boys were climbing on a stationary tank and the soldiers were trying to keep them off. Older boys were negotiating with soldiers in the shade of a building, selling their cigarettes or trading Hashish for Vodka.

Over the din of the street we could hear the occasional helicopter. Dust rose off of the ground, and looking over it all stood the majestic Hindu Kush Mountains, as fearful and remote as Allah himself.

*

9

~ ~ ~

NOMADIC LIFE

As winter turned to spring, we packed our belongings and moved from the home I grew up in, in Micro Rayan.

Our new home in Taimani was close to that of our aunt and uncle, my father's brother. We rented a three bedroom home and lived together there with the owner, who had at one time worked with my mother at Maiwand Hospital. The owner lived on the second floor of the house with her son Fraidoon who was my age. The backyard was nicely decorated and planted with roses. A large *sofha* was built onto the house and on it were a large handmade red carpet with traditional Afghan mattresses and pillows strewn across it for comfort. Our two families would sit there in the evenings drinking tea with *noqul*. From this deck rose a flight of stairs that led to a separate entrance to the second floor apartment where Fraidoon and his family lived.

Fraidoon and I became fast friends. We walked to and from school together and on my first day there, he showed me around the Taimani school building that was older than any school in Micro Rayan. The building was the old house of a foreign minister. There weren't enough chairs in the classrooms and most of the ones there were broken. The classrooms were without doors and many of the windows were without glass. There was no sewage system so a separate outhouse served as the bathroom for the entire school. There was no door on the outhouse either and only a blanket hanging over the entrance served to protect the privacy of those within. I recall the sound of a dry, hot wind making those blankets flap like flightless birds.

I noticed almost immediately that there were no girls in this new school, unlike the school in Micro Rayan where half of our class had been girls. Fraidoon smiled at this. He told me there were three girls in the entire school. They were, it turns out, hard to miss. The girls were always together, trying to ignore the teasing of the boys. They did not play at recess and I felt bad for them. One morning during a break I bought popcorn from the school kiosk and ate some of it, then took the rest over to share with the girls. They ducked their heads and walked away quickly without even thinking twice about taking what I offered.

With the exception of the girls, I made friends quickly. I began spending time after school with a boy my age named Hamed who lived on a small hill in the middle of the city. Hamed was new to the school as I was and so we quickly sought each other's company. The hill that he lived on was used mostly as a cemetery but several houses also lined the hillside. On top of the hill there was a small Russian military base that patrolled the neighboring communities; it reminded us of stories from centuries ago where the same hilltop was used by Kabulis to defend one of Kabul's many kingdoms from the enemies. It was a poor neighborhood because electricity posts reached only to the lower end of the hill and it was difficult to carry water up the hill. In the winter, the narrow paths upward became muddy and slippery. I, however, enjoyed going there and spending time with Hamed. I stayed sometimes overnight and we would sit at the top of the hill and look out over the city.

Sometimes there were lights glowing in certain parts of the city but for the most part the electricity was turned off by the government and the city of Kabul looked dark from the top of the hill. In spite of everything, there was something magical about that spot. It was a quiet, peaceful place.

In Taimani, I lost interest in soccer as did most of the boys. In school we were asked to join the Youth Democratic Organization and learned the words *democracy, communism,* and *socialism,* and were instructed in the details of the Lenin

Revolution in addition to our regular curriculum. I had all but forgotten the long-haired girl who so captivated my attention when I was but a boy.

I began noticing another young girl who spent time occasionally with my sisters and she quickly became my reason for tolerating every other change in my world. She was the only Afghan girl I had ever seen with green eyes and I somehow interpreted their gaze and an occasional chance meeting with this girl as a sign of hope. She was younger than me, I knew, but I could not shake the thought of her and each time we accidentally met in the streets of Kabul, she would smile a little and pass me by without a word, lending significance to the day that I had not known before. I found myself daydreaming of her often and the distraction helped quench the tedium of our Russian education. After school, my friends and I studied quietly and did not talk about politics in any way other than what we learned in school.

One afternoon I was at Hamed's house after school studying science for our midterm exams. I saw an old book lying in the corner of his room. I recognized it as I had seen it on the shelves in the stores I passed by and on the streets downtown where young boys were peddling books and other items to earn money to support their families. When Hamed left the room to get some tea for us, I picked up the book. Translated in Farsi on the bottom of its front cover were the words, '*A Novel by Jack London.*' I still had the book in my hand when Hamed returned. He poured black tea for us.

"I just finished reading that one," he said, "I have to return it today or I will have to pay a fine. Have you read it yet?"

"I have never read a novel."

"If you go with me when I return it you can check it out right after me."

We finished our studies and I could hardly wait to be done. We walked to the book store and inside I felt like I had earned a great privilege. I paid 10 Afghani and leased Jack

London's *Mutiny of the Elsinore*, for a week. Hamed and I parted ways outside of the store and I opened the book as I walked home and began to devour the words. I was so engrossed in the action of the story that I had nearly finished a quarter of it by the time I arrived home.

All that night I read, completely transported to the raging seas, toiling with the mutinous crew of the Elsinore. I finished the book that night and as soon as I was dismissed from school the following day, I ran to the book store where I exchanged it for another novel and walked home, once again completely transfixed.

From that day on, Hamed and I spent hours together on the hill by his home reading and talking about novels. Perhaps it was because of this that I grew to trust Hamed more than I had the luxury of trusting my other classmates. Perhaps it was because he introduced me to another world that I temporarily lost my focus on ours.

"I don't know why he was so proud to have blue eyes and blond skin," I said referring to the narrator in *The Mutiny of the Elsinore*.

Hamed looked at me, startled.

"Not that there's anything wrong with it," I covered, "I just didn't understand."

"Wouldn't you want to have blue eyes and blond skin if you were him? Sometimes I think it's almost as bad for us as it was for those slaves on that ship."

I smiled and Hamed smiled back. We were both relieved. After that we talked often about the politics of what was happening in our country. Those things that we heard from our parents or from news programs that we did not understand we would ask each other about. He would tell me what his mother had said and I would share some news I had heard from BBC radio since his family did not have access to it in their home. Our friendship was forged out of mutual trust. It was a relief to be able to talk to someone who understood what it felt like to lie each day and who was not afraid to talk honestly about what was happening around us.

It was tiring to pretend all day in school to be in support of the communist regime; to wonder if other's thought as my family did, and to worry about making a slip that would give away our political views. We could not let our guard down around our classmates but on the hill Hamed and I had no limits to the things we might talk about.

It was a time of living with ghosts and shadows. All around us people were disappearing in the middle of the night never to be seen again. And in the hills and mountains the mujahideen were expanding in number and the actions they committed in the name of religion became more and more indicative of the growing unrest in our country. Every day we heard that someone we knew had escaped and every day the realities of war slipped further into cracks in our world while truth slipped farther and farther away.

Then came the day when life as I knew it came to an end. My mother was pulling the curtains over the windows as the last light of day drained from the sky. Instead of turning the radio on as she usually did, my mother sat down at the table and she and my father held each other's hand. My sisters and I were sitting around the table.

"Your father and I have made a decision. We wish to leave the country and make a home for our family where there is no fighting. Our home is no longer safe and our friends and loved ones are fleeing the country every day. We must get out now before there is nothing left for us here at all."

Friba gasped and covered her mouth with her hand. My father had tears in his eyes and I did not understand. It sounded like good news, but there was clearly something wrong.

"I have gotten documents for myself and for Friba, and Abdul," my mother said, "We will find a place to live and I will return for your father and for Flora, Mariam and Nazima in a few months' time."

Friba started crying and my father wiped at his eyes.

"Why do they have to stay?" Friba asked.

"We just don't have the money necessary to support all of us at this time," once again it was the matter-of-factness that was terrible. "It isn't what we want, but it is what we have to do."

My mother stood then, smoothing her skirt and moving with purpose. She turned on the radio and her and father put their headphones on and no more was said on the subject then.

After school the next day I went up the hill with Hamed and I told him that I would be leaving the country. He nodded like he knew it was inevitable and then he opened his book and started reading. We spent the rest of the afternoon that way. Sometimes escape is the only answer.

I had to tell Fraidoon that I was leaving as well and he asked me hundreds of questions over the coming days.

"I wish I could go," he said and for the first time I understood that I was not to be pitied for having to leave my home, my country.

I didn't know it then, but we were fortunate. My mother obtained visas for us before the ban was placed on obtaining documents. We had an opportunity that many did not. We did not have to flee in secret at the peril of our own lives as so many did.

I told no one but Fraidoon and Hamed when my final day in Afghanistan arrived.

I walked up the hill with Hamed and when he heard that the end had finally come to our acquaintance we hugged each other and said good-bye with our eyes full of tears, swearing that friendship would not go the way of world. I told him I would not forget him and that I would write to him often. That night my mother and Friba and I said our good-byes to Fraidoon and his parents. We had a long dinner together on the *sofha* and the smell of roses was stronger that night than any other I could recall.

It was the smell of roses that drifted into my room and stained my dreams red. It was the smell of roses that hung about us as my family was divided the next morning. It was the smell of roses that clung to my nose for days, for years to come, so that I could not ever smell a rose without thinking of my father's arms around me, of the feel of him trembling as he sent his only son away, or off kissing my sister's cheeks, still warm with sleep.

It was the scent that reminded me of squeezing Friba's hand as we boarded the plane; of Kabul vanishing below us as the sun came up and painted her gold and I wanted to cry, "Wait!" because from that perspective it looked like it was all a mistake. Like maybe the night had erased the war and even the minds and hearts of men so that they changed with the light, and grew brave enough to just forgive.

We first arrived in Tehran, Iran and found an affordable hotel. The first night I woke to the sound of my mother's tears. She did not know I heard. I never saw her cry, only heard her in the night after she thought I had gone to sleep.

After a few days in Tehran it became obvious that the stability and freedom we sought was not to be had there. To my mother, who had spent years living in Shasawar, on the Caspian Sea and visited Tehran on holiday, the changes that had taken place in Iran did little justice to her memories of the place. We travelled through Iran's green cities including Aamel, Babol, Mazendaran and saw the bright light of the capital city that lured the tourists in. I too felt the lure of the city like a bright star in the night. But we did not stay long in any place.

After catching several buses from various cities and travelling through villages and deserts, I began to wonder if any place would be appropriate for us or if we would just keep travelling until we doubled back on our path. My mother was restless; on alert. She looked at her surroundings with a critical eye and I when I could not resist asking questions about our destination. She would tell me it was none of my concern and that I would be taken care of.

Friba became dreamy on the trip and would make up stories about the other passengers on the bus to pass the time. We were nearly to Turkey when the bus stopped to refill and two Afghan business men boarded. They saw us immediately as we were the only Afghans on the bus, and sat near us. It was not long before they were talking with my mother. She told them our story and the three of them did not stop talking until the bus once again pulled to a stop. I was tired and began to fall asleep in my seat but Friba pulled me by the hand and before I knew it we were walking toward the city where we would rest for the night.

The next morning my mother was up early and I woke to the sound of her repacking our bags. She led us into the marketplace downtown and Friba and I followed close behind, not understanding why we were there, but convinced by our mother's resoluteness and her hurried pace that it was not our place to know. She bought several pairs of jeans and bags of coffee and then we walked a long ways from the city to the bus stop where we started from. Friba and I kept asking her what she was doing but she did not have the energy to explain. We knew better than to press her.

We caught another bus in the same direction from which we had come the night before. After a short ride, we departed the bus and my mother told us to wait on the bench where we were. We saw her walk to a shop and we recognized the two business men from the bus the day before coming out to greet her. One man lit a cigarette and my mother gave them the goods she had bought at the market and brought the rest back with her to where we sat. When she came back to us she was smiling for the first time in weeks and she put her arms around us as we waited for the next bus.

Friba leaned her head on mother's shoulder and asked her what had happened.

"They had business here," mother said, "And did not have time to get into the city to get the items they needed for their work. Because they asked us for help I now have enough money to take us further on our journey. We will be in Istanbul by the setting of the sun."

I learned later, when my mother had time to rest and tell us the story, that the young Afghan men who got on the bus were Afghan immigrants who had escaped Afghanistan only recently. In order to support themselves and their families, they went into trade and business. They kept traveling from one city to another and from one country to another selling food, clothing, electronics and other items. The Afghan businessmen found out that my mother was trying to care for my sister and I on a small budget and recommended to her that she purchase jeans and coffee from Iran and sell them at twice the price in Istanbul. They had been doing this for months and knew how hard it was to live in a foreign country without assistance. My mother purchased just enough to cross the border without paying an additional custom tax.

As we approached the city of Istanbul, the sun was indeed setting and the mosques that rose from the hills around the city glowed orange against the green hills they seemed to have sprouted from. When we passed the water, the last of the sunlight lingered there too, as if following us on our journey. From our hotel room we had a view of an alleyway and through a space between two buildings I could just see the lights of the bridge that passed over the strait.

For weeks we lived out of the hotel in Istanbul that we landed in that first night. I could not get enough of the sights and sounds of the bustling metropolis around us. It was the largest city I had ever seen and it reminded me of the history lessons I'd participated in at school. I had learned about and memorized the works of Mawlana Jalaluddin Balkhi Rumi, the philosopher and poet who was born in the ancient city of Balkh in Afghanistan and then immigrated through Iran to Turkey where he spent the rest of his life.

From our hotel we could walk to the Black Sea and I would sit there many afternoons listening to the sound of bells and the noisy chatter of birds feeling that I might have gone back in time and feeling as though one could not live in such a place as this without harboring a soul full of poetry and a mind full of philosophy.

My mother was gone often, first in selling her jeans and coffee and then in trying to make acquaintances and secure a job. She often came home discouraged and frustrated because she could not speak the Turkish language. She was always sore and tired and did not speak to Friba and me much although she did not let us want for anything. When she was not out looking for work, she was writing letters to her numerous acquaintances outside of Afghanistan hoping that someone might say something to help guide her on her path. At last she received a reply from Dr. Rahim Nevin who ran the clinic where my mother once worked. He had resided in Germany since fleeing Afghanistan not long since.

After a few weeks of preparation, we left Istanbul and I'm afraid I left it sadly. It had been the highlight of our adventure up to that point and I had at last discovered something of the beauty of the world; of the possibility the world contained of being both magnificent and magnanimous. I could not fathom the depth of history that made places come alive. One could not be a moment in Istanbul without understanding that it is not a place but a living thing. I was sorry to leave her.

When we arrived in Austria we were greeted by a close friend of Dr. Nevin; a Mr. Malikyar who was a taller man than any I had ever seen. In the cab back to a hotel he told us that he had lived in Austria for over 20 years. His brother, once a finance minister, had been jailed in Afghanistan for trying to overthrow King Zahir and his own life had been threatened by association.

Mr. Malikyar seemed a gentle man and he looked out the window at his adopted country fondly. He was solicitous, too, of our comfort. We secured a hotel room in Wien. The wife of Mr. Malikyar arrived later and greeted us warmly. My mother visibly relaxed in the company of another woman, especially one who spoke her native dialect. The hotel sat on a rise that looked out over rolling green countryside and distant mountains. The whole expanse was unbreakably blue with white clouds drifting occasionally by. There was a balcony on which we sat while lunch and tea were served and we all talked for many hours about our experiences and about mutual acquaintances from our native Kabul, including Dr. Nevin. The cool breeze and the delicious food were enough to make Friba so drowsy that she fell asleep sitting up in her chair. I wanted to snicker, remembering how hard she yanked on my hand when I began to drowse on the bus, but I did not want to appear disrespectful so I covered my mouth with my hand to smother the laugh. Friba was embarrassed later, but in that moment it was a testament to the comfortable atmosphere and nobody minded. The trees around the hotel caught the breeze and shook it, making a sound like rushing water.

Professor Nevin called us from Germany and told my mother stories of the Afghan families living in Frankfurt. He made it sound so inviting that my mother was easily convinced that it would be a suitable final destination. I could not believe that after so much time we were to at last travelling to the place that would become our home.

*

10

~ ~ ~

JOURNEY WITHOUT AN END

We boarded a plane and flew to Frankfurt, requesting political asylum once we arrived. After a few days in a hotel in downtown Frankfurt, paid for by the German immigration office, we were transported in a mini-bus to a temporary asylum community center. We drove for hours through green hills and dozens of villages whose lights twinkled as we travelled into the night. On the bus with us were three other Afghan families whose situations were comparable to our own. All were quiet, having come to the end of a long journey.

When we disembarked from the bus, there were sudden shouts of my mother's name. Many of the Afghan families in the community center had been told of the pending arrival of recent Afghan immigrants and had waited for the bus to arrive. Before we could even retrieve our bags, my mother was hugging and kissing the women who had called her name.

Through the commotion, we finally secured our things from the driver and the bus left. As it did so, there were tears as families gathered around and Friba and I were introduced.

I recognized some of the women as they had worked with my mother at Maiwand Hospital. Others I could not remember though they recognized Friba and me.

It was exhilarating and tiring both to find at last that we were not alone, even so far from home. It had felt for a long while that we were unmoored ships bobbing about on the current, having left a home behind us and not knowing where we might end up. I knew by the look on my mother's face—having at last found something to connect her to the family she had left behind in Kabul—that we would not leave this place. We stayed in the camp for several weeks and I slept better there than I had in the rich decadence of Istanbul or the drowsy comfort of Wien. It was not long before other buses arrived carrying other families and we were waiting with the familiar pack in hopes that we might set eyes once more on a face from the past.

As time went on, we could not wait to get out of the center and finally experience life in Germany. We had heard about it back in Kabul through discreet communications from other's who had escaped. My sister had almost immediately met with a friend from school upon our arrival; one of many who had suddenly disappeared from her life. It was a time of hope and friendship for all of us, but sometimes I would wake up in the middle of the night to use the restroom and I would still hear the quiet noises of my mother as she cried.

At last we were given preference as to where we would like to live and my mother only requested that we be somewhere near the family of Professor Nevin, who was the reason we had come so far in the first place. We were driven to Luenen, a small village outside of Dortmund, and were assigned to an apartment with two other families. One was a single woman who my mother knew from working in the hospital, and the other was an old couple who were from the former King Zahir family tribe. The husband had been a pilot in Afghanistan who once flew the King's plane and proudly told us of both the dangers and the rewards of his position.

The apartment we lived in had three rooms—one for each family—and was not much different than the apartment we had lived in in Micro Rayan. The only difference was that we had to carry coal from the basement of the Luenen apartment complex in winter to keep the apartment warm.

I, too, began to settle into our new situation and discover friendship. Our nearest neighbor was an Afghan boy my age named Wahid Wahab who was in my class at school along with students from numerous other countries. There was freedom in that, in studying alongside students with diverse backgrounds who were oppressed elsewhere but who had a chance here to have a completely different future than the one awaiting them in their homeland.

At first it was exciting being in this new country. Without ever having attended 7th or 8th grade, I and Wahid were soon accepted into the 9th grade after passing German language classes and basic math tests. In my 9th grade class I met Fatih Afsin and Alois Grunert who introduced me to Thomas Hoeltman and Reinhard Hahn and several other boys who played together on a soccer team after school. I was quickly accepted into their ranks and was eager to once again play the game from my childhood that had been the foundation of so many friendships.

I had the good fortune to meet teachers, such as Herr Thomas and Frau Bartram, who were not just teachers of curriculum, but who became friends and teachers in life lessons. They taught me to be patient when involved in a struggle and to believe in myself when it seems there is little to believe in. They taught me to reach out to those in need and to focus on what I believe in to make it happen. They taught me there is grace in forgiveness and this, more than anything else, I have carried with me always.

After a year of playing soccer with my friends after school, I joined the local city soccer team, FC Luenen 74 where I met my soccer trainer, Herr Krause and many other friends. We trained four days a week and played games once per week until, in 1982 after decades of losses, we became regional champions.

When I wasn't playing soccer we were spending time at the Youth Club Center close to the school where we played foosball, table tennis, billiards, and sometimes danced to Michael Jackson's newest hits at the Youth Dance Club. It was there that I met Petra who was tall and beautiful and danced as if no one was watching her.

During the summer months I went on field trips with the other youths my age and visited the North Sea, Denmark, and Zwolle in Holland. I had the opportunity to see much of the country and to appreciate Germany's beauty. But it was the people who made Germany a haven for me. After my first year there I could not walk down the street without seeing someone I knew and stopping to talk with them. My confidence grew as I began to feel more and more at home. I felt that I could be and do anything here and success would not follow far behind. I even flirted with Petra and, what's more, she flirted with me.

By that time, Friba had gotten married and my mother returned to Afghanistan to help the rest of our family get out of the country safely. The situation had only worsened in Kabul and my father and sisters were not able to leave as planned. I was 15 years old and living alone in a new apartment above a Greek restaurant. Friba visited me once a week and I received regular letters from my father who still felt the need to direct my life over the great distance between us. He told me to quit swimming because it was dangerous and he did not want me to ride my bike through the streets of Luenen. I responded to his letters with details about my friends and about the trips I went on with the school. I wrote him of my progress and sent pictures when I could. I left out the details about the swimming competitions I had won and continued to compete in or that I rode my bike to and from school each day through the heart of Luenen. I did not want him to worry when I was so certain of my own safety.

Through all of this I could not shake off the loneliness. I thought so often about Hamed and Fraidoon and the friends I had left behind that I dreamed about them almost nightly. I thought often about a girl with green eyes who smiled at me each time we passed and never said a word.

I went to sleep one night and dreamed I was walking to the old school in Taimani. I dreamt I kicked a rock and watched it tumble over the dirt and when I raised my eyes, she was there.

She was waiting for me and I was conscious that I was no longer a boy, kicking rocks. I walked toward her and toward the beautiful smile she offered, wanting nothing more than to start a conversation with her.

You're beautiful, I said.

She laughed and turned, running away from me and looking back over her shoulder as she moved farther and farther away.

I chased after her and she laughed as the thin, white scarf of her school uniform blew behind her like wings and her hair trailed freely in the wind. When she stopped I came up behind her, nearly running into her and I saw that she was staring out at the distance ahead of us.

From where we stood on the edge of a hill I could see as far as Istanbul. I could see across oceans and the oceans were dotted with islands and each one was a world unto itself. I was so distracted by the enormity of it that I did not realize the girl had vanished from my side. It was always where I lost her in the dream. At the point where I saw the world for what it was.

*

*

"As for the rest--the weaklings and the rejected, and the dark-pigmented things, the half-castes, the mongrel-bloods, and the dregs of long-conquered races--how could they count? My heels were iron as I gazed on them in their peril and weakness. Lord! Lord! For ten thousand generations and centuries we had stamped upon their faces and enslaved them to the toil of our will." ... Jack London, from *Mutiny of the Elsinore*

*

11

~ ~ ~

OF CRADLES AND COFFINS

Momena walked home quickly, worried by the darkness. She passed at last under the sign that hung over the door and slipped inside. Her husband waited there, one of their daughters asleep on the sofa.

"She had a hard time going to sleep," he explained in a whisper, "another nightmare."

He stood and helped his wife remove her shawl, hanging it on the hook by the door. The distant sound of explosions reverberated against the walls.

"I can warm some tea," he said but she shook her head.

"I have to go back early. I needed some supplies."

In the morning, Shokour was up early but Momena was already in the kitchen trying to muffle the noises she made as she gathered towels and boiled water for tea. She unwrapped some *naan* and shared it with her husband.

"Go," he said, "I will open the shop late."

Momena hurried to gather the medicines she required and wrapped them in the towels. She placed all of the items in a bag and left the house. It was a gray morning, but the light of day made her less uneasy. She watched for a cab as she walked and two passed by before a third stopped at her signal. She directed the driver to Qalahe Zaman Khan where the clinic was.

On several occasions, Momena had been offered jobs working for the main hospitals in Kabul. Many professionals who had the means to flee their faltering country had already done so and the government tried to recruit those that were left. Joining their ranks meant that she would have to join the People's

Democratic Party and throw her support in for the communists. Instead, she remained working for the small clinic on the outskirts of Kabul, where she mostly treated patients who were in some way tied to anti-government entities or the mujahideen. When she arrived at the clinic she told the driver to wait while she ran inside to gather more tools and disinfectant.

Eventually the cab pulled up at the mouth of a dirt road and Momena exited the vehicle. She hiked along the road that led to a small village. Most of the scattered houses did not have windows or doors. She announced herself and entered one of them. An old woman came and gripped her arm, making her load heavy to carry. One of the young men standing beside the bed came and took the bag from Momena. She smiled, grateful.

"What has happened?" she asked and the old woman who clung to her began to cry and seemed to be unable to decide if she should continue hanging onto and thanking the doctor, or hold the cold towel on her daughter-in-law's forehead.

"It continued all through the night. She only began to sleep this morning, but the light came through the windows and woke her."

Momena nodded and the old woman continued crooning over her, "Bless you doctor."

The young girl on the bed moaned.

Momena spoke to her gently and told her that she would check her now. The man who stood watch beside the bed hung his head and ducked outside into the morning as the sun came and went behind the clouds. The old woman gripped her daughter's hand and rubbed it between her two leathery palms.

"She is almost ready," Momena said as she gently probed the young girl. She patted her on the knee and nodded to the old woman. She began sorting out the towels and assorted tools for the delivery of the baby. She used the disinfectant liberally and laid the things out on a clean towel. When she was finished, she slipped outside to where the young man stood leaning against the house smoking a cigarette.

"I brought some things," she said to him.

"I don't know how to thank you."

"There is no need to. Her husband deserves to see his first child. By God's grace they will both live long enough to see the child grow."

"What do I do for him?"

"I will write it down for you. Using the medications is simple, but you must also know how to disinfect and use the bandages. Too many wounds become infected out there in the mountains without proper care."

"My brother and I..."

"You do not need to explain. I know he cannot come here. I know it is also a risk for you to do so."

"Thank you, Doctor."

"I am not a doctor. I am a midwife."

"You are a savior."

Momena returned to the waiting women.

The girl moaned as waves of pain rocked her. After several hours of this, the baby was delivered and he had a healthy cry. Momena staunched the bleeding and murmured softly to the young girl while her mother-in-law looked on, helpless.

"She will be fine," Momena said when she was done and began to clear away the soiled sheets and towels. The feeling of relief she got every time it was over echoed in the long, expansive sigh of the old woman.

The man who had been holding the baby, swaddled in towels, hung back against the wall looking uncomfortable. He willingly handed the baby over to Momena who washed him and wrapped him in a blanket, placing him in the arms of his mother.

"Thank you," the woman whispered as she gazed at her child.

The woman was drowsy and she began to nod her head under waves of sleepiness as the new grandmother lifted the infant from her arms. As she did so, the young mother jerked awake at the disturbance of the child and pulled him close. Realizing it was only her mother-in-law taking the child; she relinquished her son and fell asleep.

When Momena returned home in the evening, her husband was there again after a long day of tending his store. Their two daughters were playing in the next room. Her husband's arms went around her.

"Sometimes I don't know if it's the right thing."

"If any of us knew what the right thing was, we wouldn't be in this situation."

"I worry for Abdul. I worry that he will come back here, with the things he has been writing in his letters. I think of the men out there fighting and it is so easy to separate them from their beliefs and their actions when I think of them as someone's sons. They are just boys. If Abdul were here, it might have been him."

"We are fortunate. And those boys who fight and die on the mountains are fortunate to have you as well."

"They fight but they are taught to kill too. The leaders of these militia are no better at times than the others. Who knows but that they might not end up being the most dangerous ones of all."

Mariam and Nazima ran into the room to hug their mother. She hugged them in turn and sent them back to their studies.

"I will write him a letter tonight," Momena said to her husband when the girls had left. "I will tell him in every way I can that he must not return. I delivered a baby today. The old woman who called me yesterday had three sons. One of them was killed by the Russian's and the other two went to fight with the mujahideen. I watched this woman—this mother who was so much older than her years—find out that she may be near to losing another son at the same time that she watched her grandson being born. I can't imagine such extremes of hope and despair. Our country is becoming a wasteland of dreams, but we can still look at a newborn child and believe that it will somehow be different for them in this world. There is something of God in that isn't there?"

"I should say so," Shokour said and smiled as he watched his wife. She deftly moved through the kitchen, preparing their dinner. She stood tall and proud and her husband could not believe for a second that there was anything in this world she could not bend to her will

*

12

~ ~ ~

INTO THE COLD WAR

Thinking about Kabul made me grow sick with sorrow.

As much as I loved my life in Germany, I missed being around people who understood my language, my culture, my history and never asked me where I came from. I missed the music coming from the shops and restaurants in the streets of Kabul and the noise of the vendors and the taxis. I longed to be with my extended family, gathered together as we so often did before the Russian's came, playing cards and laughing. I missed the tastes, the sights, the smells of my home and the generosity and hospitality of my people. And so it was that in the middle of a war that would soon collapse one of the greatest empires in the world, and while the rest of the young Afghans were trying to find a way to escape their country, I flew in the opposite direction and landed in Kabul airport in 1984.

It was winter in Kabul and the conflict between the Afghan communist regime, supported by the Soviet Union, and the Afghan mujahideen, supported by the U.S. and its allies was still going on strong. The U.S. considered the Afghan conflict the front line in the cold war at that time and its financial and military support to the mujahideen through the Pakistan Inter-Service Intelligence Service Agency was at its highest since the start of the conflict.

Millions of Afghans were displaced in neighboring countries, having fled their homeland in fear. Hundreds of thousands had died as a result of either fighting or fleeing. Young boys were being imprisoned by one side or drafted by the other and an unknown future awaited them. Every day hundreds of young boys fled the once innocent city of Kabul, leaving behind their beloved families, friends and shattered memories. It was the dead of winter and I was on a plane flying directly into the middle of the war that had captured the attention of the world.

I had been in Germany for four years.

During the time that I was alone, after my mother returned to Afghanistan for the rest of our family, I received many letters from them and sent several of my own that expressed my loneliness and my desires to return to the home of my youth and the family of my heart. They repeatedly told me not to come back. My father was direct in his refusal to allow such a thing but my mother tried to explain in her way.

Abdul, we understand you miss your family, but it makes little sense to think that you can change the situation on your own. It is entirely unreasonable. Let me worry about the time that has passed and let the obligation to repair our separation rest on your father and I. Please, Abdul, do not consider your loneliness as anything but what is best for you at this time. There are far worse things than loneliness. Would you believe that the school you attended in Taimani has been forced to take in such a large amount of female students that they now outnumber the boys? Please focus on your studies and do not worry about those things that cannot and should not be changed. If you doubt me, ask them Abdul. Ask your teachers to guide you in these decisions you feel are your decisions to make. I assure you they are not. I believe your teachers will tell you the same and I beg you to follow their guidance.

I was perhaps blinded by my own desires. I did not see what my mother and father meant me to see. They were afraid to openly tell me what was going on in the streets or to openly describe the horror of the situation in their letters for fear the mail would be intercepted by the government. I was too young to understand the codes they tried to pass to me in order to change my mind. I was too young and too full of the idealism that leads us to believe that nothing changes in our absence; that anything can be undone.

I did what my mother advised and I spoke with my teachers about what had become a great, undeniable need to return to my homeland. They looked at me sadly and told me they would do whatever was necessary to help me stay in Germany. They told me of the dangers that my parents could not put words to, but even then I did not waver from the decision I had already made. When Werner Krause found out about my plans to return to Kabul, he took me aside and told me he was afraid I was making a mistake.

"Abdul, I cannot make you stay," Herr Krause said, "You are practically a man and you have been through much and grown stronger for it. I will tell you that when I look at you I see a young man of ambition and potential. I have seen you succeed in all that you put your mind to and it has been my pleasure to know such a dedicated young man."

He sighed, at a loss for words I imagined, "I'm afraid if you return to Afghanistan you will be throwing away a bright future. You can accomplish so much through pursuing your studies and soccer here. You will not be free in Kabul to live a life that is worthy of your talents. It is unfortunate, but true I'm afraid."

In the end, nothing could be said or done to change my mind. Herr Krause shook my hand as I was leaving and told me if I ever needed anything to contact him. He said he would help me. I could not foresee the possibility of ever needing help. I do not know that I truly heard the anxiety in their voices or recognized the cause of their concern when they advised me against returning. Even Friba pleaded with me when I told her that I was leaving. I told her I would be fine. I had started down a path and I would not waver from reaching the end.

I told myself they had not been there and could not know what it was like in Kabul. I had lived there. My family was there.

And I would return for everything I had left behind. For Hamed and Fraidoon, for my family, for the girl with the radiant eyes. I could not shake the dream.

At last I sent the letter that told my parents I was returning and when they could expect my arrival in Kabul. There was no time for them to respond with their objections.

Below the airplane window, my city was smaller than I remembered. Kabul looked like no more than a village from the sky. I always thought it was the largest place in the world. Inside of me, there was a battle waging between excitement to see my parents and my sisters and regret that I was not returning to the place that occupied my mind throughout my years in Germany. I could tell, even from that height that it was not the same. There was a time when we left Kabul and I watched her disappear below us. It was my first time on an airplane. Kabul shrunk from view and I did not know then what the rest of the world held, or that Afghanistan was not the center of everything. I saw no similarities to the pictures I had captured in my mind of the last time I saw Kabul from the air and what I was seeing now, though it had been a meager four years since. I was only twelve then; just a boy with great expectations and dreams. I was no different now, but I thought I was. Returning at sixteen, I thought I'd learned most of what I needed to learn.

The plane landed in Kabul International airport and I walked with the rest of the passengers toward the terminal that seemed older and smaller than when I last saw it. It looked like an old train station that had neither a train nor passengers anymore. Men with suits or police uniforms stood against the walls and stared at the passengers walking past. The men in uniform all had similar thick mustaches and serious faces. I stood at the passport checking table and the immigration officer asked me a few questions as he examined my documents.

"Wait here," he said and took the passport with him to an office across from the immigration counter. As he opened the door and slipped through I saw the seated form of an apparently higher ranking official seated behind a desk inside the office. When the officer returned to the counter his hands were empty and he directed me to the baggage pick-up area. I knew then, with a sinking feeling inside of me, that this was a permanent decision I had made. I would not be leaving Kabul again.

I retrieved my bags and nurtured the anticipation of seeing my family after long years of waiting for a reunion. When I finally saw them, they rushed at me. My father, mother and sisters were all crying. I too wept with the joy of seeing their faces and feeling their arms go around me at last.

My father had already rented an old yellow and black cab and it waited for us along the curb outside of the terminal. I loaded my bags into the trunk and took my place in the back seat, beside the window. My mother gripped my hand and continued to look at me. I was divided between staring at the family that I had long missed and staring at the streets of Kabul as we drove. The sights both within and without the cab stunned me with their capacity for change. My sisters, for one thing, were four years older than the last time I saw them and they had matured into young girls who I nearly did not recognize. Although I had heard frequent news about them in the letters my mother and father sent, looking at them reminded me of how much I had missed. My father's hair was streaked with more gray than I remembered. Only my mother was unchanged but I saw in her eyes that the trial of years had caused her many worries. I saw much more in her gaze than I could understand.

I looked to the world without for answers and what I saw was enough to break my heart. The city I had dreamed of was no longer there. I could not see or feel what I once felt now that I was back. It was immediately obvious that something was missing and I could not pinpoint what it was. I looked through the windows and searched for something that would form the reason for my return, but it was not there. It was nowhere around me. The eyes of my family held questions and I—at last—had no answers.

"You see now, do you not?" My mother asked with tears brimming in her eyes.

I nodded and she had the grace not to continue. As I nodded, I was sure that she could see the realization dawning in my face that it had been a mistake to return. I understood now that any possibility of leaving the country again had been rescinded. I saw that the war had been a stealthy thief, robbing me blind of the life I'd known when last I set foot on Afghan soil.

I felt that the last four years I spent in Germany had been the dream, now I was awakened to the nightmare of my situation. And it was only going to get worse.

The house we were driven to was different from the one I had left but it was still in the neighborhood of Taimani. It was a one story mud house with a small dirt backyard. There were three bedrooms and a shared bathroom with no hallway to separate the rooms. It had become a home to my sisters and to my parents, but it was not my home. I went to sleep that night feeling that I went—in the span of one day—from having two homes to having none at all.

Late in the night I heard movement in the next room.

"Flora?" I whispered.

There was no response and then a shadow moved into the doorway, illuminated in the cold blue light of the moon through the window over my own bed. I had been lying with my hands behind my head, staring up at the blank ceiling.

"Abdul?" my sister whispered.

I sat up and made room for her on the small cold mattress.

"What is it, Abdul?" Flora shuffled closer and sat. "I want to know about our friends," I said.

She was quiet for a long moment and in the dark I could not see her face. "I told Mami to let me write to you about them but she was strict about not letting us write about the others in our letters. She said it was not our place. She did not know what I was afraid of. I was afraid you would come back for them; for some more than others." She gave me a long glance in the dark, "But I had no way of telling you not to."

"And so I have come back for them—for her, now. Why would you tell me not to?"

"Because she is not here, Abdul. None of them are here. Her whole family left, not long after you and Mami and Friba. I don't think even Friba knows what's happened to her. I always thought there was a chance you had seen her. You spent such a long time in the camp in Germany and they too were trying to get to Germany."

I hugged my knees to my chest, trying to grasp the fact that she might have passed me by. That I had done everything to get back to her and she was perhaps closer to me in Germany than she ever would be in Kabul. Life is full of cruel ironies.

"Fraidoon and his family are gone. They left and we could not afford to stay at the house without them so we came here. Since then, I don't know what's happened to anybody. Mami and Papa are angry at you for returning, but happy to see you just the same. I don't know what I feel. I'm just tired of losing people. I won't lose you too."

We sat in silence for long moments, the darkness shifting around us.

"Before you arrived, I slept in this room," Flora continued, "Look." She moved to the window and opened it slightly, waving me with her hand to come closer. I peered through the opening and there was a roost of doves on the roof beside the window. They fluttered slightly at the intrusion of our voices.

"It must be hard," Flora said at the same time I whispered, "I thought I could save her...them." The sound of our hushed laughter was as light as the dove's wings, fluttering in the dark.

The following day I rose at dawn and walked toward the city to feel the familiarity of the bitter cold against my skin and to be among the familiar people of my native land. I was sure that on foot I would be able to retrieve some feel for what I had longed for while I was away. I thought of Flora's beautiful young friend and of my old friends and imagined I might pass them by at any moment as I walked along with my hands in my pockets and my face sheltered in the raised collar of my coat against the chill. There were more military vehicles and more Afghan and Russian soldiers patrolling the streets than when I'd last been here.

I walked down to the bazaar where I had once been able to recognize the familiar vendors and everyone had seemed like family. There was no music trilling endlessly from the corner shops and restaurants. There were few vendors and many of the shops were closed. The buildings seemed smaller and older than I remembered and less clean. The city felt empty, as if the entire population were suspended in the act of waiting. The people I passed were strangers and did not smile as they once had. They did not greet me in a friendly manner or demonstrate the pride and hospitality of a people that had once defeated great empires in battle and valued hospitality above all else. I recognized only suspicion in the eyes that met mine. I recognized that they moved uniformly and were adept at adjusting their paths to move out of the way of the rushing Humvees without looking. I had mixed feelings about everything I was seeing and feeling. Through it all I had a vision of what it had been and what it might be again and the image of it overlaid the present view of my city like a ghost. I wondered if I was a ghost, too. The only stranger in a strange place.

I navigated the corners of Kabul, all of them posted with red billboards with white lettering quoting Lenin and Babrak Karmal. I moved under these toward the quieter streets. I avoided the large gatherings of soldiers that blocked some of the corners and eventually I came out of the city into the quieter roads that led toward the dusky brown hills and open skies. I was looking up at the hillsides and they too boasted billboards with pictures of farmers and factory workers. A young Afghan man was walking toward me and I thought he looked at me.

"Comrade!" he called lifting his hand in my direction.

I looked up, startled and thought perhaps I knew him. But he passed me by and I turned to see him greet another Afghan boy who walked behind me. I continued walking because I could not stop.

I thought of the friends I had missed so often and so much while I was in Germany. Now I was back and within reach of them again. I walked a long time that crisp and frosty morning, watching my breath crackle in front of me on the air. The sun was shining and glinted on the frost that clung to the rough edges of the road. I passed by the school I had left behind and the old gate was closed and locked, unsteady on its hinges. Through the gate I could see my old classroom across the school yard. It was holiday and there were no students inside. The school had not changed much except that the frames of the windows had been removed. The water well in the school yard no longer had a mechanical water pump. Instead a black rubber bucket hung from a rope that dangled over the branch of the old oak tree that stood beside the well.

Once out of the heart of the city the sky spread over me like a bowl of blue and I could see ahead the hill where I had spent long hours with Hamed when we were twelve. I walked in that direction and hiked up the hill, moving out of the narrow path to let some women pass as they made their way down the hill. The women did not carry water buckets as they once did, and two of them were wearing the non-military uniforms of the *Sepahe Enqelab*. They did not make eye contact though I offered a greeting and I could tell they moved past me with some amount of trepidation.

I could not wait to knock at the door of my friend Hamed and to surprise him with my return. I hurried the rest of the way up the hill. At the top of the hill stood a 50 by 30 foot billboard picturing a Russian and Afghan soldier standing face to face and shaking hands, smiling. White lettering on the red background read, 'The Afghan and Russian Friendship is Unbreakable!'

As I approached Hamed's house a woman came through its front door. She was fixing her skirt as she walked in the opposite direction of me. I could not see her face and did not know if she was a relative of Hamed's. I began to feel some amount of uncertainty but I moved forward regardless and knocked on the door.

Standing there I remembered that Hamed's window had been the narrow one nearest the door. He would always open it at my knock to see who was visiting. Now the window was fastened tight and the thin curtain did not stir. I raised my hand to knock again, but as I did there was movement on the other side of the door and the sound of the latch being thrown. In the opening stood an old man with a long white beard. We greeted each other and I told him I was looking for my old friend, Hamed. The man's eyes were unrecognizing and he shook his head slightly while my heart sank.

I told him that Hamed had lived here four years ago and he said, "Ah! Yes, I remember the family and the young man."

The old man looked for a moment over my shoulder, before he whispered, "They escaped to Pakistan two…maybe three years ago. How did you know him?"

"He was my classmate and my friend. I have only just returned and hoped I might find him."

"I suppose such a thing is not to be hoped for these days," the old man said with a chuckle, "Won't you come in for some tea?"

"Thank you, but I must be going. I appreciate your help."

My heart was heavy as I realized I had nowhere else to go for the moment but back home, and even that was unfamiliar. Before I left I continued to the top of the hill where I could see the sun over the Hindu Kush Mountains and the city of Kabul spread below. As I sat there, a bank of clouds rolled across the sun blotting out the light and casting Kabul in a shadow. In distant parts of the city vague lights twinkled like embers. The rooftops were the color of gray dirt and mud. I looked at my city that had been burnt and charred and still smoldered in some areas and I could not help but feel it was the loneliest place I'd ever known. It looked from above like an empty city that had tired of holding the survivors in her arms and resigned herself to her fate, turning her back on those that still had need of her; nursing her wounded pride with quiet indifference.

The Russian helicopters droned endlessly over the city and I could see the tops of the red billboards poking out among the beleaguered buildings. I thought of the poets, scholars and philosophers throughout history who had been persecuted and of the brothers of my own generation who had fled to the Hindu Kush Mountains that offered a cruel form of salvation. I was beginning to realize that not only had the landscape of my memory changed but there was no one left to populate the dream that had brought me hurrying back to claim my place in the world. At one time the whole world had been a Mecca in my mind; every moment of the future had been a destination. But now the paths that lay behind me were slowly being occluded. I did not know what to do with this unrecognizable life. I did not know if I belonged to those who fought or those who fled.

If history taught me anything it was that people reemerge and rebuild. I almost heard the noise of the bazaar, peopled once again with all the faces of the past, with joyous brotherhood. I imagined doors opening all over the city in generous hospitality and I believed that the Afghan people would someday thrive in this land again, full of welcome and ready to defeat any nation that took advantage of their trust. And I knew then that there are other ways to fight than to join sides in war.

When my mother saw me she put her hands over her heart in relief.

"I was worried, Abdul."

I had risen early in the morning as I was used to doing and had left the house while my mother slept.

"I am fine, mother. I only walked. I wanted to see the city as I remembered it."

"And did you? You cannot go into the city streets, Abdul. Not anymore. You have to avoid the crowds or they will stop you. They find any reason to stop you. You cannot comprehend the danger of what you have done."

My mother was growing angry. She stopped and put a hand to her mouth, shaking her head.

"I am sorry Abdul. It is just that I worry. It is not safe for you here. Every day boys like yourself are disappearing, captured by the mujahideen and forced to fight among their ranks, or are drafted into the army, many of them never to be seen again. Mothers are crying all over this city and I *will not* be one of them. It is not the same, Abdul. You must promise me that you will not be so foolish as to think it is. I will talk to your father," she said, closing the conversation, "We must get your school documents immediately. They will serve as some protection. You are too young to be drafted, but do not think that the mujahideen will hesitate to capture you and force you to put your life on the line for Islam."

I reached out on an impulse and hugged my mother. She quieted and her arms went around me tightly. "I'm glad to be back with you," I said, "I'm so glad you haven't changed."

Almost as soon as I arrived back home my mother and father began talking about ways to get me out of Afghanistan.

Since I was not permitted to go into the city alone and there was no one to visit besides family and even their numbers had diminished, I contented myself to staying at home with my parents and my sisters and visiting with the few relatives that had not fled the country. There was little trust to be had at that time, so families stuck together and did not mingle as we once did with neighbors on every side. In our neighborhood, as in most throughout Kabul, young boys who wanted to make money worked for the *Sepahe Enqelab* and patrolled the streets carrying AK47's, on alert for threats to security. The entire city had been transformed into a military zone.

On my third day back in Kabul, my older cousin Naheem came to see me at my home. We greeted each other with laughter and hugs and then he became serious. He sat me down and wanted to know, really, what had brought me back after I had been so fortunate as to have gotten away once. I told him I did not know anymore and he nodded as if he understood that. Naheem was a teacher of civil engineering and architecture at Kabul Polytechnic who had accommodated the Russian standards of conduct and learned Russian early on during their occupation, recognizing the benefit of blending in.

"Will you teach me to speak Russian?" I asked him.

He looked at me curiously and said with some caution, "Your mother says they will try to get you back to Germany as soon as possible. Things are not as you expected?"

I waved my hand in dismissal, "I am here now. My father says I must focus on my studies and if I excel in school I may be granted approval to study in Germany. I have applied for enrollment at the German School here, Amani High School. I can do nothing about my situation now. I only want to no longer feel like a stranger in my own home."

Naheem nodded and smiled, "I would be happy to teach you, Abdul. You have grown up so much since you went away. I am sure you will make a fine student. But you must promise me one thing," he said and his face became serious once again. "You must promise me that you will do all that you can to leave this place. So many young men of promise are being wasted every day, dying uselessly and our future dies with them. You were not meant for this. Death is no way to bring people together."

So we began my Russian lessons and I embraced them fully. I looked forward to the following days when I would be permitted to begin my studies at Amani High School and to work at building a new future. I even felt a small stir of excitement. There is nothing like an adventure; nothing like a chance to begin anew and make of the unknown world what we will.

At night, however, my thoughts turned again to the days already behind me. I thought of lost things and I wondered if I was destined to be a man who regrets the choices he made in his life. In a fit of confusion, I wrote a letter back to Germany. I addressed it to Petra, the girl who I'd danced with at the community center. I told her that I'd made a mistake in leaving. I told her I missed her and I would never know what might have been between us because I left too soon. In a fit of inspiration the following morning, I mailed the letter, certain that it was a shot in the dark and I would not hear from her again.

*

13

~ ~ ~

AMANI HIGH SCHOOL

I picked up Russian quickly, with both my cousin's assistance and by listening to those around me while I tried to remain innocuous. When school started again, my parents breathed a sigh of relief. Knowing that I was safely within the confines of the school each day gave them peace of mind. I was less likely to be stopped if I were walking to or from school with books in my arms and a document that proved I was a student.

I attended Amani High School, which was a 50 minute walk from our home in Taimani. To lessen my commute, I bought a Chinese bicycle with a bent handlebar. I was able to straighten it out and my father helped me to replace the tires so that I could ride safely. He still worried about me riding my bike as he had while I was in Germany and told me often to stick to my path. He mumbled that he would rather worry about me riding down city streets than worry about me riding across mine fields, and each afternoon when I arrived home safely, he would put a hand out to touch my shoulder as if he were checking to make sure I was real. Now that I was old enough to remember a different time, I saw that my father too was aging. He came home weary and tired after long days spent working in his store. But I always felt his eyes on me, attentive and waiting.

Twice a week, my mother served us butter, powdered milk and fresh eggs along with the usual hot tea and *naan*. She would shoo my youngest sister away from the table, saving the largest portion of these delicacies for me. When she turned her back I would wave Nazima over and give her a sip of my milk and a bit of butter for her bread. She would scurry off, giggling and happy. My mother, who pretended not to notice would say,

"You spoil her, Abdul. It is no wonder she is always hanging about you like a starved dog." Then she put a kiss on the top of my head and left me to wolf down my food and rush out the door, hop on my bike and pedal furiously toward school.

Most of the teachers at Amani were German. After my first few days there, the entire school had heard of me and were curious to know why I had returned from West Germany. Many of the students and some of the teachers asked me about my parents, thinking that I was the son of high-profile communist parents who no longer wanted their son to live in a western society and had called me home. It seemed to them that would be the only logical explanation. Either that or I was a German agent. Their curiosity did not bother me, nor did the joking tone they took when they imagined me as a spy. What bothered me was that I never had an answer when they asked me why I came back. At least not one that made any amount of sense. Not to me and not to them. Why had I returned? Because I was homesick for my family and for the ghost of a girl I did not even know?

Our teacher, Herr Schmidt, would spend the first five minutes before or after each class discussing my past in Germany. The moment we started the conversation, the class became very quiet as everyone tried to listen to our conversation in German and interpret what we were saying. They were interested in hearing how I spoke the language and in deciphering the story of my return.

In class 11A, I sat next to a boy named Farhad. He was the smallest and youngest boy in our class and probably the nicest guy at school. Everybody loved him as he smiled and talked with everyone and joked with our German teachers. Each morning as he sat down he would lean over in his seat.

"Are they really all blond, like I've heard? And tall?"

When I nodded, he leaned back in his chair with a sigh, "Ah, man. What I wouldn't give to live with *that* every day of my life. Tell me about the pretty one again. Petra. Tell me how she danced."

Farhad spoke German decently, but I still had to translate some of Herr Schmidt's jokes to him which was probably why he sat next to me in the first place. He may not have understood, but Farhad never had a problem speaking up in class and trying to throw some banter back at the teacher. For this the teachers loved him too, and I began to grow accustomed to his good-natured personality both in and out of school. Besides spending time together at school I would sometimes walk with him halfway to his home near Kohe Asmahe in downtown Kabul.

"I have one little brother," Farhad said, "Like you I am my parent's eldest son."

Then, after we had been friends for some time, "My parent's also want me to be free of this country."

Much the same as Hamed and I had once divulged our secrets, Farhad and I became quick confidants. When he was not asking me about German girls, Farhad would ask me questions about what it was like to live in Germany. He asked me how my life changed when I moved away from Afghanistan, but I knew that what he was really asking was how his own life would change if he had a chance to get away. I doubt that he understood why I came back either. I was at least honest and told him I did not have a good reason for returning; only a dozen not so good ones. He laughed at this and he was careful not to make me feel worse about my decision. He told me he was glad I returned so that we had a chance to become friends. Likewise, I tried not to repent my decision much in front of him. I understood that to young men in Afghanistan, one chance to escape would have been a miracle and to them it would seem that I had tossed a great opportunity aside.

As we walked through the dusty roads and summer turned to fall and fall into winter and the smoke from the wood-burning stoves and ovens made the air thick and gray, I told Farhad about the schools I attended in Germany, about the Luenen 74 championship soccer team and about the friends I had made, all from different places on this earth. I told him what life was like for teens just like him, living there and elsewhere in the world. While I talked he did not joke, he did not smile. He listened as if he were absorbing every single word, and he looked off into the distance as if he could see the scene I'd set.

During school breaks, Farhad and I would spend the long hours of the day together just hanging out or watching German movies together in our school theater. Farhad would never miss a new German film. He would sit and watch with rapt attention. I had been there and it did not strike me the same way, but I could see that Farhad was transported by these films and I began to understand that it was his dream to go there—to Germany; to the place I'd left behind. Farhad and I had managed to build trust with each other, which was rare enough in those times. As we walked through the broken streets to the theater, we saw an old man ahead of us yelling and waving his one good arm at two young men. His other arm hung limply at his side, useless as the past.

"Get away! You show me the respect you would show a dog on the street. This is the way young Afghan men behave? You should be ashamed! You," he pointed to the boys, "All of you!" He flung his arm in an arc and a young woman came running from a shop and quieted him as we stopped to watch. The old man was muttering to her and tears were seeping through the creases in his face. The young men had darted away and quickly vanished in the bustle of the streets. The pavement where they had been only a moment before was cracked and broken from the weight of the Russian tanks. None of the stoplights worked any longer and soldiers directed all of the traffic through the intersections. Busses, *rikshas* and army trucks alike all sped through the crowds. Old men and women were either lamenting over the loss of what used to be, or laying in the streets begging passerby for money. Sometimes they would follow us until we dropped them a coin. There was the drone of helicopters and planes and the occasional explosion raining clouds of brown dust over the city, but the scene never changed, never paused or stopped. Life just kept droning on like bees in a hive and nothing ever happened, even when it did.

Then, one afternoon that winter I came home to find a dirty envelope on our kitchen table waiting for me. It had my name on it and the return address was German. I took it to my room and opened it. The letter was a response to the one I'd written months ago, when I first arrived home. In it, Petra responded to the things I'd told her in my letter with equal regret. She wrote that she liked me too and missed the chance we might have had to know each other better. Then she went on to give me the news of what had happened there in Luenen since I left.

I stared at the letter for a long time, wondering how it been delayed in reaching me for so long. She obviously wrote it with my own letter fresh in her mind. I heard the longing in her words that echoed my own longing when I first reached out to her. I remembered how I'd felt then; desperate for something to ground me. The response had not come when I sought it, but came now when—I suddenly realized—I was no longer so lonely. My skin prickled along my arms as I thought of the irony of letters that come too late; of the many things we mean to say but never do. I wondered if I had a right to disturb her world any more than I already had. I thought of her waiting for a reply all that time while her own letter had never even reached me. I wondered what had changed for her in those months. In the end, I read the letter one last time and folded it back into its envelope. I thought for a moment I might respond in a friendly way; perhaps tell her that I was doing better now, but I never did. I once thought the world hung on her reply. Now I made the choice, consciously for the first time, to live with what I had rather than want for what I did not.

Also in my class at Amani High School was Baraymal Dost, my old friend from my boyhood days in Micro Rayan. Seeing his face when I returned was both a relief and a reminder of all that had changed between us. I remembered the days of the Russian invasion. I remembered Baraymal's father becoming Deputy of Foreign Ministry. I remembered, more importantly, the time before that when we played together and dreamed of forming a soccer team and there was nothing we could not talk about as we roamed through the streets and alleys and across the fields of our youth. Seeing him, at 16 years old, I could see that those days would never return. He remembered me and greeted me. He told me that his father was still a foreign minister. I could not help but notice that he sometimes looked at me suspiciously. And I could not ignore the way it felt when Farhad and I had to change our conversation if we saw him approaching so he would not find us talking sympathetically about the most recent plane crash or fallen village and the people lost to it.

Farhad and Wali had been in the same class for the past three years and so I was introduced to Wali. They were not particular friends, but as Farhad got along with everyone, Wali was no exception. I had not thought Wali particularly approachable at first. He secluded himself at the back of the class with a group of guys who everyone called 'The Clerks' because they shaved their beards and wore old suits and dress shoes which made them look much older than the rest of the class. They came into class together; left class together and never did their homework. They never spoke a word of German though they obviously understood it. Herr Schmidt would pose his questions in German and they would answer in Dari, then someone else would translate their answers back to German. The only reason they still spent any time at school was so they could keep the school ID cards that exempted them from the military draft.

I don't recall exactly how it happened that Wali began to separate himself from The Clerks and more and more often could be found sitting with Farhad and myself. I sensed his curiosity. I did not understand then what value he saw in associating with me, but in retrospect his intentions were clear. Anyone who spent any time with me had direct access to information about what life was like *out there*.

Wali and I lived in the same direction from the school, so when Farhad broke off to go to his house, Wali and I would continue walking or riding our bikes the rest of the way. Unlike me, Wali was the third of four brothers. His father was in the import/export business and was world-travelled and passed down to his sons a passion for business. Wali's older brothers both attended college in Moscow. Families with money were able to send their son's away; to buy their own escape. In those days, Wali's brothers would purchase electronics and kitchen appliances in Russia and send them to Wali in Kabul who would turn around and sell the useful items for a profit. He would come to school with money in his pocket, shiny shoes on his feet and new sunglasses.

It was impossible not to want to be a part of that. Wali led a life that was different from my own. While we both had the inclinations of teenage boys to get into mischief, Wali had the means to actually do it and the business sense to make it profitable. He also had the use of a car when his father was away travelling. In our class, Wali and Baraymal were among the few who were lucky enough to have access to their own set of wheels and it earned them plenty of friends.

"Come on," Wali said and took off walking away from the school without even waiting for an answer. I climbed into the front seat of his beat up Alfa Romero and he gunned the engine. Dirt spun out behind us in the parking lot of the school. Wali's brother had run a sign printing business from a small office in Qalah-e Fatullah. When he left for Russia, Wali took over as partner in the business. He had worked with his brother for a long time and was an artist in his own right. Wali walked with a kind of swagger and I fell behind as he led me to the office for the first time. It was a small, dusty shop in a larger building. The screen door clanged on its frame as we entered. Inside a small heater was turned up full-blast against the sudden winter chill that had descended on Kabul and a voice shouted from the back of the office,

"Shut the door. Quick!"

"Calm down you old *katcha.*"

"Oh, it's only you," the voice said, attaching itself to a body that appeared in the doorway, "I should have known. And look! Trouble brought a friend. I'm Najib." The young man said and shook my hand in his ink-stained one. He was perhaps twenty years old and stocky, with glasses and messy hair. The glasses slipped down on his nose a little as he looked at Wali.

"I hope you expect to get some work done while you're here this time," Najib said as he headed to the back of the office once more. It was obvious, even though he joked with Wali, that he respected him.

Wali threw our things down behind a low desk and showed me around. Before long I was watching him work over a long piece of shiny fabric that was stretched over a wooden block. He printed his letters in Dari as quickly and perfectly as if he was a machine. There was no room for error and he made none. There were no machines then for making signs and banners for shop-fronts, so businesses like Wali's relied heavily on skill and artistry. It was a dying trade in the modern world. I was captivated by the process.

"It's easy," Wali said. "I can teach you."

He tried to hand me the large brush he had been using to paint on the lettering, but I laughed and told him no way was I going to practice with that.

"All right, all right," he said. "Here! Try this then."

He found a book that had different lettering techniques in it and showed me how to follow the lines. It was all a matter of perspective, he said, of knowing how the whole thing would come together and how much space it would take. I was immediately taken in with trying to balance the strokes of each letter to make them fit precisely on a page. The hours passed quickly and Najib would peer over my shoulder occasionally, chuckling at my progress. He smoked cigarettes, one after the other and sometimes while he was working he would let the thing hang out of his mouth, but he always managed to remove it and flick off the ash just before it fell and blotted his pristine work.

After some time, Wali stopped his work and stretched. "Come on," he said looking at the clock on the wall.

We went outside through the front door of the shop which was located on a busy street. It was afternoon and the sun was casting a hazy glow. A brief rain had caused mud to gather in puddles on the side of the road. The smell of damp dirt was, oddly enough, one of the things I had missed when I thought of my homeland during my years in Germany. Being there, in the midst of it again, I had a sudden feeling that life was unpredictable but fair at least. I could not imagine being elsewhere.

"You like it?" Wali asked, gesturing with his head toward the shop.

"I do."

"Well, you're about to like it even more. Now you find out the real reason why I leave school just to come here and work."

Wali pointed down the street to where, just then, three girls in black school uniforms were rounding a corner and heading in our direction. I looked at Wali and he nodded.

"The girl's high school," he said.

I smoothed my hair and Wali assumed a casual pose leaning against the doorway. Wali was taller than me and with the money he and his family had, he dressed well. I wore jeans and a t-shirt. Before the girls reached us, they slowed somewhat. The one in the middle was taller than the other two and she looked up briefly at Wali.

"Your hair is silk," he said and though she did not meet his eyes again, the corners of her lips turned up as she passed us.

I did not have the presence of mind that day to speak to the girls, but the one on the end looked up and met my eyes. Hers were a warm brown, wide and unblinking in a pretty round face, but I could not help but feel some disappointment. I could not quite explain why I still searched in every face for the rare occurrence of those green eyes that still met me in my dreams.

The weather became harsher, and with it we spent more time indoors. When the first snow fell, I would climb up to the roof of our house and shovel the snow off with a huge *rashbill* so it wouldn't leak when the sun melted it. Wali began hosting card games in the sign shop in the evenings after Najib had left for the night. I began to notice that he would always invite the Hindu boys in our class, who he rarely spoke to either in or out of school. They were eager to be included and though they lost every time, we could always count on them to be present at the next game. I realized that they also had the deepest pockets of any of us gathered around in a circle on the floor. This, I assumed, was why they were there. My suspicions were confirmed one evening when I played a little more aggressively than I had before. I'd received a larger than normal sum of money for some work I'd done at my father's shop and I bet almost all of it on one hand of *Falaash*. Wali gave me a look over his cards and shook his head slightly so that only I saw. I assumed he was bluffing me and felt that I'd participated in enough of his games to know the way he played. But when the hand was over, Wali swept the pile of my earnings away.

"That's it for tonight, men," he said, "I don't know what to do with all this cash."

The Hindu's and the rest of the group left, dejected, but I stayed behind. Wali was quiet as we picked up the cards and pushed chairs and tables back to their places.

"You set me up," I finally said.

"Didn't you see me shaking my head? I *told* you not to place that bet."

"You can't possibly win so much on luck alone. Tell me how you do it."

"Aww, come on. I'll give you your money back Abdul."

"I don't care about the money. I just want to know how you do it."

"Why? Are you going to help me?" He looked at me sideways, assessing my potential.

"Maybe."

"All right," he finally conceded and we sat back down while he dealt the cards and showed me how he kept three cards out and substituted them into the hand he'd been dealt. "It's easy really."

He let me try it but my hands were not quick enough and more often than not I dropped the cards I was supposed to be concealing.

"Here," he said, "I'll take the cards out and you just deal. With both of us doing it, no one will suspect a thing. We can split the money we make. You'll be rich!"

In the end he kept the money I'd lost that night, but the lesson proved more profitable for me than one night's losses. The following day I used what little money I'd kept and bought a used pack of cards off of one of the Hindu traders who set up near the school. I went home and practiced until the pads of my thumbs were raw from sliding the cards into my palm, but I finally was able to do the trick as seamlessly as Wali had shown me.

It was a week or two later that we ended up at the home of a friend after school while his parents were out. We sat again in a circle, this time on thin mattresses that were laid across the dirt floor where the family would later sleep. I employed my new skills after Wali won the second hand. When I won the hand, Wali's head snapped up and he looked at me sharply. He called the game for the day and said we had to leave. We walked in silence some way back toward Taimani. I did not know if he was angry. Wali was always able to keep a straight face that revealed no emotion. Then he punched me in the arm, not hard but in the way that guys do.

"I see I'm going to have to keep you on my side," he said.

*

14

~ ~ ~

TO SAY GOODBYE

When my father learned that I was playing cards with Wali, he was furious. I did not understand his anger at first. It was some years later that his older brother, my uncle, told me that my father had lost the home he'd inherited from their father during a game of cards before he met my mother. These were the two things my father would repeat often after that: "My son, you should not drink alcohol or gamble ever. It destroys your life and takes away everything you have earned." The second was, "A good woman will make a better man of you than you could ever be on your own."

With the money I won at cards, I went to Shor-bazaar and bought a used Russian camera from an old man who repaired and sold used electronics of all kinds. I had become fascinated with television since we had first gathered around one year before in our home in Micro Rayan. Since then, TV had become more popular, and while the Russian's claimed that it was their influence that brought this modern marvel into the homes of Afghans, I knew better. Still, I was held captive by the way pictures and information was transported from distant places through nothing but a thin antenna. It was fascinating and I had acquired a desire to somehow understand this mysterious world of images and information. A camera was the only option as it was the only one I could afford. The man who sold me the camera knew my father and so he threw in an extra role of film for free and showed me how to remove the film only in the dark. I was as excited as a child when I left the shop. I ran nearly all the way home, cradling the prize under one arm.

In school I brought the camera out to show the guys and they were thrilled to pose for pictures. I only took four pictures, afraid of using too much of the precious film. But when I finished taking pictures of the guys, Farhad said, "Here, you need to be in one of the pictures. Have Wali take one of you and me."

We stood in the sunlight that streamed through the window from the high afternoon sun. The heat on my back was warming. Herr Schmidt walked in then and saw us but said nothing. I smiled because Farhad could be permitted anything, even a brief disruption of the class. I looked up briefly just as the picture was taken. Farhad remained steadily smiling. The good-humor and liveliness of his personality shone out through his eyes and his unwavering smile. It was only a moment in time, a frozen memory. I am left now to remember the context of the world in which that picture was taken, but then I was a smiling innocent. I could not know then what would come of us.

In time, the Russian government would recognize the yearning that had overtaken the youth of our country to escape our once familiar and now unrecognizable homeland. They became aware that the German movies they played, and the influence of German teachers they hired, had instilled in many a dream to travel to that country. In recognizing this they did the only thing they knew how to do: remove the sources of the information. They took away the German movies and forced the German teachers to resign from their positions in our schools. But they could not take away the real cause of dissatisfaction unless they removed themselves from the picture and that was not to happen for some time. And so the spark of a dream stayed alive in people like Farhad, who would always hold out hope that the world was something better than it was.

Unlike Farhad and so many other young men in Kabul who longed to get away, Baraymal had seen much of the world since we had been children together in Micro Rayan. He had lived in New York for a time when his father served as a representative for the United Nations. Since I had returned to Kabul it took him some time to warm up to me again. But after several months, the look of suspicion dropped from his face and he began to speak to me as a friend once more. The topic we started on was soccer of course. He asked me if I had played since we were children. I was grateful for his efforts at friendship and I told him of the time I spent playing soccer in Germany. He was interested in my stories of how we'd won the championship and how Herr Krause had taught us that soccer was more than just a game. It was not long before Baraymal, Wali, Farhad and myself were spending time together both in and out of school.

We were all so different, but there were ties that connected us. Perhaps nothing connected all three of us directly, but there were links that we each shared with one or another. Friendship is a strange thing in that regard. One can never predict it or define it. Friendship is incidental to life. Without one or the other we are nothing.

The weather warmed again as another winter passed and the late frost vanished from the ground. I could not be still. If I stayed in one spot too long, I risked the vague notion of capture that my parents felt lurked around every corner. Those travelling by car were not stopped as people walking the streets were, and so I felt safer when I was with Baraymal or Wali. Baraymal had the added protection of knowing the right people due to his father's involvement with the government, and Wali had the protection of his father's wealth so, all in all, I was able to enjoy some leisure with them.

One afternoon, Baraymal suggested that we go to Qargha Lake to enjoy the warm weather. Wali immediately agreed and I said I would go too, although I had my reservations about the trip. Qargha Lake had once been a peaceful destination where the entire population of the city would go in nice weather to enjoy outdoor recreation. There was little money back then, but the Kabuli people embraced their culture and sense of community and the community embraced them in return. That was before the Russian's came.

Eight of us piled into the Volkswagen Bug that day, with Wali behind the wheel. Only Farhad declined to come. He was the youngest of our group of friends, but also the most responsible. He was honest with his parents and if they told him not to do something, he did not do it. That was Farhad and he did not claim to be other than what he was. The others may have joked about his being too scared to join us, but it did not go beyond that. We all respected Farhad and wished we had something more of his good-will and conviction.

We stopped first at the park near the high school to pick up a few dozen Kebab orders from *Hotal-e Dad Khodai Charikari*. The restaurants along the park played Ahmad Zahir songs and they could be heard from a distance, under the trees. A few blocks south of the park was Ahmad Zahir's old apartment. I was not sure who lived there now that he was gone. The park had been popular since before the Russian's came. It was built previous to the invasion to accommodate the dining and leisure needs of the foreigners who lived and worked in the nearby embassies. The park was in an upscale neighborhood of Kabul and it was an especially popular hangout for young people who would stay out until midnight. Now we knew to be out of the park before dark.

When we arrived at the lake, it was deserted. The wind blew a fine dust through the open windows of the car. We parked near one of the restaurants that lined the lake. Once these *hotals* had thrived, but now their facades were riddled with bullet holes and there were only open gaps where the windows had once been. They had long since been abandoned and the vacant skeletons of what remained made me think of the ghost towns in the Wild West movies that sometimes played at the Zaynab Nendare Theater.

Wali picked up a rock and threw it into the empty shell of one of the buildings. The sound of it clattering dully against a wall echoed back to us. Our laughter was unnatural in the desolation of that place. Baraymal pulled a bottle of vodka out from behind one of the seats in the car and we walked to the lake across grass that had not been cut in many months. The wind caused ripples on the surface of the water. I remember now the distinct, uninterrupted view of the sky, the long brown line of the surrounding hills, and the nearly transparent green of the lake. The wind blew softly, stirring memories of the times we had come to the lake when I was a child. It was saddening to see it differently, and I had a vision of what it once was—what it might be again. Of course I had no idea then, as a teenager, what the future would hold. I have been back since but I cannot say that my hope for that place has lived up to my youthful expectations. Qargha Lake is now surrounded by the million dollar homes of drug lords. The restaurants are once again occupied, but no one goes there as they once did. Money has come to Kabul, but the long lost atmosphere of peace has not come with it.

That afternoon we sat in the dense sand beside the water. Wali and Baraymal and some of the others passed around the vodka until it was nearly gone. We laughed as the sun beat down, but all the while I had the odd feeling of being watched. We were idle in a place where we had not the luxury of being idle. In the hills all around us and perhaps closer than that, the mujahideen set their camps. At any moment we might be approached, sitting as we were, conspicuously in the open. In spite of these feelings of unease, I felt a sort of possessiveness for that place. It was my lake, my home, my friends that surrounded me. They could not take that from me though they would try.

The Democratic Party in control of the government demanded that students from all around the city of Kabul march in front of the Presidential Palace every few months in support of the government and its policies. They handed out pro-government banners for us to carry and there was no choice in the matter, for if it was discovered that we did not participate, punishment would follow.

Farhad and myself, being of the same mind in the matter of politics, attended these events together and not without some planning. Our plan had several steps. We discovered quickly that the first trick was to avoid that part of the crowd that received the banners. By hanging around the outskirts of the group, we could make a show of our presence and still have the most chance for an early escape. Second, we avoided Baraymal at all costs. He was known to be an advocate of the government and as such would stay until the very end of every walk. Third, we knew that there was no point in trying to leave within the first hour or so of the gathering. During this time, the organizers maintained an eagle-eye watch on participants to make sure there were no dissenters.

During that time, we showed outright enthusiasm for the cause. Farhad was the one who taught me to use my powers of observation and to recognize the opportunity for escape. There was always a point where the individual school groups would merge to form a larger group. There was general disorganization at this time, which made the possibility of escape much more accessible. We would take the opportunity to hide our books under our shirts and pretend to be organizers rather than students and skirted our way to the edge of the crowd. From there it was fairly easy to blend into the regular population on the sidewalk. We would typically head to the dark seclusion of the movie theater then, where images of a different life would play in Farhad's eyes. I sometimes fell asleep in the cool, sweet peace of the theater until he shook me and told me it was time to go.

Ours was not the first government to force their ideology on its people, nor would it be the last. They had many ways of doing this. I did not recognize it at the time, nor was I intended to, but now I see that propaganda was infused into each aspect of our lives. Our socialization as teenagers was heavily influenced by the government at the time. The Russian's, for all intents and purposes, did their best to distract the youthful population of Afghanistan by enticing us with a social freedom and cultural diversity that had not been accessible to previous generations of Afghans. In the modern Afghanistan of the time, boys and girls were allowed to interact in ways that our culture had once deemed unacceptable.

Amani High School had a concert hall that held regular events for the students of both ours and other schools in the area. All that this meant to the male students of Amani was that the girls of Zarghona and Malalai High School were often in attendance at the events. Our interactions with girls were still respectful above all else. Wali had continued to exchange brief comments with Aria each day when she walked by his signage shop after school. She would raise her eyes, and give him a smile to let him know it was acceptable for him to continue to pay his regards in such a way. Eventually, she would make a comment in return, and these comments would turn into brief conversations. When I was with him at the shop, she refrained from speaking and her moon-faced sister would smile at me. I tried not to encourage her and often waited inside so Wali could talk to his girl alone. The relationship progressed after several months to their walking together to the street corner while the two other girls walked on ahead of their friend. It was not permissible then that a boy and girl show affection in public or openly acknowledge that they were forging a relationship. Although I would, once in a while, see a boy and girl holding hands in the relative safety of the shade trees at the park, even this intimacy would be dropped quickly if they knew they were observed. We all lived in fear that our parents or relatives might recognize our attentions to girls as inappropriate and restrict our freedom.

126

Wali, for all his street-wise bravado, kept his hands in his pockets and a good distance between himself and Aria when they talked. He suddenly became the first of my friends to suggest going to the concerts when they were held. We would attend as a group. Typically these concerts were performed by various local entertainers. Some of them were singers and musicians known in the Afghan community, and others were groups of guys from our own or other schools who would sing songs in Dari or Hindi and play the traditional harmonica, table and *rebab*, or the more modern keyboard, guitar and drums. We would inch closer to the girls we admired, though it was sometimes difficult to tell them apart in their matching uniforms of black dress and black socks, with white scarves draped not over their hair, but over their shoulders. I often scanned the crowd without noticing any girl in particular. When I was with Wali, I mostly tried to avoid the moon-faced girl who was always nearby. Then one afternoon I was listening to the strains of a traditional Hindi song being played on the *rebab*. It drifted through the audience like it had wings. Perhaps I romanticize it in hindsight, but I think I felt for a moment that I was caught in a dream of the past. Perhaps it is simply what happened next that gives the memory a dreamlike quality. At that moment I met the eyes of a girl across the crowded room. This particular girl was in conversation with a friend, and happened to turn at the exact moment that my own eyes alighted on her. She stopped then—time itself stood still—her mouth open with a half-formed word on perfect pink lips. But it was not that which held me entranced. It was rather that the world fell away and all that remained was her eyes. Green as the water of Qargha and iridescent as a dragonfly's wing.

When we were all together in Comdish restaurant, Farhad, Wali and I, we would share the dream that we might meet someday at a café in Frankfurt or at a college in New York.

The Comdish restaurant, as one of our favorite gathering places, was a constant reminder of courage in the face of warfare. Comdish was a village in the Nooristan province of Afghanistan. The people of Comdish continued their fight against Arab invaders for centuries without ever giving up their ancient religion, culture and traditions. Just like every corner of Afghanistan has its own story of invasions, defeats and survival, Comdish was no exception. For many years, the Arabs called Nooristan not by its name but rather by the name *Kafiristan*, or 'land of infidels.' We had been taught by our history teacher, Mr. Wafa that there were still people in Nooristan that held on to their ancestors ancient religion of Zoroastrianism that had been around for almost four thousand years in the region of Afghanistan. I wondered then if the owner of Comdish restaurant, who was always kind to us boys, had built the restaurant there in the heart of Kabul to remind not just the local residents, but the foreigners as well who enjoyed the atmosphere and peace of the restaurant, that there is no greater opponent than the courage of the down-trodden.

"You know," said Farhad, "anything is possible if you believe in it."

Our time at Amani High School was soon to be over and with that, we would lose our school ID's which meant that we could be stopped at any time and subjected to either fight among the ranks of the Afghan army or alongside the mujahideen depending on who got to us first. Unless of course we chose to escape. It was the often unspoken subject that hung on the air between my interactions with friends and family. Time whittled the days down to hours and we were caught between boyhood and manhood. My parents, I knew, thought about the possibility of me escaping as much as Farhad and Wali and I did. It gradually became a certainty rather than a possibility that the day would come when each of us would have to find our way free of this country, whatever the dangers may be.

"Have you been practicing the verses of the Quran?" Wali asked.

"My dad has been drilling me. He yells every time I mess one up and goes on about how it is going to be the end of me," I said

"My parents are uptight too," said Farhad, "They are just worried."

"It is no joke," said Wali, "As soon as we are on the mujahideen territory they are going to ask us the verses and you better know your prayers as well. If you get captured by a moderate group they might let you go, but if Hezbe Islami captures you, they either kill you or make you fight with them. Either way, you die."

"How can you tell which group is which?" I asked.

"By if you are dead or not," Wali said, laughing. "You will not know which is Hezbe Islami. You just hope you get lucky."

Each month one or more of our classmates would stop showing up in class and eventually someone would receive a letter saying that they had gotten safely to Pakistan or Iran. Sometimes there was no letter at all and we were left with nothing but the hope that they were still alive. Each time I heard that one of our friends had escaped Kabul, I felt completely empty and alone. Occasionally Farhad or Wali would fail to show up in class and I would not be able to concentrate all day on anything beyond the frozen ball of fear that sat in my chest. We had promised to tell each other if we meant to escape, so there was that at least to cling to, but with the amount of secrecy we had to maintain it would not be surprising if one of them were whisked away by their families, unannounced. There were any number of reasons an opportunity to escape might suddenly become available and they would have to jump at it without a second thought to the trivial detail of telling me. I oscillated between terror that Wali or Farhad had escaped, and hope that they had.

So it was that we lost friends, neighbors, classmates and even relatives who mostly left in the early mornings while the rest of us still slept. It could take days, weeks or sometimes months to successfully cross the border out of Afghanistan. Some left their house lights on and wouldn't bother to sell their belongings so no one would notice their escape until they were safely away. Others had no choice but to sell their appliances and furniture at low prices just to have enough money to pay for their passage to another country and start a new life once there. There were any number of monetary costs associated with fleeing. The safest way to escape the country was to get a guarantee letter from a mujahideen commander or a smuggler, but it was also the most expensive. Many of the mujahideen soldiers saw the financial opportunity associated with turning toward smuggling and demanded high payments for their services. Once a mode of escape was secured, the dangers one faced were numerous. In addition to the threat of mine explosions and bombings by Russian planes, we heard of many horrible incidences involving robbery, rape, torture and killing that gave us more than one moment of pause in which to think twice about what lay before us. Those with money and connections would go to Pakistan or Iran and then move on to Europe, Australia or North America. Those without would simply hope to start a new life in one of the neighboring countries. That was the thing: the promise of a new life— wherever it might be—kept most of us dreaming of taking one risky path or another out of Afghanistan.

If escape was not the topic of conversation in my home or among my friends, it was at least always on our mind. I was constantly creating different scenarios about my own escape. I imagined getting captured by Russians, the Afghan government, the mujahideen or the Hezbe Islami Gulbuddin, and asked myself how I would get out of each situation. I lay awake at night staring out of my window. The pigeons flew effortlessly through the dark, alighting sometimes on the roof and then flying away. Prey to cats, they would only imperil themselves if they nested for a night. They were forced to be industrious, self-preserving creatures. The black sky that hung over my city stretched as far as I could see and then vanished behind the towering peaks of the Hindu Kush. I wondered who out there was doing what I dared only to think of at that moment. I thought of the Hezbe Islami hiding in their caves with the blood of a thousand innocent Afghans on their hands. I thought of the Russian army, boldly occupying our city and demanding much but giving little. There was little difference between one and the other. Both were extreme sides of a battle that had been fought before and would be fought again, without there ever being a clear winner. When my mind was finally exhausted with the possibilities, I tried to close my eyes and hear only the sounds of the restless birds.

Each morning I rode my Chinese bicycle to school with Wali. After school he went to work at the sign shop and I walked with Farhad most of the way home.

One day we left school together and the sky was overcast. We were both tired from a long, gray day and walked slowly, but Farhad asked if we could take a different route home. All day he had been quiet and it seemed that something was on his mind. He shifted the books in his arms and when we were out on the road where no one else was walking, he told me his news. He would be making his escape that night and would not be coming to school anymore. We were passing by the embassies then that housed the government personnel and we stopped on that road in front of the foreign ministry so that I might absorb what he had said and to ultimately say our good-byes. As much as I had thought about this eventuality, it did not feel real now that it had come. We hugged each other and tried to wipe our tears. I had a hard time believing I would ever see him again, but I would have had a harder time believing what would actually occur so many years later. Not wishing to prolong inevitable sorrow, we parted ways there and Farhad walked away waving toward me as I went to grab my bicycle where it lay against a tree.

*

15

~ ~ ~

THE KUCHI

A year passed and I did not know where Farhad was. I didn't hear from him and I had nothing to do but pray that he was alive as I had done for so many of our other classmates. One evening as it was getting dark, I was sitting at home thinking about my future when there was a knock at the door. I knew it was Wali by the secret knock we used between ourselves.

"We don't have much time," he said, "I want you to come with me tomorrow morning, to Pakistan. I found a way for us to get away."

I was so shocked I forgot to invite him inside. He pushed past me and I shut the door. He pulled his thin coat tighter across his chest but in truth it was quite warm both outside and in. He told me then that a truck was ready to take us to Peshawar. It was a smuggler's truck, designed so that two people could hide themselves easily without attracting notice.

"My father already paid him," Wali said, "All you have to do is come with me."

I had more questions than there were answers and I did not know how to respond to him.

"We will stay a few days in Jalalabad and then go on to Peshawar through the main border at Torkham. I've been waiting for this opportunity for months, Abdul; it could be your opportunity too."

I asked him if I could think about it before I gave him an answer. He told me he'd wait and I offered to have him wait in the house while I talked with my parents, but he said he would rather wait outside and have a cigarette.

I took the news to my parents, who were as startled as I was and sat down with me at the kitchen table. I told them everything Wali had told me and they, too, had many questions. After a long discussion, I walked outside to meet my friend. Darkness had completely fallen and I picked out Wali by the glowing end of his cigarette. He was sitting on a low wall nearby, staring at the distant hills where faint lights glowed.

"I am not able to go with you, Wali."

He dropped his cigarette and ground it under his foot. He nodded.

"Man, I hope I don't get captured," was all he said, and then we hugged each other quickly. I watched him walk down the dirt road away from my house; a shadow moving through the darkness until he disappeared among it and was gone.

Wali had made up his mind, and carried through with his plan. I didn't tell him why I decided not to go. I didn't want to hang my reasons like an excuse between us. Wali probably knew, anyways, that our situations were different. His father was wealthy and well-connected. If the son of such a man were to be captured, he could easily influence Wali's freedom. I could not hope for so much.

It was a month before I heard from him, and during that time I lost all interest in school and friends. It seemed such a pointless existence to be trapped in; worrying at every moment about the next day and how to begin it. There was one thing only that kept me grounded during those long days and I did not know how to find her or how to make her understand what she was to me. On the day that Wali's letter arrived I also made a decision.

In the letter, he wrote that he had reached Islamabad. Although he had been captured and held by the border officers, he had carried enough money with him to bribe them in exchange for safe crossing.

"I'm waiting for my Visa and then I'll fly to Germany where my mom and younger brother live. I met a few of our friends in Pakistan," he wrote, "So you can tell everyone that they are well."

I thought of Wali and our other classmates who had left without warning all gathered in Pakistan, greeting each other like old friends and I felt more alone than ever. I felt that every moment I spent in Kabul was just a preface to the time when my life would really begin. And so I tried to think of those things that I came back for and of those things that I would be leaving behind again and my thoughts came to the green-eyed girl. I decided two things: One, I would have to leave my country. Two, I would see her before I'd go. The only place I had seen her since we were children long ago at the pool in Micro Rayan, was at the concert held at Amani High School. So I would go back there. I would find her.

I attended many concerts as the school year drew to a close. I arrived at each one early and did not leave until late. I scanned each face in the crowd to see if I might fall upon those eyes again, but for many weeks I did not. Then one evening I sat alone in the back of the hall, slouched down in my chair and trying to avoid Baraymal who would try to talk me into walking with him at the last political rally of the year. My hands were in my pockets and my hair fell across my forehead like a partial shield. I was listening to a conversation taking place behind me when the music suddenly stopped. The conversation halted too. There was some commotion and the crowd that had been standing in front of me parted only a little and I saw her, just as the music started up again. She was standing with two other girls, both of whom looked taller and older than her. She still had the petite look of a younger girl. As luck would have it, one of the girls she stood with was in conversation with Baraymal. I jumped out of my seat and made my way forward, recognizing an opportunity when I saw one.

"Baraymal!" I called when I got close. He was talking to all three of the girls and I couldn't help but notice that his eyes kept lingering on the girl with green eyes. I also noticed, to my satisfaction, that she looked bored and only smiled politely where the other girls laughed loudly.

Baraymal turned at the sound of his name.

"Abdul, I was looking for you. I thought you got away."

"Not a chance."

Baraymal turned to me then, to the exclusion of the girls, "I wanted to make sure we could finally walk together next week at the embassy."

"Baraymal, I would not miss it for the world. I will not interrupt your conversation. I only wanted to say hello. Forgive me." I said more to the girls than anyone.

"Let me introduce you. This is Abdul," Baraymal said by way of introduction, "We have been friends since we played soccer together as boys."

It was just as well that the taller girls were more interested in what Baraymal had to say, as it allowed me the opportunity to shift closer to the green eyes that waited for me and to strike up a conversation.

"I know you," I said.

"We have not met."

"We are meeting now. But I remember you from the pool when we were children."

"Do you?"

"I was gone a long time. I think that maybe I came back for you."

"That was foolish."

"Was it?"

She cast her eyes down.

"I am leaving again," I said.

"Leaving for where?"

"For another country, another world maybe," I smiled.

She looked up and gave me a shy smile. That one smile buoyed my spirits and made me feel that anything could be made possible. I felt a sudden rush of daring that flowed into my words.

"My name is Abdul Nasser and I am the only son of Quabela Momena of Taimani and I am confident that you will find me somewhere out there, if I don't find you first. I'm not letting my friends go. Not one of them. And we are friends now."

"Are we?" She laughed and her laughter was like bells.

"Yes. We are."

"I wish you luck, Abdul Nasser of Taimani," she said, still smiling.

"Abdul Nasser of the world," I responded confidently, "I will tell you all about it when next we meet," I said and already I was walking away, having done what I was meant to do and feeling the magnetic pull of the world sweeping me away into whatever might be.

I went home with renewed faith in pursuing my escape out of Kabul. It was what I then devoted myself with total commitment to succeeding. My parents, I think, were encouraged by my enthusiasm in putting a plan into place and we talked about the options more frequently. My mother told me later that during those last few months she began to think more often about the good that would come from my escape and what it might mean for my future.

Survival makes optimists of us all, she would said, *I like to think I chose to see the positive side of things but truly I think I could not bring myself to fear the worst. I could not have lived with such thoughts in my heart. I could not have let you do what needed to be done.*

No longer having a school ID, I was forced to become adept at evading the Army Search Crews who waited at every street corner, stopping and questioning young, male Afghans. I learned to escape easily each time I was stopped and questioned. I jumped twice from a moving truck to escape a search crew and learned to blend in with the crowds as I knew the soldiers were not allowed to start shooting on the main streets. I was captured only once before and taken to Kandake Tajamo which was a semi military camp that was used for the temporary holding of captured Afghans before they were flown to remote provinces to fight the mujahideen. The Afghan Army and the intelligence department held on to the new recruits that were captured on the street of Kabul for only 48 hours before their departure. During that limited time, I knew I had to find a way out. The new recruits in Kandake Tajamo would be flown to the most dangerous war zones and most likely would end up dead. I decided to keep one of my eyes shut and pretend that it was injured so that I could delay my departure. I knew they would need to send me to the military hospital to verify the "damage" in my eye. The soldiers and intelligence personnel knew I had intentionally closed one of my eyes, but they had no choice but to get the approval from the hospital before sending me to fight. I threw myself from the running truck while being taken to the military hospital.

During this time, my parents struggled to put together money and to make connections with other families in similar positions who might be able to pass along useful information. Many of the claims that families made endorsing one smuggler or another proved to be false or the smuggler's themselves would take our money to secure my escape and then not show up at the time of departure.

My mother spoke to a former co-worker who had three daughters and a young boy. The eldest of the daughters was the beautiful girl who sat next to me in the first grade. All those years ago, I had not realized who she was. They made arrangements for a smuggler to take their family out of the country and arranged for me to go along with them. My mother spoke to the father of this family and was assured that they knew the contact well and we were practically guaranteed safety.

Hours before we were due to leave, my mother was told that a different mujahideen smuggler would be accompanying us instead of the original, planned contact. The other family was worried as they did not know this smuggler, but it was their chance to escape and they took it. On the recommendation of my mother's better instinct, I did not.

I found out later that they were robbed by the mujahideen and were kept like prisoners for months until the girls and their mother escaped to a neighboring village where they found shelter. The father and son were not able to join the family nor even protect the women during the long imprisonment. We learned much later of the trials they endured. But theirs is another story.

The right opportunity to escape was difficult to come by and I was quickly wearing out my welcome in Kabul. The local soldiers began to recognize me after I evaded them enough times and it became more and more difficult to hide. My parents became desperate to find a way to get me out of the country, and I too began to worry that if enough time went by I would be forced to take any chance at escape rather than doing it the way I wanted.

Early one morning a search crew came to our house. We could tell by the loud banging on the door that it was no one we knew. They pushed the front door open and began to look through the house for me. Someone had given them information as to my whereabouts. Fortunately I had planned for such a situation and as soon as I heard the knocking and my father looked up at me with sudden fear in his eyes, I ran out the back door of the house and scaled the six foot wall in our backyard, dropping into the neighbor's yard and hiding behind a wall. The neighbor there knew of me. She was a woman living alone since her husband and son had been taken to government prison, so she sympathized with my plight. Before long I was jumping into her yard every time there was a knock on our door—sometimes multiple times in one day—and waiting until I heard my sister at the back wall whispering that it was clear for me to return.

Most of the rest of the time I spent indoors reading books. I became a prisoner in my own home. I could not work since I would be quickly turned in or recognized or otherwise dragged into a cause I did not believe in or want to die for. The communist government was losing its popularity every day. More and more Kabulis were becoming disenchanted and losing trust in both the government and the mujahideen to fight a war that was becoming nothing more than a power struggle. It became widely recognized that most of the mujahideen leaders were using religion as a front to gain power. The mujahideen efforts were largely funded by neighboring countries—including Arabs and the western block—to break the knee of the communist regime backed by Russia.

Meanwhile, we were constantly finding different smugglers who offered to help and took our money and expensive goods in exchange for their promised services and then were never heard from again. There was little trust and little enough hope for an honest opportunity but we had no choice but to keep trying.

In the winter of 1987, one of my parent's old friends came to visit us. His name was Dadmir and I recalled his previous visits with my family. Dadmir was a *Kuchi*, a nomad who lived in a village in Jalalabad called Gerde Ghauss. As a young boy I listened to his stories about the *Kuchi* with whom he and his ancestors had lived and travelled across ancient lands.

In our culture, connections between friends were as strong often as those between families. Connections are maintained over long periods of time. We might not see each other for years and then meet again with open arms and hearts. It had been years since my father and mother had seen Dadmir and years more since my mother had delivered Dadmir's wife of their first son. Through that association, and through long-standing traditions of gratitude and hospitality, our families had remained connected in spite of time and distance. Here was Dadmir again, staying in our home and eating the best food that my parents could afford to set on the table; telling us stories again until I felt my cares slipping from my shoulders and believed I was not so different now from the boy I had been.

One of my favorites was the story he told about the time his family made enough money to build their first permanent residence. They built a mud house in Gerde Ghauss so that his mother and sisters could stay and care for the family while the adult males continued their trade routes by traveling from city to city and country to country on camels, horses or donkeys. As a young boy, Dadmir had been happy that he could stay in one place and attend classes and meet other boys. He said that his grandmother carried him, at the age of seven years old, on her shoulders for hours to a nearby village where he waited for hours along with dozens of other boys for a teacher to arrive. The teacher was a volunteer from Jalalabad who took a bus every day for fifty minutes to gather the children under the shade of a tree and teach them on a small blackboard. The board was almost white from nearly constant use. They did not have pencils to write with or paper to write on, but relied on memory to learn what the teacher taught.

When Dadmir grew up and took the lead of his father's caravan and trade route, he sold the camels, horses and donkeys and bought two new trucks with money he had spent years in saving. He let the women take care of the flocks of sheep and goats in their village and he got into the business of rice, flour and tea which ended up changing the life of Dadmir and of his entire village. The new industry he developed meant that the men of the village no longer had to travel by animal for weeks or months. Most of the males in the village took his lead and bought trucks. Their trade route was now between Pakistan and Afghanistan. When Dadmir's wife was pregnant, he drove her to Kabul where my mother delivered their first boy after three girls. He remembered a time when one third of the births in the Kuchi village resulted in the loss of the mother or the baby.

At the time when Dadmir visited us in 1987, most of the Kuchi in his village were successful businesspeople that were able to hire their own teachers to come and teach literacy to the children of the village. It made me wonder at the power of education to transform a small village and I have never forgotten the idea that if education has the power to elevate the status of groups of people in remote villages, it might do the same and more for an entire nation.

Dadmir was grateful to his grandmother for carrying him on her shoulder every day to take him to his teacher. He praised her for her tireless commitment to her family and he sang the praises of the volunteer teacher as well, who truly wanted to help his country to become independent and free. Such devotion and personal conviction, Dadmir said, is a rare thing to find.

When Dadmir told the story again on this visit, it inevitably brought him to the topic of politics. The government, even when he was a child in the 1970's, did not care to provide a teacher for hundreds of Kuchi boys to learn the basics of literacy. There was not war at that time, but government indifference that meant a man had to make the choice to travel so far and teach these children. Dadmir blamed the Russian invasion mostly on the prior administrations, especially King Zahir who created the situation that made it so easy for the Russians to invade.

"If he did not spend so much time in foreign countries and in entertainment and focused on the needs of his own country, we would not be in this situation where the sons of our nation are the very ones that help the enemy to invade," said Dadmir.

As the conversation and the night wore on, the topic turned to more serious subjects. As nomads, Dadmir's sons were not subject to the army draft and they were relatively safe in their small, remote village. Dadmir however, was aware of the precarious situation of young men in my position. My parents further elaborated on our struggles to secure a mode of escape. Dadmir grew quiet and then he said,

"If you come to my village, I can help you escape across the border. My village, Gerde Ghauss is near the Torkham border."

My parents were grateful for his offer and he acknowledged their friendship in kind. I went to bed that night as I did every night, beside the window so that I could escape easily if the search crews came in the night. I thought for a long time about the prospect Dadmir had laid before me. I heard everything he and my parents had discussed and I heard also the hushed tones they used when they spoke of the Khyber Pass. I would have to cross it after I reached Dadmir in Gerde Ghauss. I knew of the Khyber Pass, and of its long and bloody history as a trade route and a strategic military location, dangerously cutting through the Hindu Kush Mountains. I began to understand the full range of dangers that awaited me. I fell into a dreamless sleep.

One evening a week or two later, I was running from a search crew and one of our neighbors saw me hiding in his yard and opened his door for me. He worked as a clerk, I knew, in one of the military bases on the outskirts of Kabul. He had almost lost one of his legs when a Russian plane bombed their village in Panjsher two years before and still had a piece of metal shrapnel in his left leg that he was proud to show to people.

"Ah," he said when I ducked inside, "It is the savior of Kabul!"

I'd come to know him well since my return from Germany and he often joked that I must be a savior if I dared leave my comfortable life in Germany to return to a wasted city.

"It seems Kabul is not in the mood to be saved tonight," I said.

"No, she is *in the mood* every night," he laughed, "It is only that these men rape her before the honest men ever have a chance."

Sharif was an intelligent man. He worked at the military base out of necessity, as he had a wife and four children to support. We sat and talked for some time that evening and I told him about Dadmir's offer to secure my passage across the border.

"You did not ask me first?" he said, surprised.

"I did not want to make trouble for you."

"Bah!" he waved his hand as a dismissal of trouble, "*you* don't make trouble for me. The *Russian's* make trouble for me. I've waited a long time to get my revenge on them. I do it slowly, you see."

He provided me then with the missing link in our plan to get me to Dadmir's village. Sharif told me that he could obtain fake documents so that the joint Afghan government and Russian checkpoints would let me pass. I questioned him again to see if he was serious and then I went home to tell my parents. They displayed a mix of emotions and for the next few days we all waited without talking about it to see if at last my opportunity would come through.

*

16

~ ~ ~

ROAD TO JALALABAD

A few days passed as my parents seemed to hover over me in anticipation. I read my books and tried not to entertain any expectations about my future. A week passed and I began to suspect that my conversation with Sharif meant nothing. Perhaps I had misunderstood and he was only being hospitable; trying to pacify me in my worried state. On the eighth night after our conversation, there was a knock at the door. My mother and father exchanged a look and my mother nodded. I stuffed my book under the couch cushion and headed for the back door. Once outside, I ducked under the open window to hear the conversation inside. The voices were muffled, and I strained to hear them. After a moment there was silence and the sound of the door closing. I waited for someone to tell me it was okay to come back inside. Just then, the back door burst open and a loud, male voice shouted at me.

"Aha!" it cried and my heart pounded in fear that I had been discovered by the search crews who had been dogging me for months.

"Aha!" the voice cried again, and I looked up in fear only to see Sharif standing there smiling like a madman and waving a handful of papers at me. I broke into a broad smile and jumped up, shaking his hand and wiping my brow theatrically. He laughed and patted me on the back as we stepped back inside the house.

"Boy, have I got something for you!" He said.

My parents were waiting by the kitchen table. My mother's eyes were averted, but I could sense her anticipation in the way she held her body. She would tell me later it was more than that. It was—she would say—a combination of hope and fear; of love and horror. *I pray you never know what I mean, but you will. When you have children of your own, you will.* When I watched Omar walk away from me on his first day of school, I felt a taste of what she must have felt and I have felt it many times since, for each of my sons.

In the kitchen that night, my father stood smiling uncomfortably. Sharif slapped the papers down on the table in front of us.

"I did it, didn't I? Just like I said I would. Right under their noses!" he laughed again. "You are a military man now, brother."

For a brief moment, I was struck with fear that he had somehow misconstrued my intentions and enlisted me as a soldier in the Afghan army, but he continued.

"At least according to these. The papers here say that you are a soldier and this one…" He pulled another from the stack, "These give you permission to visit your ill uncle in Jalalabad for 3 days."

He turned serious now. Out of the corner of my eye, I saw my mother put a hand to her mouth.

"These documents alone are not enough to secure your escape. You have heard stories about those who have been caught?"

I nodded. He spoke now to my mother and father as much as to me, "I must give you all of the information you need to answer their questions successfully. They will ask questions at the checkpoints. You must ensure that they do not detain you. That is when the real trouble begins."

We nodded solemnly and Sharif tried to put on a happy face again, but I think it was suddenly very real for my parents and myself and we had a hard time mustering up more than a gracious 'thank you,' and watched as Sharif hobbled to the door and left us alone.

For the next few days, Sharif visited us each evening and spent time with me, explaining the base, its officers and other important facts about a soldier's life that I must be able to answer immediately if questioned. I would have to be convincing in my role as a soldier since those who questioned me would be soldiers themselves. I tried not to be nervous thinking about this. On the fourth day of his instruction, Sharif asked me several questions that I might be faced with and I answered all of them with minimal hesitation. He drilled me for another hour and then stood up to leave. I heard him inhale deeply and when I looked up at him, he was nodding.

"I think you are ready, Savior of Kabul."

I shook his hand and he seemed about to say something more, but my father approached and shook his hand as well. Sharif turned to him and muttered something against the Russians that sounded like something about them being "dirtier than the pots they piss in." Ordinarily I would have chuckled, but not that night. When he was halfway out the door, Sharif turned and hollered over his shoulder at me, "Keep her with you!" and patted himself on the heart. I lifted a hand to wave. It was the last time I saw him.

When the day came, I woke at four o'clock in the morning. I dressed in comfortable, traditional Afghan clothing, including a loose *payraan tumbaan* and vest with a *pakol* hat and a *patu* for warmth. The sky was not yet warmed by the sun and my things were piled by the door, waiting. In my travel sack were the fake documents, a change of clothes and a novel I had not yet finished reading. We determined that I would catch the earliest bus from Pule Kheshti Mosque and travel from there to Jalalabad where I would attempt to find Dadmir. From there the plans were unclear, but we were confident that our old friend would help. My mother was going to write to him as soon as I left to let him know that I would be arriving soon at his home.

My parents and my sisters were all waiting for me as I went through my things one last time to make sure I had everything I would need. They stood motionless. When I looked at my father, I saw that he was no longer able to hold his tears in. I could not imagine their anguish, nor can I imagine it now. They would have no way of knowing if I was alive or dead until they received word from me that I was safe in Peshawar. And if that letter never came…well, it had happened to others.

My sister Maryam held a Quran in her hand and had me walk under it three times. I hugged my father who gripped me in a tight hug. A slight sob escaped his mouth as he let me go. My mother crossed her arms around me and said, "God be with you at all times my son."

A taxi was waiting on the curb in front of our house in the cool, pre-dawn darkness. I climbed inside and we drove in silence toward downtown Kabul where I paid the taxi-driver and got into a mini bus heading for Jalalabad. I found a seat near the back of the bus, which was hardly an inconspicuous spot given the size of the vehicle. The engine was running and I watched as the other passengers boarded. Each of them looked tired and unencumbered by worry. I realized they all had legitimate reasons for being on the bus. I was sure that none of them were in the midst of escaping as I was. I envied them their routines; their annoyance at having to be awake so early for a day of travel.

I watched the familiar sights of Kabul slip by the window as we drove. Slowly at first, and then they were flying past and I wondered if I should ever see them again. In my sadness at leaving my home and my family, it occurred to me that life is simply the view from a series of windows. There is nothing we can do to change the view. We simply move on. Realizing the negative turn of my thoughts I closed my eyes and tried to clear my mind. When I opened them again, we were on the outskirts of Kabul and in the distance I saw a grey heron just taking flight over the Kabul River. I watched it soar low over the glistening water until it disappeared in the tall river grass on the far shore.

The bus began to slow and with the grinding sounds of the engine, my muscles began to tense. I knew we were approaching the first checkpoint. I leaned as close as I could to the window and saw the army vehicles parked ahead. I fought the urge to sink down in my seat, knowing that in my role as a soldier I had to appear confident. We ground to a stop and the bus doors opened. An Afghan soldier boarded the bus with his gun slung over his shoulder. He exchanged some words with the driver and then glanced around. I had been watching him as discreetly as possible from the corner of my eye, but I averted my gaze quickly when he turned. I heard his footsteps, slow and measured as he approached me. I was the only young man on the bus and I knew his attention would be drawn to me. I looked up at him and smiled as casually as I could.

At this time, another soldier boarded the bus and spoke to the driver. He looked back and saw his buddy talking with me. Our eyes met for an instant and though I looked away, I could feel his gaze on me. The soldier standing next to me asked me for my documents and I produced them. He looked them over slowly, asking me where I was stationed and why I was travelling. I spit out my answers seamlessly. He spent another moment in examining the papers before he handed them back to me. The soldier at the front of the bus was laughing now with the driver and leaning casually against the dashboard. The first soldier looked around at the other passengers before he made his way slowly to the front of the bus. He said a word to his comrade, who looked at me briefly. The bus driver said something to the soldiers to cause them to laugh again. Then they turned in unison and exited the bus.

As soon as they left, the engine roared to life again and I let out a relieved breath. The loud engine of the bus seemed to hum now with reassurances. My confidence soared after passing this first checkpoint. I knew now that my papers would pass inspection and that I could convincingly answer the questions posed to me. With the bus moving again, I settled into my seat and stared out the window as the sun rose over the hills and coaxed the surrounding landscape to life. A flock of warblers wheeled in the fresh blue morning. Throughout the bus, windows were lowered and a cool breeze stirred through the vehicle. The road ahead of us began to climb toward the mountains, still cast in shadow. The rays of the sun were spilling on me, but I shivered in spite of their warmth.

After about an hour of driving into the mountains, we were close to Sorubi Dam. Our bus was stopped for the second time. Being later in the morning, there were more soldiers milling around at this checkpoint than the last. Once again, two men boarded the bus. The first was clearly an Afghan soldier, but the second wore no distinguishing uniform and stood at the front of the bus with his arms crossed, looking narrowly at each passenger. Unlike the first checkpoint, these men did not speak to the driver. Desperate for something to focus my eyes on, I locked my gaze on the driver who sat staring straight ahead. I was leaning back, head rested on the seat to appear unconcerned. I looked the soldier in the eye as he approached me and demanded my documents. As he took them, the non-uniformed officer ordered the soldier to bring my papers outside. They departed the bus and I struggled to appear indifferent. After a moment, the soldier stepped back onto the bus and waved at me to step outside. I stood and followed. Once outside, I stood and waited for instruction. The man who wore no uniform was staring intently at my documents. Behind him stood a rigid soldier with a gun in his hands and two more on his person. Looking up from my papers, the officer—who I suspected was an Afghan Secret Service Agent—began questioning me about my status in the army.

I answered his questions as I had practiced and while I did so, his eyes bore through me. When he was finished, I was unsure if I had answered satisfactorily because he told me then that he would have to verify my documents.

"Sir, I am afraid the bus will become late and I will not make it to Jalalabad today if I am detained much longer," I spoke up.

He looked at me carefully and nodded. He walked to the bus and leaned inside. I overheard him instruct the driver to continue on his route without me. My heart sank in my chest.

"There," he said with a smirk. "Good of you to not wish to detain those passengers."

"I am worried about my uncle."

"There will be another bus. Until then, I will have time to verify these."

He waved my papers in the air.

"Put him in the booth," he said to the armed soldier that stood behind him.

The bus remained idling behind us as the driver jumped down to retrieve my bag from the roof. As he threw it on the ground at my feet, I tried to catch his eye in a last attempt at rescue. I knew if the officer left to verify my documents, he would only confirm that they were fakes. Instead of looking at me, the driver looked over my shoulder to where a distant shout could be heard.

"*Hawan!*"

Nearer to us, someone yelled, "*Prot!*"

We all dropped to the floor at this command. Seconds later, a resounding explosion was heard. As I raised my head, I could see huge clouds of dust a hundred feet away. The soldiers started scrambling and the officer stood up, ordering his men to their positions. One of the soldiers turned to us and told the bus driver (who was already scrambling back aboard) to move the bus to shelter. I could tell by the look on the drivers face he would not be waiting around for me and I debated whether to follow him or to wait and try to retrieve my documents.

There was more shouting then and I crawled behind a pile of stone blocks, unsure if I was making the right move. The second explosion was louder and closer. Shards of debris and clumps of dirt rained down on us. I stood up and the non-uniformed agent was standing up nearby.

"Let me go on my way," I shouted at him, "There will be no more buses anytime soon now."

Around us, the soldiers had burst into action. The agent looked at me and then at the site of the most recent explosion, mere yards away. He shook his head and moved to grab my wrist with his hand, but I shook it off and grabbed instead for the papers he held. I pulled them from his grip and started running toward the bus as it gathered speed. I shouted and the bus slowed enough for me to jump on, documents in hand. The rest of the passengers stared around themselves, uncertainly. Fortunately they were too concerned about the explosions to care much for what I did. As the driver pulled away we heard the sound of machine guns rattling behind us. The explosions and shooting continued as we drove for at least another mile, throughout which we all huddled in our seats with our heads down. After some distance, silence invaded the bus again and we sat up, one by one with great sighs of relief and murmured conversation.

Every few miles or so on the journey through the winding mountain roads, there would be burned out Russian tanks or trucks on either side of the narrow road. It was often unclear if we were in an area controlled by the mujahideen or the Russians. Steep mountains rose up on either side of us and occasionally we would dip into a valley. I kept my eye on those tall mountain peaks, looking for signs of the mujahideen. I was afraid they would attack and take control of our bus. I knew that if that happened I would surely be captured. They would have no need for the old men and women and children and would likely let them go. I only hoped that the mujahideen would attempt to verify my documents as their enemies had. Only then would I have any chance of escape.

For the next hour, our speed did not exceed fifteen or twenty miles per hour. The slowness of our progression was excruciating. I was waiting for the attack to come at any moment. Then the bus began to slow even further. Up ahead there were two Russian tanks stopped by the side of the road. Similar to the previous checkpoints, soldiers scanned the assembled passengers and I was asked to step out of the bus.

A similar scene played out in which a uniformed soldier examined my documents and informed me they would have to be verified. I used the Russian I knew to explain to them that I was in a hurry to get to Jalalabad, but once again I realized that I would have no choice but to follow their plan. The bus was waved on, my bag was thrown at my feet and the driver took off, probably thankful to be rid of me. The soldier took my papers to one of their booths where several military personnel were encamped. I looked around me, feeling suddenly alone and vulnerable as the tail-end of the bus grew farther and farther away.

A Russian soldier who had been standing nearby observing nodded at me and asked me if I had a cigarette. I pulled a pack out and handed it to him. He took one and then held it back out to me.

"You keep it. I'm too worried to smoke. My uncle, he's sick and I can't seem to get where I need to go," I said in Russian.

He thanked me by saying, *'Tashakoor,'* and lit his cigarette. I asked him his name and he told me it was Sacha. I told him mine was Abdul. He looked impressed that I spoke Russian so well.

"Where are you going?" he asked.

"Jalalabad," I said, "I just can't seem to get there. I only have three days but I don't know if I'll make it. This is the second time they've had to verify my documents and sent my bus ahead."

"You seem like a good guy," he said, pocketing the pack of cigarettes, "You say you already had your papers verified?"

"Back at the Sorubi Dam checkpoint," I said nodding at the road we had come in on.

Sacha told me to wait and walked to the booth where the first soldier had retreated with my papers. A moment later, Sacha returned with another man, an Afghan soldier this time. The Afghan was carrying my documents and when he approached me, he spoke to me in Russian and asked me where in Kabul I performed my military duty. I answered the questions the same way I had when I was previously asked. He handed me the documents and told me to wait for the next car to Jalalabad.

I thanked him and I thanked Sacha who talked with me while I waited. Before long a truck pulled up to the checkpoint and stopped. The truck bed was loaded with boxes, but Sacha approached and asked the driver if there was space for me.

"He says get in back and hold on tight," Sacha said.

I climbed into the bed of the truck and thanked Sacha again, waving at the Russian and Afghan soldiers as the truck lurched forward and moved toward the city.

Alone in the back of the truck with nothing but boxes and open air around me, I had time to think about the journey I was on. I already felt that I was far from home and I did not know what awaited me on the path ahead. I had mixed feelings about my decision to leave the city that had given birth to me. Already the journey had been fraught with peril and it had barely begun. I began to consider turning around and going back. I thought about my parents and what would happen to them if they lost their only son. I told myself it wouldn't be so bad to go back to them and join the military in Kabul. After a few years I would be able to attend Kabul University and at least I could be with the people I loved most in the world. I thought about the city I deserted; about what it meant to live in a place where you are both understanding and understood. As I thought these things I began to feel the weight of my fatigue. I leaned back on a box and closed my eyes. I was kept warm by the thought that I might go back there, surrender myself to the flow of life. Then I fell asleep.

When I dreamed it was about the past. It was not a dream so much as a memory of faces. I saw Farhad and Wali. I saw the other friends and relatives that had gone before me. I saw the face of my sister and my friends in Germany who I had also left behind for the irresistible pull of Kabul. I saw Baraymal and myself as children, and Hamed on the hill where we once read our novels, I saw eyes as green as spring grass and cream-white skin.

As the truck bounced along the rutted road, I opened my eyes on a beautiful sky that spanned the distance of the world. I knew in that moment that there was nothing more beautiful in life than to be free. How else would I change the lives of those I loved than to be in charge of my own destiny? The flow of life is a funny thing. Sometimes you cannot tell if you flow through it, or if it flows through you. In the midst of so much thought and imagination, the truck finally slowed to a stop and I sat up to see that the world around me had changed while I stared at the sky. I had arrived at my destination: downtown Jalalabad.

*

17

~ ~ ~

PLUMES OF SMOKE

I jumped from the truck in downtown Jalalabad and tried to brush the gathered dust from my clothes. I immediately began looking for the bus to Torkham that would travel through Gerde Ghauss. The sun was high in the sky and I darted through the crowds of people along the streets. I asked a few passersby in Pushto if they knew where I could catch the bus to Torkham. The first man gestured to the location where I would find the bus depot. Another woman told me the next bus to Torkham would not leave until the following morning. I continued walking, hurrying now to the bus depot. When I arrived, it was only to confirm that the bus to Torkham had already left and that I would be stranded in Jalalabad overnight. I began to formulate a plan to find a motel in which to sleep. I wandered the city, at a slower pace now. The sun was beginning its descent. I stopped the occasional pedestrian to ask where I might find a place to sleep for the night. Eventually I came across a young man, only a little older than myself, who had a dirty satchel slung over his shoulder. His clothes were well-worn but his face was friendly.

"Ah!" he said when I asked him for the address of a motel.

He nodded his head and took me by the arm, leading me in the opposite direction of that in which I had been walking. We turned down a narrow side street and he took the lead, turning once to smile at me. We finally arrived at a *kota*, a big open room, where many travelers slept. It was close to the bus stop, so it was an attractive place for bus and truck drivers, or weary visitors to spend the night. The young man nodded and I thanked him.

"We are on the same journey, my friend," he said. I was surprised by this, but before I could ask him what he meant, he vanished into the shadows of an alleyway. Once I established where I would spend the night, I set out to find something to eat. The smell of the local restaurants made my mouth water, but I knew I could not afford to eat a fine meal. I did not know what expenses I would face as I travelled. I passed by a restaurant whose windows and doors were open, letting out delicious scents and the sound of laughter from those gathered within. Beside this building was a smaller, humbler stand and I ducked into it to purchase my meal. I did not realize how hungry I was until the meal was finished and my stomach continued to growl. I thanked the boy behind the counter, who had been apparently daydreaming as he stared into the night outside.

The night was balmy and still retained the heat of the day. I walked back to the *kota*, my clothes sticking to my skin and my skin prickling from being under the sun all day in the back of the truck and on foot. I entered the open room where I would sleep and found an empty spot on the floor. As most of the other travelers had, I took my *waskat* and folded it many times to make a pillow and pulled my *patu* over me to serve as a thin blanket. By the time I settled in, there were five strangers in the room, trying to rest. I began to think of how the following day might unfold, but it was only a moment before all thoughts ceased and sleep descended on me.

I woke up at 4:00 the next morning, the world outside just beginning to gray in the high windows. I drank some black tea, *naan* and sugar for my breakfast served by the *kota*. I participated in the Morning Prayer and made my way to the bus stop. The conductor who sold me the ticket informed me that the ride to Torkham would take two hours since the driver would be required to stop for a length of time at each military checkpoint. This news concerned me since my fake documents only allowed for my being in Jalalabad. I didn't know what reason I should give to the checkpoint officers for my travel beyond the city. As I waited for the bus, I tried to come up with a new story that would explain my travel. I sat with my head down and the squeal of the brakes roused me from my thoughts. The bus doors opened and I watched as the other passengers boarded. It was mostly filled with older men and women when I entered. I realized they were all looking at me as I tried to find a seat. I took a window seat in the middle of the bus next to an old man with a long, white beard. I started to talk with the old man and just as the bus began to move, I told him in broken Pushto that I was feeling very ill and needed to sleep. I hoped that by faking sleep I might be able to avoid communications at the checkpoints.

There was no hope for me actually sleeping. My insides were turning with apprehension. I listened to the sounds of the bus engine grinding, the low hum of conversation among the other passengers. I followed these sounds for signs that we were approaching a checkpoint. At the first sound of the engine winding down for a stop, my heart began pounding. I listened as the bus doors opened and questions were asked of the bus driver. The soldiers did not come aboard and we were allowed to pass with little interest taken on their part of the passengers inside. The same thing happened at the following checkpoint. I could hardly believe that my luck would continue.

At the third checkpoint, I listened as one of the soldiers boarded the bus. I heard him at the front of the bus, asking questions of each of the passengers. I had my eyes closed and my *patu* around my head. I used the hand I was laying on to cover part of my face. I dared not move and tried to keep my breath as regular as possible. I heard the soldier's footsteps coming closer; his voice growing nearer. I heard another soldier at the front of the bus, talking with the driver. I felt rather than saw when the soldier was next to me. He asked me in Pushto where I was going. I kept my eyes closed and did not move.

With a hand on my shoulder, he shook me and raised his voice to ask the question a second time. I realized it would not be possible to continue pretending to be asleep and I was just about to begin stirring and open my eyes when the old man next to me raised his voice.

"Go away!" he grumbled, "This man is ill. Let him sleep."

There was silence for a moment and I'm afraid I held my breath. In another moment, I heard his footsteps move on as he continued questioning the remaining passengers. Slowly, I let my breath escape and opened my eyes to peer through my *patu*.

The soldiers finally exited the bus, but the driver did not move. In another moment, three uniformed soldiers got on the bus. I noticed with relief that these men did not carry weapons. From their conversation with the driver, I gathered that they needed a ride to the Torkham border, most likely to resume their duties after a break.

I began to wonder how long this ride might continue. I was not able to check the time and since I had been pretending to sleep since Jalalabad, it seemed like an eternity that I had been aboard that bus. When we stopped again, a single solder climbed the steps of the bus but when he saw the off-duty soldiers, they merely confirmed that the bus had already been checked and that no new passengers boarded since the last checkpoint. We continued and in each of the following checkpoints, much the same scenario played out. After what must have been nearly two hours, the driver stopped and shouted the announcement that we had arrived in Gerde Ghauss. I had actually begun to doze off, but with this news, I lifted my head and shouted back that I would like to get off.

The three army soldiers at the front of the bus looked back at me and started to whisper to each other. I threw my bag over my shoulder and made my way to the front of the bus. The soldiers grew silent as I approached and I could feel every eye on me. I quickly descended the steps and was in the street. It was obviously too late for them to detain me, regardless of what they suspected, and they had no weapons since they weren't on duty. The bus pulled away and I immediately found a quiet road that led to the heart of the village. Quickly, I removed my fake documents from my bag and tore them up. I had been instructed by Sharif that since Gerde Ghauss was a nomad village it would be in complete control of the mujahideen after dark. It would be dangerous for me if the mujahid soldiers suspected that I was an army soldier.

It was a beautiful morning and the sun had just risen fully over the hills around the village. There were no cars in sight and ahead of me stretched an asphalt road that ran parallel to a river. The landscape all around was barren and monochromatic. Ahead of me, the village looked deserted. I began to feel that I had been dropped in the middle of a foreign landscape; near a village that had been vacated after some disaster. I felt completely isolated and alone.

I remembered the Kuchi from my childhood. There was a time when I was a young boy and I travelled from Kabul to Kandahar, and then through Farah to Herat with my family. We bought dozens of boxes of matches and threw them from the window of the bus at 70 miles per hour to the Kuchi boys standing on the side of the street. Along the drive, we passed several Kuchi camps. We passed their caravans as they moved from one place to another or saw them sometimes settled in the middle of nowhere. All through that long drive we came across these living, travelling nomads and I remember that my mind was occupied for hours in thinking about their lives. My father told me stories of the Kuchi when we sat on the balcony of our apartment in Micro Rayan and watched them in the interminable distance, building their tents. It was always when the weather was mild and the rains came infrequently that they would establish themselves near Kabul. I remember watching as they approached over the desert landscape, attended by camels, dogs, chickens, sheep, cows and flocks of birds I'd never seen before— as though they brought with them the exotic memory of other worlds. It may have been the first time I realized that the world extended far beyond what I knew of it. I watched as the large black tents were hoisted over the camp and flapped in the breeze, and as the Kuchi people moved about, as small as toys from where I stood. I think I even envied them for they were not removed from the greater world, but a part of it.

Looking out over the village of Gerde Ghauss now, there was not a tent in sight. Unlike those traditional kuchi villages of my memories, this one was made up of actual houses built with traditional construction materials such as mud and straw. The village looked much the same as that of Shor Bazaar where my mother's parents and grandparents lived, and which had been built hundreds of years ago. Unlike Shor Bazaar where all of the houses were two or three levels, these houses sat close to the ground. I stared so long at the kuchi village from the road that its flat brown color nearly blended into the surrounding landscape and gave the illusion that it might disappear altogether. As I grew closer, I was gradually able to see thin plumes of smoke rising from scattered chimneys; evidence of life after all.

I did not know how to find Dadmir now that I was finally in the village. I walked among the houses that were closest to the road. An old man with a wild, gray beard and two women with their faces covered stepped from one of the homes and walked toward me. The man walked ten feet ahead of the women and I could tell that it was for protection. I was a stranger to his village. He did not take his eyes off me as we closed the distance between us. When I was near enough to be heard, I said, "*Salaam Alaikom*," and told him I was looking for the home of Dadmir.

The old man's voice was low and rough as he said, "*Walaikom Asalaam*." The women had come up behind him and all three of them looked me over from head to toe. The old man finally turned and pointed me ahead. He told me in his native Pushto language to ask for Dadmir once I got there. I continued walking in the direction he had indicated and I came across some children with bare feet playing in the dirt. When I got close to them, they stopped what they were doing and stared at me as if they had not ever seen a stranger. One of them ran away to a nearby home as soon as he saw me approaching. I asked the remaining children where Dadmir lived. One of the boys, who was about five or six years old, stepped forward from his friends and grabbed my hand. He began pulling me with surprising enthusiasm and I followed. He then told me that Dadmir was his father. I wanted to laugh out loud. I suddenly knew that this was the child my mother had brought into the world. This was the child that Dadmir had been so thankful to her for. I felt safer in that moment than I had in as long as I could remember. I felt tears pricking at my dry eyes and hastily wiped them away with a dirty sleeve.

I found myself standing before a house that did not have a traditional door. Instead, the opening was covered with several pieces of cloth that had been carefully sewed together. A moment later, a hand swept the cloth aside and Dadmir ducked through the opening. He hugged me as soon as he saw me and started laughing. He stepped back and looked at me, his face warm and friendly. He had never before seen me with a *patu* and *pakool*, and this seemed to be the cause of his laughter for he told me then that I looked very much like a nomad of Gerde Ghauss.

"Stay," he said. "Live in the village with us and get married. Your father wants you to get married anyway," he continued chuckling as he put a hand on my back and guided me through the doorway into his home.

The doorway opened into a modest room that was barely large enough to hold a mattress spread with a clean *destar khwan* on which the food would be served. On the mattress a feast was laid and my stomach became noisy at the sight of so much food.

"Breakfast!" Dadmir announced and gestured for me to sit. I sat and he followed but I did not touch the food. I assumed that with so much food we would be joined by at least ten others.

"Eat, eat," he said. "It is all for you."

I did not wait a moment longer but dug into the food as it had been weeks rather than hours since I had eaten. The food was delicious, the robust laughter of Dadmir was welcoming, and even the small, dirty faced that peeked through the curtain occasionally with wide eyes, made me feel all the comforts of home. When we were through with our meal, Dadmir introduced me to the rest of his family. It seemed that he was related to most of the village and I could hardly keep the names straight of each of the brothers, cousins and nephews that came and went from that small house. I began to grow tired from my long journey, but I would not think of removing myself from the welcoming conversation of Dadmir's kin. My stomach was still full from our breakfast when it was time to eat again. This time, the women ceremoniously went outside and killed a sheep on my behalf. As a guest, this was meant to honor me, and I expressed my gratefulness for their abundant hospitality. While more food was being prepared, I waited in a small room with Dadmir's brother and cousin, while Dadmir himself discussed plans for me in the larger room at the front of the house. He came to me and I was told that I could join a caravan that was leaving Gerde Ghauss that evening, before sunset. As much as I wanted to conclude my journey, I was not yet ready to leave the unexpected welcome of Dadmir and his family.

A few hours before the long trip through the Khyber Mountains would begin, Dadmir's brother showed me around their village. It no longer looked like the flat, empty prospect I had seen from the road. Now it was teeming with life and the joys of a shared community.

We walked to the river, just a few minutes from Dadmir's home. At the edge of the water, young women were filling up their *koza* and chatting with each other, laughing and glancing in our direction without fear or modesty at having their faces uncovered. They stared at us and giggled, and I had the unique feeling of being an exotic stranger in this place. From the river we walked along the edge of the village to where the mountains began their steep ascent. As the day gradually began to slip away and the temperature cooled the songs of moorhens and kestrels drifted on the air, as sweet as women's laughter. I occasionally caught a glimpse of the darting shadows of the birds, as if it were a game to dart among the waters and the slender trees.

It was soon time to turn back and prepare to meet the caravan. It was with regret that I had to leave that place. Dadmir's brother pointed to the distant, towering mountains of Khyber and Tora Bora. Their shadows were just beginning to lengthen over the village.

"Those are the mountains you will soon cross," he said. "I have not walked those mountains yet, but my ancestors have been doing business through the passes there for many years. My uncles know the routes in their sleep. People say that some of the high peaks are still controlled by Russians and it may be true. It is certain that sometimes caravans are attacked. But I do not know if it is the Russians or... others... who prove most dangerous to travelers."

He gave me a look that told me we would discuss it no further and we walked on in silence. Already the atmosphere had changed. I noticed those men who walked through the streets with purpose and these I took to be the mujahideen soldiers who patrolled the village at night.

Just as darkness was about to take over the village, Dadmir walked me to the caravan site which was about fifteen minutes away. I had left my bag, including my change of clothing and novel, with Dadmir who agreed to bring it to me when we met again in Landi Kotal. He had already handled the details with the smuggler and when we arrived, he slipped some money to the man leading the caravan. I saw then that I would not be alone in the journey. There were some women standing to one side who were speaking in Dari to each other. The various ages of the women suggested that they were of the same family and I guessed that they were escaping as I was. The youngest woman must have been only slightly older than me and she was trying to load her belongings on one of the donkeys. The donkey kept moving under her efforts and the woman groaned in exasperation. I moved over to help her, but she looked at me with disgust and shooed me away with the bundle in her arms.

"Let us alone," she snapped at me. "I don't need any help from *Khadist*."

She spat the final word out with distaste and I backed up, unsure why she would mistake me for a secret agent of the Afghan communist regime. I feared that her comments would draw the attention of the rest of the group, so I backed away and slouched on the fringes of the group with Dadmir, not wanting to be suspected of communist sympathies.

Within ten minutes, the donkeys had been loaded and the caravan was ready to move. Dadmir and I had already worked out that I would write to him to confirm my safety once I was able to cross the border into Landi Kotal. He would take the letter to my parents in Kabul, and collect his reimbursement from them. After we confirmed these details, I moved into place at the rear of the caravan where I would hopefully attract the least attention. Dadmir called after me, quietly, reminding me not to fall behind as it would be easy to lose my way in the dark.

I saw the practicality of this advice as we moved upward into the hills and darkness closed in around us. I wasn't able to see more than the next step in front of me in the pale moonlight and there was not a sound besides the occasional "*arr*" of the donkeys and the muted whispers of the women. I was amazed that the donkeys seemed to know the path without any direction from the smuggler who led our pack. These animals and their ancestors as well had probably walked this road for generations. The animals dictated our pace and direction and after a long stretch of quiet, I began to wonder if the smuggler was actually with us any longer. I gathered from the noises of the women that they were complaining about the darkness and the uneven path. Apparently reducing herself to communicating with me, one of the women—I was not sure which one, but I knew it was not the young one because I heard her protesting as her relative turned to speak with me—asked me when we might arrive and how long the walk was. I had no way of knowing and told her so.

I had been walking for five hours without stopping and I wished I had rented a donkey as the others had. The women in the party were not perched on top of their animals and possibly sleeping for all I knew. I kept my eyes on what I could see of the donkey in front of me and did not stray from the path he set. Before we left, the smuggler had giving us only one warning and that was to follow the path that was set for us unless we wanted to stumble over a land mine. With this he had given a sadistic little laugh. The caravan leader was an old man with a gray beard and weathered face. He was missing several teeth and wore a traditional Afghan turban. All of a sudden, he muttered something to the donkeys and the entire party came to an abrupt halt. I barely avoided colliding with the rear of the animal in front of me and waited in silence. The smuggler made his way back along the line of travelers, explaining to us in a whispered voice that we must remain completely quiet for the next two hours as we would be passing Russian and Afghan army posts. He warned us that they would not hesitate to shoot us if we gave away our presence there. I wondered if the old man was wearing his ragged grin in the dark and a chill ran down my spine.

At this point, I realized we were not even close to where we needed to be. I was frightened at first that one of the donkeys might bray and blow our cover, but I was soon shocked at their absolute quiet. I could barely hear them breathing whereas before they had snorted and puffed away freely. For the first time, I felt true appreciation for the beast in front of me, who also sensed that his life was in danger.

Far ahead of us I noticed a light and as we drew closer I was able to discern the movement of bodies in the glow it cast. I began to feel worried that we were moving in the same direction as the light. We passed within 150 feet of the light and the soldiers that were on post there. The danger had never felt so real as when I looked at those men, unaware of our passage only yards away. It was surreal to see them and to hear their voices as the talked back and forth, and to know that the slightest sound would give us away. I felt like a ghost in the dark, only facing a much realer threat than any spirit. When we finally passed the encampment, my breath did not come any easier. I kept expecting an attack from behind and my ears were alert to any noise. It was in this way that I continued walking, shivering from both cold and fear.

I spent the following thirty minutes alone with my thoughts and hoping that we wouldn't face further danger. I knew that we had barely begun our journey since we had not yet encountered the rough terrains that the Khyber Pass was known for. It was odd to be one of a group, but with the inability to see or feel or hear those around me. Much the same as when I stood at the top of the road looking into Gerde Ghauss, it was easy to imagine that the world had changed around me; that I was anywhere with anyone in the dark. It was with thoughts such as these that I thought of Farhad and Wali and the many classmates who may have walked this same path. I thought of my parents and my sisters, who did not know that I was fleeing our country in this way. I was sure they would not have let me go if they knew that Dadmir would not be with me throughout the journey. Lastly, I recalled the look of lucid green eyes and tried to imagine that the owner of that steady, dreaming gaze was with me on this journey. Perhaps only a foot away in the dark. Even with the fatigue and discomfort from walking so far over rocky ground having had only scant hours of sleep in days, I felt that I could walk ten times as far to find my own place in the world.

I almost believed that the light that grew ahead of us was part of my imagination, until the caravan stopped again. This time, there was no warning from the smuggler since we were all fully aware of the danger it represented. We started moving again and the garrison light grew ahead of us. I saw no soldiers on post under it and I hoped that this was a good sign that we would pass unnoticed. We were just passing by it when the donkeys picked up their pace and we were nearly jogging. I was afraid that the sounds of our progress over the rocks would alert the soldiers, but it turned out I did not need to worry. The donkeys had sensed the danger even before we even knew what lay ahead.

"Salaam Alaikom, brothers!"

A voice tore free of the night at the head of the caravan and I was sure that any peace left in the world was shattered at that moment.

A lantern flared to life and we were all caught blinking in the sudden blaze of light. The donkeys stamped their feet and let out pathetic, dejected noises. I felt hope draining from my body as I saw in the glow of the lantern that we were surrounded by a different kind of soldier, many with their guns drawn and leveled at us.

"Welcome to the land of the mujahideen," said the leader and the lantern swung from his hand.

*

18

~ ~ ~

THE NO MAN LAND

There was not another sound for what felt like several long minutes. The crazy light swung over the surrounding faces, casting them in grisly shadow. We were surrounded by a dozen men. The one who stood nearest me was carrying a kalashnikov and reached out to grab my shoulder. His grip was brutal. One of the other men shone his flashlight on me and in its light I saw for the first time the face of a mujahid soldier. His face was covered in a full, black beard and only his long white teeth and the whites of his eyes were visible in the darkness.

"You have a gun with you?" He asked, giving me a rough shake to show he meant it.

"No," I said and my voice broke from being unused for so many hours.

He pulled me out of the line of the caravan and the rest of the soldiers swung their lights over the assembled travelers. Finding that they were all women and old men, no one else was challenged. The soldier slung his rifle over his shoulder and began to search me while two other soldiers trained their guns on me.

"Show me your papers," the soldier said.

"I don't have papers."

My voice struggled and I could barely hear myself speak over the pounding of my heart. I cleared my throat and repeated the answer. I looked into the faces of the mujahideen around me and tried to gather comfort from their uncertainty. The leader who held the lantern walked back to where I was being questioned. He grinned treacherously and addressed the soldiers.

"The Khadist has come on his own feet to surrender!"

The soldiers chuckled and I felt the pang of recognition. I dared not turn around, but I thought of the woman on her donkey behind me who had made a similar comment when I joined the caravan. I wondered what she had told the leader to throw his suspicion so resolutely on me. I knew the truth was my only option at this point.

"Brother mujahid, I am not a Khadist. I refused to join the government so I am traveling this route to immigrate to Pakistan.''

There was silence for a moment while they tried to assess the truth in this statement.

"We'll find out soon enough if he speaks the truth," said the leader, again addressing his soldiers.

There were more snickers from the assembled men and I could see them relaxing slightly. My own heart rate slowed somewhat as the reality of the situation washed over me. I was at least relieved that we had not been overcome by Russian's. I tried to look at the men and consider that these were my brothers, however different their choices had been. These were the men of my country in our various beliefs and we maintained some common reasoning. I remained concerned however that I had no way of proving that I was not a khadist. Equally I could not imagine how to convince them that my family and I were against the communist regime.

One soldier seemed assigned to guard me after that and kept his gun relaxed in his grip, but it was clearly leveled in my direction. The rest of the soldiers lowered their weapons.

The travelers in our group dismounted their donkeys and accepted water that was offered by the mujahideen. I looked at my fellow travelers but none of them made eye contact with me. It was a terrible time of mixed feelings. I questioned again my decision to escape and wondered what would come of these recent developments. My destiny was, in that moment, resting in the hands of a group of men who lived in the mountains and had likely received no other education other than learning the ways of war and religion.

I gathered from the first moments with this group that they were not of the extremist factions known as the Hezbe Islami. I only hoped that I was correct in these assumptions. From what I had heard of the extremist groups, there would be no mercy shown; those who were captured would surely be kept and forced to fight or be killed if they refused to do so. My mind was racing, trying to process the possible solutions to the situation I now found myself in. The moments moved quickly and I was not able to discern the intentions of these men, or find an appropriate solution. Each moment came quickly upon the next and I was unable to anticipate what might happen next.

The group suddenly split and the soldiers gathered together. The travelers joined the animals again and I could see that the group was preparing to leave. The soldier guarding me made no move and I dared not be the first to break my position. Suddenly a rough hand came down on my shoulder and I turned to see the leader grinning at me.

"You will be coming with us. We will put an end to the question of who—or what—you are."

He patted me firmly on the back and I stumbled forward a little. The leader turned and shouted to his men and we began to move. I turned and looked back at the group I had spent the long night traveling with. The dark began to shroud them in its cover, but the last thing I saw before they were concealed completely were the eyes of the woman who had twice accused me. They burned with a hatred that was not meant for me, but for a thousand men I might have been. I took some comfort from this. I realized none of us are in control of our own destinies. We make the best of the moments we are given. We learn to die by hatred or survive by hope. I made my choice. I followed the men who led me, determined to live.

After an hour of walking over the uneven terrain, we reached an area that was tucked into the base of a tall black mountain. I could only make out the looming silhouette where it blocked the dim and distant stars. The men who walked with me told me we would climb the mountain. The camp was there in the high ridges. I was told that the Russians no longer had control of this area anymore. It unnerved me that they said this as though I may already be aware of it.

We began to ascend and I could not discern any path ahead of me. I only saw the darting shapes of the others moving rapidly ahead. I had to struggle to keep up and half crawled as quickly as I could to try to keep my balance. One of the men was just behind me the entire time and he laughed as I faltered. It was clear that these men knew the paths through the hills like the back of their hands. My eyes strained on the ground directly in front of me and did not waver. I felt my hands and knees becoming torn and bloodied.

"Once you are here for a few months with us, you will be able to run up and down this road with bullets raining down on you."

I tried not to think about his comment, but continued climbing. How long we spent on that road I cannot guess. Finally a voice from the front of the group told the some of the men to take me to rest. I was led exhausted into a deep cave in the mountainside. I was given a place to sleep and I collapsed there. I meant to stay awake to assure myself of my safety, but instead I slept immediately. In the morning, I was awakened by a firm shake. I rose quickly, uncertain of where I was but knowing instinctively that the situation was precarious. I stood against the protesting pain in my body and let myself be led out of the cave by the soldiers. We spent the day climbing the mountains and stopping only briefly for minimal food and water. Sometimes the men would talk to me. They asked me questions about how I had come to join the caravan and asked me where I was from on several occasions as if they expected me to give a different answer. I did not stray from the truth and for the time being, this seemed to satisfy them. By the light of day, I was able to climb without using my hands which were battered from the previous night's climb. The road rose steeply and I was still much slower than the soldiers. Only two of them stayed close by me and I was at least comforted by the fact that I was not heavily guarded. I did not doubt for a moment, though, that were I too break away it would be quite easy for them to stop me dead in my attempt to escape.

When darkness fell again, I was able to continue walking upright, but had to force my feet to make each step as exhausted as I was.

It was near three o'clock in the morning when we reached the base of the mujahideen camp at the peak of the mountain. I was guided into another cave there by the two soldiers who seemed to be assigned to my watch and once again fell deeply asleep.

The following morning I was awakened at five by the voice of one of the soldiers. I felt as though I had only just fallen asleep and could have slept for days, but I knew I could not refuse to say the Morning Prayer with my captors. I followed where they led and washed my hands, feet, mouth and face as dictated. The soldiers did the same and then told me where the Qebla or prayer direction was. As soon as I was done with the prayer, one of the soldiers took me by the arm and pulled me away from the rest.

"I am to take you to Qomandan Shersha," he said.

None of the soldiers were particularly rough with me and their casual treatment gave me some hope that I was in a neutral camp. I felt both fear and relief at meeting the man who would determine my fate. The soldier led me through the cave system and into the new morning outside where the mujahideen commander sat on a big stone block with his legs crossed. He had a *pakol* on and looked to be European with his blue eyes and brown beard. He started to speak in Pushto and I recognized the inflection of a fellow native Afghan.

"My name is Shersha," he said, "And I have been a freedom fighter in these hills for eight years."

This man's voice was oddly comforting. He looked fresh as though he had just come from the shower. He was clean and good looking; his voice mild.

"Tell me who you are," he said.

I told him my name and where I was from. I told him in truth what I was doing in the caravan crossing the Khyber Pass in the middle of the night. He posed several questions which I answered faithfully and after some time of give and take in the conversation, I could see that Qomandan Shersha was becoming convinced that I posed no threat to him or his men.

"You are only hours away from the border. It is providence that you were detained here, Abdul. You are *Kabuli Asseel*, a native son of this country like myself. It is your duty to fight, to defend your mother country from the enemy of Islam."

Shersha watched me as he spoke, assessing my reaction to his words. I composed my face so as not to betray any feeling for what he was saying.

"I have been living and fighting in these mountains for eight years, away from family and friends and the comforts of home."

He pointed to the highest peak rising above us.

"The Russian's controlled those peaks and used their position to advantage against us. It was not without the bloodshed of our brothers that we took these mountains back. I lost many mujahideen brothers in the long fight, but here we sit, in our rightful place. Look around you. We can hit the Russian's in Jalalabad from here. They are not safe at any distance."

I could hear the pride written in his words.

"It is your duty and our honor to give you a part in this story," he continued, "You do not yet know what opportunities are before us. You do not recognize that the life of Islam and Afghanistan is so much more valuable than any individual life. There is no sacrifice too great to be laid down on the altar of Truth. You will stay with us, Abdul, and you will learn. There is so much to be learned."

He gazed out over the ridges and peaks that spread across the horizon. All I could think was that there must be some way to convince him otherwise. I understood now that Shersha was good and fair man. I felt that I might reason with him.

"Qomandan Shersha," I began, "I am expected. My family will not know what has become of me if I do not cross the border and send a letter."

Shersha listened and it was a moment before he spoke. I followed his gaze down the sloping hillside that stretched thousands of feet into the dip of the Khyber Pass. I was sitting on a stone block by Shersha now. We were clearly on the highest peak in the region. I imagined the restless and worried sleep of my parents; the nightmares they must be suffering. I thought of how much worse those visions would get when the letter I was meant to send did not arrive. I pictured Dadmir and then my parents traveling to Pakistan, only to find that I had never arrived and my heart broke for them. For myself, I was less afraid. I understood that this mujahideen group was not an extremist faction. But I also knew that I would be forced to fight against the Afghan army and the Russians who defended the communist regime, and I knew that if I stayed, my life would be in danger.

Qomandan Shersha spoke again and told me that it was my duty to stay and fight.

"For at least six months," he said, "You will do your duty by Islam and fight for our freedom. It is no more than our right to ask this of you."

I tried in vain to convince the commander otherwise, but it was clear that his mind was made up. I imagine this made him a good commander, but for me it was a fearful sentence. The only thing that encouraged me was that my sentence was at least defined. I hoped that in staying with the mujahideen, I may be able to convince Qomandan Shersha to lessen my time there and allow me to move on to Pakistan. I tried, as I sat there looking at the view and listening to stories of war, to understand what motivated these young and old men alike to spend so many years in the mountains. I had read of brave Afghans throughout history and I knew that this was how my people had fought the Arabs, Alexander the Great, and the British Empire so many years ago. Now I would be part of the long history, whether I wanted to or not. I was stirred from my deep thoughts by the grip of a soldier's hand on my arm.

"Follow me," he said, and I was led away from Qomandan Shersha who had delivered his intentions on me and had nothing more to say.

We passed a tent on the hillside under which four mujahideen were playing cards.

"Hey *Cherk*," one of the men shouted, referring to the man who led me as 'dirty.'

"Are you going to serve their breakfast now?" The other men chuckled.

"Of course," my leader shouted back.

We climbed the mountain even higher. After thirty minutes of climbing, we reached another cave where rockets were piled taller than a man. The soldier took five rockets from the stockpile and laid them one at a time on the ground outside of the cave, pointing in the direction of Jalalabad, from where I had travelled. There were wires attached to the back of the rockets and he waved me over to watch as he adjusted these. He held his arm out and told me to stand aside.

"Allah O Akbar!" He shouted and fired off the first rocket. He repeated the process four more times and I watched in disbelief.

"Where do they go?" I asked when the rockets were gone, "What is the target?"

"It is up to Allah that they will land on the homes of infidels," he said, without any doubt that this was the truth.

I nodded my head in confirmation, but inside I said a prayer asking God to forgive me for the innocents that were likely harmed by those weapons. There was no coordination of any kind to ensure the targets of those rockets. In some haste, we stumbled back down the mountain to the original camp in case the Russians started bombing the location from where the rockets originated.

While the serving of "breakfast" that first day had nothing to do with food, I did learn over the following weeks to cook for the men. I was taught to bake breads and run up and down the narrow roads until they were so familiar I might have been able to accomplish the errands in my sleep. I joined the mujahideen in the night *gazma* and played cards with them during the day. I met an old man who brought meat and oil and various supplies on the back of a donkey each day. It was my job to descend the mountain to the road and pick up the goods he brought. I never went alone, but we often rested at the bottom and spoke with the old man before returning to the camp.

One day, after I had been with the mujahideen for three weeks, I was on one of these errands to meet the delivery. The old man dropped the bags and hugged his brother mujahideen in greeting. I sat on a cool stone and took a drink of water. Several other men were talking with the old man. After a moment, he approached me where I sat.

"You must make yourself ready to go to Landi Kotal. I will take you," he said.

Landi Kotal was the town across the border in Pakistan that I was in route to when our caravan was detained. I looked up at him, confused. The other soldiers spoke to each other in a small group. Another man approached.

"We must take you up to meet Qomandan Shersha," he said to the old man.

Together, we hiked up the mountain and the old man was taken in to speak with the commander. They spent some time alone in conversation and then I was called in to join them. I waited nervously, trying to judge by their faces what was being discussed. Then Shersha began to speak.

"Our friend has requested that he be allowed to take you across the border to Landi Kotal," he said. "It was Allah that brought you here. I hope you see the importance of what we fight for. It is for Islam that we shed our blood on these mountains. There are infidels in the world and it is likely safer here than out in the world among those would betray you and destroy you without a care."

I began to fear from his speech that I would not be permitted to leave. He continued talking about the cause that they were fighting for. And then finally, he told me I was to be permitted to leave with the old man. I did not know what had taken place to convince Shersha to release me, but I stood and hugged him as was the tradition, and thanked him for his kindness.

I said good-bye to the men I had come to know in the past weeks and the old man followed me down the familiar path along the mountain. I could hardly wait to begin walking toward my destination. In the broad light of day I felt free of everything and though the journey to the border took another six hours on foot, there was nothing in me that regretted the ache in my feet or the exhaustion that began to take its toll. The sun was beginning its descent in the pale, vacant sky when I crossed the border at last. I nearly fell to my knees with relief.

The old man and the donkey separated from me and I felt for the first time the reality of my situation. I was free of the mujahideen. I was free of Afghanistan. But I stood now in the lawless land of Landi Kotal. It has been said that the only way to stay safe in Landi Kotal is not to go there. The streets surrounding me were crawling with people and children. Boys as young as ten years old were carrying guns on their shoulders. Hashish warehouses festered among the open bazaar where weapons were the specialty. Nearby I saw makeshift factories where young children worked with their bare hands, making breech blocks and weapons for sale to the masses.

I thought of all the times I had stood on a pinnacle in my dreams, looking out into the wide world. We never know what to expect. We hope for one thing or dream of another. But what awaits us is a bit like the streets of Landi Kotal; a free-for-all where the laws of truth and nature cease to exist. In a moment of glimmering hope, I caught sight again of the man and his donkey weaving through the crowd. Instinctively I knew to follow him and did so. I darted amongst the people; the dirty, impoverished and the wealthy alike. The city was a cacophony of tinny shouts and ringing bells, the clang of money and wares changing hands. The sun set in a western sky that drifted from pink to orange. I kept my eyes on the back of the old man's head, feeling for the first time in a long time that absolutely anything was possible.

I traversed the dusty paths through the "Smuggler's Bazaar" behind the old man and came at last to a grocer. I saw the old man stop and it looked as though he were speaking to someone. As I approached, the old man moved and I saw behind him the familiar face of Dadmir. I shouted to him and he looked up, relief washing over his haggard features. He rushed forward and held me at arm's length, assuring himself of my safety. I was smiling so hard that the tears were kept at bay. The look of exhaustion and worry on his face suddenly suffused into a smile of his own and we hugged each other gratefully.

Dadmir turned and I saw that the old man waited expectantly. Dadmir pulled the rupees from his pocket and paid the old man. After the old man continued on his way, and Dadmir and I began to walk, he told me that he promised the old man 1500 rupees to release me from the mujahideen. I did not hear the story in its entirety until some time later. Dadmir told me then that he would take me to the hotel where we would sleep that night and handed me the bag with my belongings in it that I had left with him in Gerde Ghauss. I was suddenly beyond tired and suspected that Dadmir himself was exhausted, for we walked through the streets in silence.

We stayed that night in a *kota* a few blocks from where we met at the bazaar. As I sat in one of the corners of the *kota sarai*, I wrote a hasty note to my parents notifying them that I was safe and sound in Landi Kotal, Pakistan. I gave the note to Dadmir and I was so tired I didn't remember falling asleep until I woke the next morning. My goal was to get to Peshawar where I could secure my immigration documents and then to find my way to Islamabad where we had relatives that I might stay with. I hoped that in spite of the time that passed since they left, I might find Wali or Farhad in Islamabad. Once there, and in possession of a Visa I would be able to contact my sister in California and eventually secure a flight to Europe or the U.S. I felt that I was finally nearing the end of my journey. It is this false sense of security that fools us all, in time.

Dadmir and I rose with the sun and began walking again. We came to the bus stop where I would catch the bus to Peshawar. He reassured me that he would inform my parents that I was safe and together we went over my plan to reach Peshawar and Islamabad. When the bus opened its doors, I hugged Dadmir and thanked him. Then I was on my way to Peshawar.

The bus was packed with immigrants and off-duty mujahideen. I began to doze off as the bus lurched and swayed over the uneven roads. We were about twenty-five kilometers from Peshawar when the mini bus stopped at a check point. I sat up straighter to look out the window and see what we were meeting with. Two Pakistani police officers got on the bus and spoke to the driver. I was sitting near the front of the bus and overheard them asking him for his party affiliation and ID, which he quickly provided. I sunk lower in my seat, hoping that the officers would only scan the assembled passengers with their eyes and ask no further questions. One of the officers looked up and the other handed the ID back to the driver and departed. I turned my gaze back out the window so as not to meet the officer's gaze. Just when I thought he was sure to leave the bus, I heard him ask the passengers in the front row for their ID's and my heart thudded in my chest. He gradually moved through the rows until he reached me.

"What is your mujahideen affiliation?" He asked.

"I have no affiliation as of yet," I responded.

"ID?"

I shook my head. His eyes narrowed.

"Why not?"

"I will get my ID in the next couple of days. I am on my way to Peshawar to obtain it. I just came from inside," I said, referring to my escape from Afghanistan.

He stared at me a moment and then motioned for me to stand.

"Come. Step outside."

I followed him off of the bus. As soon as I was outside, another officer stuck his head through the doors and ordered the driver to move on. The officer who had detained me ordered two other men in uniform nearby to take me to *Tana* and find out more about me. These officers led me away and pushed me into the backseat of a car. We drove in the opposite direction from which I had been traveling on the bus. The sun beat through the dusty windows of the car and the vinyl seats made me sweat until my shirt was stuck to my back. I dared not ask to roll the window down. We drove for fifteen minutes until we came to a low building and I was ushered inside. The artificial lights in the office flickered and buzzed. I was led into a room and told to wait. For several hours I sat there as different officers came in and questioned me. They wanted to know who I was and where I came from. I answered each question truthfully. They did not give me any information as to why I was there or when I might be released.

At that time, there were over forty-five groups and parties that were fighting against the Russian's and their installed government. Most Afghan immigrants were involved in one or more of these groups and were required to carry the ID that identified them as an affiliate with these mujahideen groups. Hezb was the shortened name for the Hezbe Islami Gulbudin, which was one of the most influential and the most dangerous of these groups. At best, they simply did not follow strict Islamic law. At worst, they were volatile extremists.

After being held for hours in the Pakistani Tana, an officer came into the room and guided me out of the building. I blinked in the harsh sunlight. For a moment, I thought I was being released and may have a chance to finally reach Peshawar. Then I saw the group that awaited me outside.

Two men, obviously mujahideen soldiers, approached the officers who held me. Two other men stood by a Toyota Corolla parked in the sparse shadow of a tree nearby. I was quickly seized from the officers by the mujahideen and led to the waiting car. They shoved me roughly in the back seat and the two remaining men slid in on either side of me. Almost immediately they grabbed the *patu* I wore and pulled it up to cover my face. I gasped and tried to pull it back down but they held my hands down and ordered me not to move. They told me I would have to remain with my face covered until we reached our destination.

My breath came rapidly and my eyes darted around in the dark. I heard only the voices of the men talking with the officers just before they climbed into the front seats and started the engine. From their words came the sudden confirmation that I had, after so many harrowing moments and ordeals—and on the verge of safe arrival in Peshawar—been released into the hands of the Hezbe Islami Hekmatyar.

*

19

~ ~ ~

TEN THOUSAND PRAYERS

Throughout the Soviet occupation of Afghanistan, Gulbuddin Hekmatyar gained power as an anti-soviet military commander. Popularity did not necessarily coincide with power and he was often wayward in his loyalties. Hekmatyar founded the Hezbe Islami group in 1977 and was largely funded—through ISI Pakistan—with monetary aid from anti-soviet supporters, of which the U.S. was one of the most generous contributors. Hekmatyar alternately fought with and allied with other anti-soviet factions in Afghanistan to no apparent gain but his own and employed questionable tactics to strip various mujahideen groups of their power while bolstering his own. He fought not only against the hated soviet enemy, but against his own kinsmen; both civilian and otherwise. Along the way, his group—with its strict Islamic laws—made many enemies both inside and outside of Afghanistan. It only fueled Hekmatyar's viciousness; he could not be sated with taking revenge.

In the backseat of the car, with my face covered and my hands restrained, I perceived that we stopped at two checkpoints before proceeding. Only when we arrived at our destination were my coverings removed. I looked around me, overwhelmed by the sudden sense of sight and tried to drink in every detail of my physical situation. We were at a post in the high mountains. All around us was dirt and brush against the gray and brown rocky terrain. There were scattered tents and men performing the duties of their various posts. The sudden light hitting my eyes made me blink several times. I was grabbed by the elbow by one of my captors and led into a comparatively dark room where I was thrust into a chair.

Here too, I surveyed my surroundings. The men around me all had long black beards and most were seated with their legs crossed on mattresses on the floor, talking to each other. Several of them stopped their conversations at my entrance and stared. Although I was fearful, I accomplished the customary Afghan greetings. An older man, who looked to have some ranking, stood and gestured to the men to move me to sit next to him. He told the men he had been speaking with to depart and make room for the new arrival. These men stood and stared at me as they departed. I sensed that they were trying to learn something of me by my appearance alone and I wondered what their observations told them. The mujahid that originally detained me leant over by the other man and whispered in his ear. I knew he was giving him a briefing about me. I sat still and tried to look innocent of whatever wrongdoing they might imagine.

After a moment the older man gave a wave of his hand that told the mujahid to stop.

"Yes, yes," he said, and then he looked at me closely, "It will at least wait till after the evening prayer."

He said nothing more, but stood and took me by the arm. He handed me off to a guard who waited outside the room and from there I was taken to a large room where the men gathered for prayer. I participated in these rituals and all the while my thoughts flew about without any hope of settling. I was uncomfortable having not been given the opportunity to discuss at once my capture and my intentions, and to perhaps plead my case. At the same time, I tried to think of ways to use the opportunity to learn more about the group that captured me so that I might find a better way to make a plea for release. At the back of my mind was the memory of Wali—normally so carefree and recalcitrant—drilling Farhad and myself on the Islamic prayers and the Quran and cautioning us to avoid the Hezbe Islami at all costs.

When the prayers were finished, two young men entered the room and spread a white cloth across the ground. I looked around me at the other men gathered in that room—apparently military officers. They seemed to have only the slightest interest in me and I gathered by their familiarity with the routines that many of them had been there for a long time. I don't think they noticed or cared who I was. At this time, two other men entered and began serving dinner. We ate quietly and drank black and green tea that was watered down excessively. During the drinking of the tea, a few of the mujahideen who joined us carried on a conversation about politics. They were apparently discussing a number of men in their group that were currently inside Afghanistan running an attack. One mujahid with a black beard and dark eyes with blackening around them came and sat next to me. Over his meal, he sat writing on a piece of paper. I did not pay much attention to him since I was trying to overhear the conversation instead. When he finished writing, I was surprised to find him handing the paper to me. He nodded at me to take it and I did.

"Answer the questions," he said and handed me a pen also.

I looked at the long list. The questions were written in Dari and it was popular knowledge that the Hezbe Islami generally don't like those who speak Dari. My stomach twisted in a knot as I read.

The first question was, "Who is the leader of the Sholeh-e Jawid Party?"

From this I guessed they had probably mistaken me for someone else; someone who knew such things. The black-eyed man remained a fixture beside me but did not look at me when I glanced up. I read on.

"Which Khad department gave you the order to come to Pakistan to work for them?"

The questions continued in this vein and I confidently took the pen and answered truthfully that I did not know. The rest of the questions alluded to my background and I answered those honestly as well, with the exception of mentioning the time I spent living in Germany. I did not see how that would help my situation since the Hekmatayar and his followers notoriously hated western society despite the fact that so much of their funding came from that block.

I tried to answer the questions quickly so the man beside me would know that I was not fabricating the answers, but by the time I was finished it was 10:00 pm and the room had cleared. I handed him the paper and he glanced down briefly before ordering one of the guards at the door to remove me. Once I was in the hallway, another man flanked my other side and one fell into step behind us. In the shadows, this man directed me with curt instructions and occasionally nudged me roughly with the tip of his gun to guide me. I felt the cool night air wash over me as we stepped outside. From our vantage point in the hills I could see garrison lights visible in the distance, glowing intermittently across the slopes.

We eventually arrived at a low building that was built independent of the mountain. I was ordered to sleep there for the night. I crouched through the doorway and found a mattress laying on the rough floor. I knew from the low voices that continued outside the building that I was not to be left alone that night. I barely had time to think before I fell asleep, but even in my dreams I ran through the possibilities of what the morning might bring. In the first dream I imagined I was freed and allowed to continue on my way to Peshawar where I could take care of my business at last. It was the last happy dream I had.

It was still dark out when a rough hand grabbed me by the hair and pulled me up off the floor. I hardly had time to register where I was before I was dragged from the mattress and thrown upon the floor. I blinked for a moment, unsure what had happened and only certain that it was not a dream by the persistent pain in my head. In trying to accustom myself to the dark, my eyes landed on the rectangle of pale moonlight shining through the doorway. The opening was interrupted by the shadow of a man. As my focus cleared I saw that this was the same man who sat beside me the previous night and wrote me the questions. From somewhere outside, lanterns flared and cast a dim glow into the room. The man's beard was long and streaked with gray. His eyes were darkened black the same as before. I stood, unsure what I was expected to do, but certain that it would not be in my interest to stay on the floor. He darted at me then and hit me around the face and head. I tried to block his attack with my arms, but the onslaught was combined with equally vicious yelling from the man and I could not comprehend or defend either.

"You lie! You are a filthy Khadist!" He screamed at me.

In a moment he had beaten me back onto the mattress and seeing that I was well beaten, he dragged a chair across the uneven dirt floor and sat on it, glowering down at me. He took his gun from his shoulder and lay it across his lap, then leaned back in the chair as if it was his pleasure to be there. The look on his face—when I was finally able to blink off the dizzying effects of the punches and look at him—was smug and superior. Two men stepped through the doorway and these proved to be the bearers of the lanterns. They stood just inside the doorway and the black-eyed man began to speak. His voice was one of authority as he asked me about some verses of the Quran and then asked me to recite some prayers in Arabic.

For only a moment I paused, remembering the last time I had worked so tirelessly to remember the words. It had seemed so inconsequential at that time, with my friends beside me. I looked down at the mattress as I gave my recitations and I pictured Wali's face in my mind, fiercely serious as he demanded me to repeat the lines one more time.

Seeing me pause once more under the pressure of the situation, one of the men who stood guard moved behind me and grasped my hands behind my back. He pulled up until I could barely breathe. I forced the words from my mouth as the black-eyed man smiled and the assailant behind me remained in his pose.

When I finished, the black-eyed man stood slowly and deliberately, carrying his gun in his hands. He walked slowly across the room in front of me. He handed off his gun to the other man who had now released my hands and then doubled back to face me. He said nothing, but stood over me and I felt the full threat of his presence.

Without saying a word, he once again laid an onslaught of punches on me and then, just as quickly, left the room.

"Take him to the cell," he ordered on his way out.

I was left alone then with the two men. I bled profusely from the cuts on my face and I could not tell how many there were or how bad they were. One particular injury on my forehead bled into my eye and I had to blink rapidly and lean my head to one side as the men hoisted me up and pulled me from that room. It was difficult to see where I was going in this manner and I stumbled several times over the rough path. We ascended a smaller hill that was adjacent to the larger peak where the camp was and where I had gone for dinner and prayer. This smaller peak lay in view of the camp and as we approached the top, I made out a sturdy building of stone and some mud that was Warzek jail.

I was ushered into a rough room along a row of six seemingly similar rooms. When the door was opened, I saw there were a several other prisoners that lay in various states of degradation. One of the guards hit me between the shoulder blades with the butt of his rifle and I fell to my knees inside the doorway. Before I could turn around the heavy doors and bars were closed and bolted behind me. I felt humiliation wash over me as I looked up and met the hopeless faces of my fellow inmates. In spite of the pain, I shuffled to a vacant corner and sat with my back against the wall, not wishing to draw any further attention. I breathed deeply and for the first time since my arrival, I felt relief at being at least out of the way of an unsuspecting attack. I was fairly certain now that the Hezbe Islami leaders had no intention of letting me go. Lost in thought, I half consciously tried to wipe the blood from my face with my shirt.

An old man stood and spoke something through the high, barred window. A few moments later a hand reached in and the man took what was offered. He made his way through the bodies and knelt beside me, handing me a cold, wet towel. I took it and thanked him with a nod. He retreated back to his corner of the room without further acknowledgement.

Throughout the rest of the day, there were not many hours that we were left without interruption in the cell. After my arrival—which woke many of those who slept—the inmates rose and tried to assemble themselves with some sort of order. I noticed that the ages of the prisoners varied. Some of them dragged themselves to standing as if it were a great physical exertion. Some rose more quickly and these I could tell were still motivated by fear rather than dejection. Some of the men did not rise at all and by observing them I saw that there existed an unspoken communication between them and the others. For each man that did not rise, another came to kneel beside him, poised with a hand on the elbow and eyes on the door.

I joined the rest in an ill-formed line along one side of the room, having had no time to rest further that morning. In a moment, the sounds of the cell doors unlocking could be heard. At this time, the resting men were hoisted to their feet by their accomplices and blended into the uniform line. When the soldiers entered they walked among us briefly before ordering us out to wash for Morning Prayer. We shuffled from the room. Some had obvious difficulty walking and they were discreetly assisted by their fellow prisoners when possible. More than once, I saw a guard interject the butt of his gun into the line to discourage such help from being given.

The rest of the day passed in much the same way. We were only allowed to leave the cell to wash for prayer. This occurred five times each day. There were two bathrooms constructed of mountain stone blocks and mud behind the main building. On the top of each of these sat a guard. I soon learned that these guards were posted there all day every day until the last prayer preparation, which was at 10:00 pm. From there, the guards would step down; lock the bathroom doors, double check that all of the cell doors were locked and retreat to the guards' room which was just across from the row of cells. There was a barred opening in the door and during the first several hours, I made a habit of observing my captors. I watched them retreat into the room and heard them talking and laughing when they left us. I did not know what to expect next from any front. After the last prayer, one of the guards entered and watched over us as we prepared for bed. I followed the other prisoners in my cell as they retrieved thin dirty mattresses from a pile in the corner. I selected one for myself that appeared to not have been washed in years. Like the others, I selected a clear spot on the dirt floor and laid down the mattress. Laying on it revealed the uneven ground and prominent stones beneath. I did not have time to reflect on this however, because the guard that watched us was now at my back.

"Not so fast *batche patloone* cowboy," he said, "Mawlawi asks for you to join him."

The faces around me turned at the sound of this name and then darted quickly away, apparently not wanting to call down the same judgment upon themselves. I stood quickly.

"You are in a hurry?" The guard laughed and turned, leading me out.

Warzek Jail was comprised of multiple buildings. The largest was the one I was being housed in, but there were two more that stood nearby. It was to these that we walked. These rooms appeared to be the jail offices and I heard voices issuing from other rooms.

"I have the *batche patloone* cowboy," the guard said as he presented me into one of the rooms.

Although I wore traditional clothing, he was alluding to the wearing of jeans; an un-Islamic practice according to the Hezbe Islami. The men in the room laughed. All except one. The man with the blackened eyes stood staring at me. I gathered from their further conversation that this was *"Mawlawi,"* the religious teacher. I was left in the room and the door shut behind me. The room consisted of a table on which were a small stack of papers and pens. The floor was dirt as in all of the crude buildings and the lighting was dim. Three guards flanked Mawlawi and in one corner of the room stood a tall post that looked to be the side of a dismantled ladder and a steel weapon covered in black leather. These I took to be the implements of torture and my eyes wavered over them. Mawlawi saw the direction of my gaze and his own followed. He walked to the devices and stood beside them.

"Sit," he directed and the three men moved quickly to gather a chair and put me in it.

Mawlawi pulled a piece of paper from the table and I recognized it as the questions he had given me on the night of my arrival.

"You have beautiful writing," he said, "It is a shame you waste your skill on the *Shohle Jawid*."

I was afraid I would be punished for speaking, and I said nothing.

"You do not deny it, then?"

"I do...deny it. I am not with the *Shohle Jawid*."

Mawlawi feigned a look of disappointment.

192

"I thought you might save yourself the trouble of lying," he said and his hand with its long fingernails went down to seize the steel weapon.

"I am not lying."

"We will see."

He waved his free hand to the guards who took me up under the arms and directed me to the corner. Instead of using the steel instrument on me, Mawlawi placed it out of reach against the far wall and walked around the table to face me. I could not resist the strength of the three men who held me. One of the men knelt behind me as the other two pushed me to a sitting position on the floor. My hands were grasped and tied behind me to the wooden pole. The man behind me remained there, his knees digging into my back as he held the pole in place. The two remaining men stood, waiting for instruction from their leader.

Mawlawi pulled up a chair and sat in the same manner as he had before; at his leisure to interrogate me. He began asking his questions. Most of them were related to evolution, democracy, *Khad* and the *Shohle Jawid*. I answered his questions faithfully and honestly, but the answers were not what he wanted to hear. He made a motion to the guards and they reached down to grab each of my legs. They situated themselves in front of me and each began to pull my feet toward them. My body would not give to the pressure they exerted and I could not maneuver myself into a better position with my hands tied behind my back. I began to sweat as profusely as if I were stepping into a shower.

"What sport do you play?" Mawlawi asked.

"Soccer."

"Aha…I thought so. Pull harder, men."

I wanted to scream in agony, but my teeth were gripped too tightly together to permit air to escape. Through all of this, Mawlawi continued to fire questions at me. Each time I was given a brief reprieve from the leg stretching, but with each answer that did not satisfy him of my guilt, the guards were once again directed to pull at my limbs.

That night I believe I was tortured to admit that I was a Shohle Jawid party affiliate. For many nights after that, the questioning and the subsequent torture were the same. I often passed out from the pain after returning to my cell and woke to find that I could not walk. I became one of the men who could not rise in the morning. The old man who helped me to clean myself on the day of my arrival proved himself willing to assist me often. When I could not rise to my feet for the morning prayer, he knelt beside me and waited patiently to hoist me to my feet at the sound of the guards.

"You are just a boy. They should be ashamed," he said.

I looked him in his watery brown eyes, afraid to trust. He seemed to understand my need for silence and he said nothing more. The nights that followed proved to be much the same, except that occasionally I was left alone. It seemed to me this was only a fear tactic they used. They were never predictable, never consistent, and as a result I was constantly filled with dull hope and sharp fear. One night I passed out in the chamber during the torture and when I came to after a brutal kick from Mawlawi, he slid a paper across the table in my direction.

"Are you ready to sign?" he asked, "We all know you are a member of *Sholeh Jawid*. All you have to do to stop the pain is sign the paper. Then you will be allowed to leave Warzek."

During the time we spent in the cell, I had listened to the other prisoners talking. I knew from their comments that those who confessed to involvement with the *Shohle Jawid* or *Khad* were transported to the stricter prison of *Shamshatu,* or as they sarcastically called it, "Little America," where no sunshine was visible for months or years. Signing the papers would be signing away my future with little hope of escape.

"For where?" I asked.

Mawlawi laughed and then before he could fully choke off his mirth, he began kicking and hitting me. He screamed all the while that he knew what I was. That I would end up in Shamshatu anyway.

After that night, I was left alone for two. In that space, the old man came and sat beside me.

"I am Naseem," he said.

"Abdullah," I answered.

I was leaning against the wall, my body aching.

"I have seen many come and go before you," he said.

"For how long?"

"I have been here seven years. There are those who have been here longer; many who have been here less."

I leaned my head back on the wall and closed my eyes.

"My children were grown. I had many years with my wife. I was fortunate, I think. Many young men have been taken from young families. You are married?"

I shook my head.

"Small blessings," he said, nodding.

In the following nights I began to hear the stories of Naseem and my fellow prisoners. Many of them spoke of their children; the last time they saw them, how old they would be now. Each had a different story about their capture. Some were mujahideen fighters who were caught performing actions inconsistent with *Jihad*. Others were civilian Afghan immigrants who were simply taken from the streets of Pakistan. In other cells there were officers of the People's Democratic Party, Khadist's and PDP soldiers.

I told them my story as honestly as I told it in the torture cell. It was a mantra against the corruption that I felt was being enacted against me. I felt as though my past was the only solid, real thing I had to cling to. If I told my story often enough, they may eventually believe me. Naseem felt otherwise.

"You have been tortured almost nightly. It starts that way. They have not made up their mind what to do with you yet. But they have made up their mind of one thing: they will not believe you."

For another two nights, my torturers did not call for me. I recovered the ability to walk, but not without extreme pain. Naseem guided me to the window in the cell door and pointed out the guards to me. We watched as they put *Nasswar* under their tongues and played their cards. I learned that Mohammed Sakhi was the guard who handed the wet towel into the cell for me when I arrived. The guards were on a rotation between the three cell buildings and many of them spoke to us readily if their officers were not around. When the officers arrived in our building, the cards were quickly hidden and all conversation stopped.

There was one other window in our cell and I would put my face up to the fresh that stirred through the bars from the outside world. I stood there motionless at the opening, breathing the cool mountain air. While I stood thus, a small black bird landed on the ledge of the opening and hopped in and out between the bars that divided the inside of the cell from the world he roamed in. I dared not move and disturb him, but watched as he darted about, barely a foot from my face.

"The Black Drongo," Naseem said.

Naseem knew his birds and told me that this one was a regular visitor to our cell. He dug into the pocket of his loose pants and withdrew a handful of crumbs that he must have pilfered from his breakfast. He spread the crumbs on the window ledge with shaking hands. The small bird sprung on them, grateful and I continued to watch in silence. Sudden emotion made me wordless; the smallness of both the life and the gesture before me gave me thoughts that I could not put to words then and find that I can do no better now.

After two weeks at Warzek, I began to settle into their routines. At each meal our food was dropped into the room. Sometimes the guards would linger and often Nasseem would strike up conversations with them. Seeing that Nasseem was acquainted with me, they asked me questions about my past. I did not feel that they were seeking intelligence, but were motivated by curiosity alone. More often than not, the conversations revolved around politics. The guards clearly supported the fight for Islamic Law. They had such pride in the Hezbe Islami, touting its success stories and praising the organization of the group. They were eager to impart their faith in the religious beliefs they held and praised the educated stature of so many of their party affiliates. They did not see any of the other mujahideen groups as true Muslims.

"I will give you only one warning," Nasseem said, "They will not let you rest. They are afraid of the truth's they do not understand. Control is a funny thing. Those who truly have it do not feel the need to exert it. It is all a matter of politics. The men who torture you want you to sign a paper simply because their superior officers demand it. The more confessed prisoners they have, the more justifiable their role in this war."

"Do they never cease their torture?"

Nasseem shrugged, "In time, spirits grow weary on either side of a never-ending battle. I have been here for four years; I was tortured for two."

The old man adjusted his body on the hard floor.

"My warning," he said, as if suddenly remembering the point he meant to make, "This cell is clean, but there are many that are not. Do not stray from your story. They put their men in the cells to pose as prisoners and they will try to befriend you, ease you into betraying your secrets."

"I am telling the truth."

"Can you even be sure anymore?"

Nasseem rolled over in the dark and spoke no more. I blinked in the pitch blackness of the cell until despair overwhelmed me and I slept. The following day, after Morning Prayer, I was not allowed to return to my cell. I was taken by two guards who told me on the way that I was being assigned to a different cell.

I was taken to the building next to the torture and interrogation building. The men in my cell did not speak to me that first day and no one came for me that night. When the guards opened the door, they pulled one of the other men from our small room and the door was locked behind. All through the night I heard the anguished screams issuing from the building next to us and I did not think I slept until the sound of our cell door opening woke me and watery sunlight filtered into the room. The prisoner they had taken the night before was thrust into the room and he did not move for the rest of that day or the next.

On the second night in my new cell, it was my turn again. I was pushed to the floor in front of Mawlawi and another man who picked grime from under his fingernails. It was the second man who spoke.

"You see, Abdullah, that we do not take lightly our duty as Muslims. You do. For that you will be punished, by God and by the instruments of God."

He took the steel tool up and inspected it.

The night that followed was perhaps the worst of my time with the Hezbe Islami. There was little method to their questioning and little restraint in their beatings. They accused me at once of being *Khadist*, of being a PDP official and of denying my affiliate with *Shohe Jawid*. Each hit was a nearly unbearable pain and each question an incomprehensible riddle that was meant to either put words in my mouth or wear down my mental strength until I stumbled into a confession. When I did not speak from pain or confusion, Mawlawi would commence beating me with his fists. There were only two blessings that night. The first was that the beatings, while merciless, were at least not carried out with the intention of breaking bones and mutilating the bodies of their victims. The second was that my interrogators did not ask me if I had ever been out of Afghanistan before. Had they found out about my time in Germany, they would have surely seen it as irrefutable evidence of my suspected affiliations.

The torturous interrogations continued almost nightly. Sometimes the nights they didn't come for me were worse than those when they did. I found little comfort in my fellow inmates as I had in my previous cell. When these men began to tell me their stories it was clear that I had been placed in a cell with decoy prisoners. These men tried to garner my sympathy with their tales but I could easily see that they lied. I had met true prisoners in the previous cell and I could see the truth of their harrowed lives in their eyes, hear it in their voices and feel it in their emotion. These men lacked the qualities of those that honestly suffered hardship and I knew almost immediately that I had been placed in a cell with the enemy who wanted nothing more than to extract a confession from me.

My only friend seemed to be the guard Mohammed Sakhi. When his rounds brought him to our building, he would bring me the magazines and newspapers he had saved for that purpose. They were all published by the Hezbe Islami publishing organization in Peshawar and consisted of Hekmatayar's speeches and articles detailing the history of the organization. The Hezbe Islami originated as The Muslim Brotherhood at the Kabul University, and since led a reign of terror. With the help of ISI Pakistan, the group was responsible for assassinating vast numbers of educated Afghan immigrants during the soviet occupation, throwing acid in the faces of Afghan girls who weren't wearing hijabs and killing thousands of young Afghans like myself who tried to leave or were captured during the war. The stories, while they horrified me, were written in such a way that they praised Hekmatayar and his cause, celebrating their conviction that God was with them as they defeated the infidels.

Out of my homeland; my prison, there must have been ten-thousand prayers for every one that was heard. The Hezbe Islami Gulbuddin was only one of the brands of enemy that thrives on terror. The true Islam they promoted was fear, ignorance, cruelty and oppression. These enemies were much crueler than any of the invading armies of the past. While those armies fought courageously on open battlefields, these cowards hid in the dark and lashed out blindly in an effort to destroy and hijack culture, history and civilization. In the name of religion, they kill indiscriminately and torture the innocent; all for the sake of power. Similar groups like the Haqqani and Taliban remain the axes wielded by Afghanistan's invaders of darkness. No enemy of Afghanistan has ever been so cruel.

Even Mohammed Sakhi, while he seemed to be my only friend, took every opportunity to confirm his objectives and repeat to me the words of Hekmatayar's speeches that he had memorized. During that time, Hekmatyar gave many speeches to his followers in that camp and I was told with great pride of his visits. Sometimes Mohammed Sakhi and the other guards would ask me about the schoolgirls in Kabul. They would joke about the young women who wore no hijab, but I could tell from their questions that they wondered what it would be like to marry a literate girl with an independent mind.

In my mind I had already defeated their dark ideology and ignorance almost 40 years ago when my mother was among the first 6 women in Afghanistan to throw away her *burqa*. Her legacy was mine and belonged to many others as well. It was her gift to the Afghan women to embrace their first freedom and never be afraid of those who would try to take that freedom. With all the pain and suffering I endured at Warzek, I felt more strength when I remembered my grandma's stories about my mom and I imagined how courageous my mother was at that young age, daring to walk the streets of Kabul despite the dangers that awaited her and every woman. The memory of those sweet stories and thoughts from my grandma produced the only smile that touched my lips during that long imprisonment. All the while tears of pride were rolling down my wounded cheeks without interruption.

I grew more and more despondent as time went on and lost hope that I would ever see my way out of Warzek. One night I was taken to the torture chamber where Mawlawi waited. He and I were alone in the room.

"I grow tired of you," he said.

I perceived over the last several weeks that we had reached a stalemate in the interrogations. The officers were neither able to gain new information from me nor break me entirely.

Mawlawi picked up the steel tool.

"Tonight I think I will give you fifty hits, unless you decide to speak."

I said nothing and Mawlawi proceeded to pace around me, deciding where to place his first blow while I waited in the agony of anticipation. The first one came from behind and landed hard on my shoulder. I winced in pain.

"Count!" Mawlawi shouted.

I counted each of the next eighteen hits as they came while he shouted at me to speak louder. At that point, one of the other officers entered the room and told Mawlawi that he was needed outside. Mawlawi checked to make sure I was still secured to the wooden pole and left the room. He was gone for what I estimate was ten minutes. When he came back in he took up the steel weapon.

"How many hits so far, *batche sarake qeer*?" It was the name they sarcastically called me, meaning that I grew up on an asphalt street. I did not grow facial hair quickly and although my hair had grown longer in three months of captivity, my relatively clean appearance was a constant reminder to my tormentors that I was not one of them.

"Twenty-five," I said.

Mawlawi turned toward me and I saw his grip tighten on the steel shaft of the device he held.

"No," he said, "It has been exactly nineteen. And now I know you are the lying infidel we always suspected you of being. We will start over. This time you will count to seventy-five."

The beating continued and all the while Mawlawi yelled that I was not to be trusted. He would no longer believe a word out of my mouth. I effectively proved to him that everything I said before had been a lie.

After that night I knew that the tortures would continue with renewed ferocity. The following day, even Mohammed Sakhi proved his allegiance to his cause. He visited me under the guise of being on his normal rounds, even though I knew he was not assigned that day to watch my cell. I lay most of the day unable to move and Sakhi spoke to me through the barred window. He tried to express sympathy for me. He told me he wanted to see my handwriting because he had heard I was talented.

"You want me to sign the papers," I said, seeing through his ploy.

He was silent for a moment.

"They will let you go if you sign."

"They will never let me go. They will send me to Shamshatu."

"You will be lucky to get away with your life. If you don't sign, you will die here."

I knew then that Sakhi was no different than the others. His primary goal was to satisfy his superior officers by turning in the required amount of documents to keep his position.

"Show me your papers," I said.

In the oblivion of pain that gripped my body, I could barely move. My chest hurt with the effort of breathing and it was painful even to blink my eyes. But suddenly, with nothing to lose, I felt for the first time in my life what it is to be in control.

Sakhi entered the cell and showed me the documents they wished me to sign. I had him hold them up for me as I read. I selected those that did not directly align me to their most hated enemies and I signed them. I wanted them to know that they had me where they wanted me. I was ready to be compliant. At least, that is what I wanted Sakhi to believe so that he might tell the rest of my sudden change of heart. When one is beaten badly enough, before it truly breaks the spirit, it enlivens it. In that moment I knew that I must find a way to escape. I only hoped to buy myself a little time.

*

20

~ ~ ~

ESCAPING THE RELIGIOUS EXTREMIST

In all the time I spent at Warzek, we had been told that behind the bathrooms was the utter edge of the mountain peak which resolved in deep ditches 150 feet below.

For the past several weeks, each time I visited the bathroom with my escort, I poked a series of small holes in the back wall of the bathroom to see where we were actually situated. What I was able to determine from that vantage point was that the bathrooms were, in fact, at the edge of the peak. But the drop below was only about thirty feet. What was more; in the distance I could see what appeared to be refugee camp. There were no buildings or military posts in sight, but rather thousands of crude houses.

I observed all of this and thought about the possibility that I might be transported to Shamshatu where my fate would not be known for years. I had no choice but to try to escape from Warzek while I had a chance. My only other option was to wait and hope to be released, but the chances of that happening grew smaller by the day. I began to exercise in anticipation of enacting the second option.

During the week after I decided to try to escape, I was still dragged to the interrogation room. I prayed each time that they would not perform the leg-stretching as it would delay my escape for the time necessary to recover mobility. I was almost relieved when Mawlawi picked up the steel bat. Since the counting incident, he seemed to relish beating me with that instrument.

"You like this one," he said, "You asked for more last time, no?"

He and the guards laughed at my expense and while they inflicted their torture, I formulated my plan. I had observed that the guard would descend from the bathroom roof before the last of the prisoners used it and would begin making his rounds of locking up. We were well in hand with the other guards as our escorts and the only time we were left alone was in the bathroom itself.

One night, after dinner had been dropped into our cell and we awaited the call for the final prayer wash of the night, I lay down on my mattress and pretended to sleep. When the door clanked open and the guards called us, I did not move at first, but waited to stir myself until the others had taken their turns so that I might be the last to use the bathroom. Unlike other nights, I wore my shoes. I had taken care to lace them tightly and roll down my *pakul*. I followed the guard to the bathroom door. As usual at that late hour, the guard was ready for prayer and was not carrying his gun. The rooftop guard was always armed. I looked up expecting to find the space on the roof empty, but instead I saw the silhouette of the guard hunched in his position. My heart hammered in my chest. For a moment I thought I must not attempt the escape under such conditions, but in the next moment I realized that this might be my last chance. I did not know what tortures would come next nor what condition my body might be in to travel on another night. I could not stay a moment longer at Warzek, with my future uncertain. I decided I would have to try to carry out an escape anyway.

Once inside the bathroom, I climbed up the wall over the hole in the floor by gaining purchase in the rough stones and hoisted my body through the small hole near the top of the roof. It was mainly an opening for ventilation and I had a moment of fear in which I thought I might not fit through it. Fortunately, the opening was wider than it was tall and I was able to maneuver my body through it. I dropped out on the other side and hung for a moment to the lip of the opening, feeling the cold night air on my body, before I dropped to my feet. At the back of the nearest building was a block wall that butted nearly to the edge of the steep drop. I took off running immediately, hoping to get behind it before I was observed. I was not so lucky. The rooftop guard heard me and began shouting. He leaped down from his perch and a moment later I heard several footsteps in pursuit. From the sound of it, they were nearly upon me.

I darted behind the wall and looked for a place to jump, but I could see nothing in the ground. The guard shouted at me to stop and by now I could hear that they commotion had alerted the others. I jumped blindly, just as the gunshots rang out behind me. I landed a few seconds later and the force of the jump caused me to roll a few more yards until I came to rest at the bottom of the incline. I stood quickly and looked around, trying to orient myself and then began running away from the sounds of my pursuers. I didn't feel any pain as I ran and jumped over those stones that I was able to see. I could still hear the shouting of the guards and the gunshots behind me, although I hoped and assumed that in the darkness they were merely shooting blindly. Shortly I was able to see the lights from the refugee camp and I focused on it as I ran. I stumbled and fell a few more times, but rose quickly and continued running. The further I got, the brighter the road became and the sounds receded behind me. It must have taken me twenty minutes of running and finally walking before I found myself at the edge of the village. Here the mud houses were connected to each other and I was reminded of Dadmir's home in Gherde Ghauss.

I was not sure where to go or what to do. I stopped next to a wall, took a deep breath, brushed off my clothes and adjusted the *pakul*. I set off into the village and came across small groups of people who seemed to be exiting their homes and heading out in the same direction that I walked. I saw a mosque ahead and followed the groups that moved toward it to perform the evening prayer that I had missed. I thought I might go there and blend into the crowd. I knew the guards would come here soon to find me. I spotted a young boy with a white hat entering the mosque.

"Brother," I said, addressing him politely in Pushto, "Where is the gate to the camp to go out?"

"The gates closed at 7:00," he said and looked up at me with wide eyes. "If you need to get out tonight, you can use the back route." He pointed.

I thanked him and quickly followed in the direction he indicated. When I was far enough from the crowd at the mosque, I broke into a run. As I left the village and continued running, I only prayed I did not step on a landmine. Ahead of me another light bloomed on the horizon and I drove myself steadily toward it.

It was another half hour at least before I came to an asphalt street, but there were no cars or buses in sight. I moved on into the small city, where some of the shops were still open but there were not many people out. After questioning a few of the shopkeepers, an old man in one of the stores said that if I didn't have a place to stay that night I could sleep in the back of his store for 10 Rupees. I agreed to this and asked him when the earliest buses left for Peshawar. He informed me that I would be able to board before the Morning Prayer and be on my way.

I gratefully accepted his hospitality, not wishing to continue moving through the streets and risk drawing more attention. I did not know how I would pay him his fee in the morning. The old man closed his shop and I watched through the window as he walked to his home on the other side of the street. I couldn't sleep almost the entire night and what little rest I did get was fitful. Not only did I have fears of being found by my jailors, but I was also plagued by pain now that my body was at rest for the ordeal I had suffered. I finally roused myself for good at 3 am and prepared myself to catch the bus although it would not leave for another two hours. I walked to the front of the store and sat behind the glass watching the city wake outside.

A few immigrants walked slowly down the street toward the bus stop which stood a block away from me. As the sky turned gray and the stars completely disappeared, the numbers of immigrants increased until there were hundreds of them walking past the window and down the street. I waited anxiously for the shopkeeper to return and unlock the door.

Before long, I saw his gray head bobbing toward me. Once out of the building I ran for the bus stop. The mini buses were waiting to be filled with passengers and *tongas* were unloading and loading new passengers to take them to their destination. The conductors shouted their destinations.

"Peshawar! Room for one more!"

I whipped around and darted for the bus.

The conductor smiled, "Peshawar?"

"I don't have money to pay now, but I need to get to Peshawar."

"You are from Kabul!" the driver said, recognizing my broken Pushto. He responded in Dari.

"Get in and have a seat before someone else takes it."

I thanked him and took the only seat left; in the last row of the bus. I nearly cried from relief when the bus began moving forward, but exhaustion made it impossible and I slept instead. My body still ached and each movement of the bus over the rough road was a reminder of my ordeal. Regardless, I was able to get some rest and woke after we had been on the road for 2 hours. When I looked out the window I was greeted with the sights of Peshawar. We moved slowly down a busy street, thick with people, and into the heart of the city. When the bus finally stopped, I thanked the driver again and descended into the city that I had struggled hard and long to get to. This time, my eyes did well with tears, but I could not indulge in idleness. I had more to accomplish.

My first objective was to find the Habib Hotel. My mother knew the owner, who I had never met and was known by me only as Kaka. He was one of the many people that my mother new in her career and who retained much respect for her. Before I left Kabul, my parents and I had gone over the plan many times. I was to find Kaka and leave a message for my parents that I had arrived safely. He would then see that the letter was carried back to Kabul by a traveler. The Habib Hotel was a popular hotel and I was able to get directions to it from the first person I asked on the street. The city itself was much bigger than Kabul and its streets more crowded. The streets here were wide and had more room for traffic. People walked on the same street with the cars, trucks, *riksha* and even *tongas*. Unlike Kabul, the driver's seat was on the right of the cars in the British tradition.

I walked for ten minutes before I came to the large structure of the Habib Hotel. A sign hung from the side of the building, beckoning me and I ran the rest of the way up the street to its front door. In the lobby I asked for Kaka but the man behind the desk did not recognize the name. I told him he was the owner of the hotel. The man looked at me suspiciously for a moment and then told me to wait on one of the couches behind me. He said the owner would be there in a few moments.

A few minutes later, a passenger car stopped in front of the hotel and a man with a white beard and freshly ironed traditional Peshawari clothing got out of the vehicle. The guard at the front entrance opened the door for him. He approached the front desk and the man I had previously spoken to indicated to me and must have told him that I was waiting to speak with him. The elderly man turned and looked at me, not unfriendly, but curious. I stood to greet him.

"Salam Alaikom," I began in Pushto, "My name is Abdul and I am the son of Qabela Momena who worked for your nephew, Professor Nevin."

Without any hesitation, the man began to laugh and drew me into his arms.

"Abdul, I am so glad to see you! Have you been to see your mother yet?"

"I have not. I only just arrived. I escaped from Warzek jail where I was held for over three months.

"Yes, I know. You have not heard then. We know all about your capture. Your mother is here, Abdul. She has tried to secure your release many times but was unsuccessful."

I must have stared at him, incredulous. I could not believe that my mother was there, in Peshawar. Suddenly the tears that threatened before were released and streamed noiselessly down my cheeks.

"Come, come," said Kaka, with a hand around my shoulders.

"I will give you a room to rest in before your mother returns. She works ceaselessly to find a way to help you. She has gone again to speak with your captors. I cannot imagine her surprise when she learns that you are safe."

Kaka laughed again. I was deposited in the room and slept much over the next hours. I was checked on frequently and food was brought. When I finally felt that I could sleep no more, I showered for the first time in three months and ventured from my room and into the lobby. I spoke with Kaka more and we agreed that it would not be wise for me to leave the hotel since I had no documents and could easily be taken from the streets.

For three days and nights, I waited for my mother. Kaka proved to be a worthy friend and he kept me full on good food and conversation. On the third afternoon, I was finishing my lunch in the dining room when my mother entered the room and stared at me in disbelief. I jumped to my feet and she ran to me, gathering me in her arms. My mother was a very strong woman but I could see that her eyes were nearly out of tears.

"I did not believe them," she sobbed as she held me, "I thought you were dead and they only told me you escaped."

My mother stepped back and looked at me. She wore a traditional black scarf and her face looked tired; older than I remembered. I could not stop smiling at her. We went to her room and sat together, telling each other our stories. I did not mention the torture I endured. For her part, it seemed that Dadmir had informed my mother of my capture. The bus driver at Landi Kotal informed Dadmir when he came to check on my arrival that I had been taken by the Pakistani Police. My mother had gone to them and learned that I had been turned over to the Hezbe Islami and it was with them that she proceeded to try to negotiate for my release, with no success.

My mother told me that my father and sisters weren't aware that I had been taken hostage. Only she had been privy to this information and did not reveal anything to my father for fear that his heart condition would weaken. Her story became even more heartbreaking. She had been told by the Hezbe Islami that the only way to secure the release of her only son was to detonate a bomb in the city of Kabul.

"I told them I was a doctor and that I have spent my own life giving life to others. I could not take another life, even if it cost me my only son."

Still she promised herself that she would do everything in her power to free me and that she would never return to Kabul without me. In spite of the trials I went through—the tortures I endured—her strength was unimaginable.

After we exhausted ourselves with these tales of suffering and rejoiced in our ultimate redemption, my mother dried her eyes once and for all and took charge.

"We have to move to a different hotel," she said, "I come and go from Kaka's hotel often. They will eventually come looking for you here."

As we packed our few belongings, I began thinking about my next step. As grateful as I was to see my mother and feel peace and safety in her company, I knew I would not be able to rest easy if I left my journey unfinished. I told her that I must continue to Islamabad and obtain my papers. At first she insisted on travelling with me that far, but I made her see the reason in returning without me to inform my father and sisters of our safety. She finally consented to this and it was with great difficulty that we parted after being with each other for only a week. It was heartbreaking to part from her. We held each other for a long time and I kissed her on the cheek. I was already thinking of the road ahead and she, I imagine, was thinking of the one behind; and wondering how many times a soul can endure saying good-bye.

*

21

~ ~ ~

SAVE THE CHILDREN

I travelled first by *riksha*, and then by a crowded mini-bus called a "flying couch" to Islamabad. I arrived first in Rawalpindi, which was about thirty minutes outside of the city and from there I travelled on foot to the heart of Islamabad. Once in Islamabad, I found the Afghan Clinic for Refugees in G9/4 where one of my distant relatives, Jawad worked as a nurse. Jawad was a few years older than me and we had seen each other only a few times at family gatherings. While he and his family had lived for some time in Kabul, I did not hang out with Jawad there. It was the first time we had seen each other in over two years and we were quickly reacquainted. He wanted to hear about my journey and I wanted to hear about his. We laughed and agreed that our stories would be told, in time. First we had to discuss practical issues.

When his workday was done, Jawad took me to his home which was a few miles from the clinic in the G8/4 area of Islamabad.   The area was predominantly home to Afghan immigrants who were waiting for their immigration documents from the European countries, Canada or the U.S. Jawad's home there consisted of two single beds in a room that was no bigger than a ten by twelve foot box. He offered me a fresh set of his own clothes as mine were dirty and travel-worn. When we finally settled comfortably at his home, I told him some of my ordeal. He in turn said that my timing could not have been better since he would be leaving within a matter of weeks. His immigration to live with his sister in Australia had been approved and he was waiting only for his visa to arrive before leaving. I felt the implied urgency of my situation; I would have to find a job and a place to live in that brief time.

Jawad and I stayed up late talking about our various travels. He explained to me what life was like in Islamabad. He had met friends here, some he had known in Kabul and others he only met since his arrival. This news renewed my faith that I might run across a familiar face in the city. Perhaps one of my old friends was still camped in the city, despite the passage of time. I fell asleep in the midst of retelling some account of my escape to Jawad and he let me sleep. When we woke in the morning, we went to the bazaar in G9/1 and Jawad bought me some new clothes and basic necessities to get me started. After this he went to his job at the clinic and I remained on my own to traverse the city.

In the course of the morning, I found my way to the office of the United Nations High Commissioner for Refugees in Islamabad. I waited in a still office for some time while music was piped through the speakers and cool, gentle air was recirculated throughout the building. These amenities that I had been long without soothed my nerves and nearly relaxed me into a trance. I was finally granted an audience with the Commissioner's appointees and I was able to sit before them and explain my situation. I told them of my life in Kabul and my escape. Everything from my multiple captures to my eventual arrival in Islamabad came pouring out. They had likely heard this story before; I could not imagine how many times. Each face in this city was another story like mine, another plea for help. I was humbled after this meeting. I was told that I would be provided with temporary documents so the Pakistani Police would not detain me.

Shortly after this meeting I was contacted by one of the Commissioner's officers in the Peshawar office. She said she had been assigned to help me obtain my permanent documents and asked me to visit her in Peshawar to provide her with one of the ID cards the Afghan mujahideen group had issued to me. I was not about to go back to Peshawar and I was concerned that the solution she had in mind was to reinstate me with the mujahideen. I determined not to accept her help and thanked her for her time, but told her I would be staying in Islamabad.

I wore the same outfit of jeans and a shirt on a daily basis, washing it regularly in the utilities provided where Jawad lived. Most of the days I spent travelling the city and trying to speak to those who might help me. When I was stopped by the Pakistani Police officers, I showed them my expired UNHCR letter. It was a long letter, written in English with a UNHCR stamp. I responded to the officers in my limited English and between my passable English, the UNHCR official stamp and my jeans, I was typically not hassled.

There were many mixed-use complexes in Islamabad for the Afghan immigrants and I patronized these often. I was finally able to establish contact with my old soccer trainer, Herr Krause, in Germany and with my sister in the U.S. Herr Krause sent me a check for one hundred deutsche mark in his first correspondence. I did not learn until much later that he sent money often but for one reason or another, the mail did not reach me. One afternoon I was at a loss for what to do next and I was looking around me at the shabby condition of the city and its inhabitants. The city itself was swarming with bodies of displaced souls. In every corner of Islamabad, construction was underway to build an infrastructure to support the influx of Afghan immigrants. I stared at the degradation around me, where every manner of human foibles was personified. There was hopelessness, dejection, weakness, frenzy, desperation and I knew not what else. It made me wonder where I would find myself. What sort of stasis might I come to here? What future awaited me?

Somewhere in the recesses of my mind I heard the voice that called my name. But really, there had to be any number of men here with the same name. The urgency of the voice; some memory of it stirred me from my darker thoughts. I turned to the sound of it and saw a young man I did not recognize. An older woman, probably his mother, was smiling beside him. He was most certainly calling my name and approaching me quickly.

"It is you!" he called. As I stood to greet the stranger, I was suddenly flooded with memory.

"Hamed!" I yelled back.

He closed the distance between us and we hugged. I could not believe that this was my old friend from Kabul. My initiator into the world of novels that gave me so much of an understanding of—a longing for—the larger world. I felt in that moment he threw me a rope once again. My uncertain future was stabilized by the familiar face of the past. I greeted his mother and nearly begged them to stay and pass an hour or more with me. We walked some distance and found a park to sit in. The fresh air and good company cleared my mind and renewed my faith. Hamed told me that he had met with Wali just before my other old friend flew to Frankfurt where his mother waited. I asked about Farhad, but Hamed did not know him personally and so he promised to take me to Jinah Super, another park where most of the young Kabuli guys spent their free time when they weren't being taken to the *tana* by Pakistani Police for questioning.

From what I had seen of the lifestyle there and from Hamed's own stories, I began to see how truly hard life was for Afghan immigrants in Islamabad. Every day the police would stop the Afghan refugees. They would detain, search and question them without reason. Hamed warned me that he had lost more than one acquaintance because the police would drop hashish in the pockets of the young men they detained. In this way they could create a case against the perpetrator and get paid. For those who were lucky enough to evade the police and their traps, life was a waiting game. Only the wealthy were able to secure fake documents or smuggle themselves out of the country.

The rest of us had to wait for the chain of command to pass down the verdict on our futures. There was little to occupy our time, meanwhile since schools and colleges were too expensive for poor immigrants to attend.

I parted with Hamed exchanging promises on both sides that we would meet again. He took me, on one occasion, to the Jinah Super where I searched for a familiar face, but was a stranger to the young men we found there. In the meantime, Herr Krause continued to send letters to me on a weekly basis, promising that he would help me to secure a visa to Germany.

At that time, I was able to make contact with Wali who was living in Germany. He said he was glad to hear from me and told me he would try to send money to help me. I was happy to hear that he was living well, but instead of sending money he sent along a German passport that was due to expire in six months. The passport belonged to a Turk who was born in Germany and was the same age as myself. Wali advised me to pay for a photo change, an entry stamp from Karachi and buy tickets to fly to Germany if all else failed. The prospect of that seemed enormously unattainable. The expense was beyond anything I could imagine. My sister also sent letters frequently and she too was trying to start the process for my immigration to the U.S., which typically took around two years to accomplish. I realized then that leaving Islamabad any time in the next few months would be impossible. The embassies I visited simply rejected my immigration to their country, including Germany where I had lived and gone to school. Between the little money Herr Krause was able to send me and a small amount sent by my sister I only had enough to buy occasional meals and launder my clothes. I saw that I needed to find a job.

One day I walked alone as I did most days, only returning exhausted at night to sleep in Jawad's airless room. As I walked I thought about many things, going over the sparse options for work that lay before me. I was distracted enough not to notice that I was being followed until it was too late. I felt a small tug and before I knew it the young boy was darting away down an alley behind me. I turned in time to see him and felt at my back pocket to know that he had run off with my wallet before I set chase. I did not get far before a Pakistani officer detained me. Fortunately I kept my UNHCR letter separately and was able to show him this, but the thief got away. With no money, I had no choice but to write to my sister in San Leandro California and explain the situation. While I waited her response, the time came to say good-bye to my old friend Hamed again. I learned that Jawad, too, would be leaving for Australia in a matter of days. He offered to let me rent his room after he was gone, but I could obviously not afford it. Instead I went around asking if anyone had room for me. That was when I met Baba Farid.

Baba Farid was in his late forties and wore a long gray beard. His hair was long and he tied it back in a ponytail when he was inside. He wore jeans and when I first met him, he told me he was a mujahideen commander. He told me that he spent five years fighting the Russians and that after he was wounded; he relocated to Islamabad where he had been for the past three years. I later learned that this was not the truth. It was the story he gave to everyone he met. I don't know what his real story was. I let him have his lie. In exchange, he did not ask me questions either and agreed to take me in as a roommate. Jawad soon left for Australia and at about the same time I received a letter from my sister with fifty dollars in it and a promise to send the same amount monthly to help me out. I was at least able to pay Baba my share of the rent and spend the rest of my time looking for work.

Baba worked as a driver for the Save the Children office and spent most of his salary on drinking alcohol. He had to drive to Lahor as part of his job and he would buy his drinks there, carrying them around in a plastic bag. He smoked hashish almost constantly with one of his friends, Ghulam, who pretty much lived with us although his real home—and his wife and many children—was only a block away. Most of the jobs I could get were in Peshawar and my return to that city was out of the question since it was also the nearest home of the Hezbe Islami. It gradually came to be that my sister's contribution to my finances, though extremely generous, was barely enough to survive on.

Baba told me that their office needed a bookkeeper for their branch of one of the largest refugee camps in the world in Mianwali. The camp was about a five hour drive from Islamabad. Despite its distance, I was thankful for any opportunity that took me in the opposite direction of Peshawar and I jumped at the chance to interview for the position. There were at least ten other immigrants who applied for the job. After several interviews with the American and Pakistani managers, and math and English exams, I was offered the job with a base salary of 5,000 rupees, which was about $100 per month.

Baba Farid drove me and my meager belongings to the camp, which was located in the foothills of the mountains in the Punjab province. Over 120,000 Afghan families from every province of Afghanistan lived in the camp. Besides myself, there were twenty-two employees at the Mianwali branch of the Save the Children office inside the camp. After I had been there several months, the supervisor in the office was threatened by one of the tribal leaders within the camp and decided to go to work in the main office in Islamabad. Since I spoke better English than the other employees and I managed the budget for the camp, Mary Werntz, the General Manager of the office made me the supervisor in his place. Shortly after my appointment, Mary called me on the phone from the main office in Islamabad. She invited me to take part in a computer training class in Islamabad over the course of several weeks. I was eager to improve myself and told her I would be there. In addition to selling the rugs in Islamabad each weekend, I also attended computer training courses, courtesy of the Save the Children Foundation. I saw my first IBM computer during that time and learned how to load programs, run finance applications and perform daily activities, save them on a disk, print and send them to the main office.

The gratitude I felt for this opportunity was soon challenged. My responsibilities more than doubled as I was called on the handle issues both inside and outside of the camp. On more than one occasion the situations I dealt with were life-threatening. Our branch had multiple projects for the refugees including literacy, embroidery and carpet weaving. Children from ages 5 to 12 were involved in the literacy and carpet projects, while women did the embroidery. Every day I distributed 10,000 to 15,000 rupees amongst the camp coordinators to pay for the jobs the refugees performed.

Sometimes we would distribute third-party food or clothing to the refugees when the original donors didn't have the ability to do it themselves. These third-party donations were sometimes more trouble than they were worth. There was never enough of the goods provided to reach each family in the camp, creating constant obstacles in our attempts to keep the peace. On one occasion, 500 pairs of sandals were shipped in for distribution by our office. The coordinator who was put in charge of distribution went through the camp, randomly giving out the sandals to those he passed in his route. A few days later, one of the tribal leaders sent armed men to the office and we were ordered to shut down the office and discontinue our services since the coordinator had failed to distribute a single pair of sandals to anyone in this particular tribe. As the supervisor, it was my job to ease the tension of the situation. I invited the tribal leader to meet me for lunch during which I apologized for what happened and promised to take care of his tribe when we received future donations. It was neither the first nor the last time we had to deal with such situations of unrest. Later we decided to reject third-party donations to avoid the power-struggles that ensued.

There were at least forty-five groups comprised of mujahideen families living among the other refugee groups in the camp. The mujahideen soldiers visited their relatives during their breaks. When they returned from the war, many maintained the war mentality even though they had returned to a civilian refugee camp and this contributed to some of the unrest that we saw. There were some commanders that reminded me of old war movies in which the British warriors returned from battle on their horses to the exultant kingdom. The citizens of Mianwali greeted their returning heroes with cheers and waves as they passed on the roads. The difference here was that these men returned to a refugee camp in a foreign land, they returned always with a few less comrades each time and the war was nowhere near over. Some of the commanders had been at war against each other, fighting inside Afghanistan over party affiliation, ethnic differences, or simply for control of a territory. When they returned to the camp, fights would break out once again and a week did not go by that someone wasn't killed as a result.

Instead of focusing on the bookkeeping and management of the office and staff, I had to drive almost daily into the camp to deal with the daily issues of the ethnic elders, political affiliates, mujahideen commanders, and other disgruntled residents. The collection of so many tribes, ethnicities, languages, regions, and political affiliations in one place gave me the opportunity to learn in depth about my own background and current affairs, and to recognize the complexity of the Afghan plight that seemed huge, but not impossible to solve.

Some corners of the camp were so dangerous that our coordinators would not travel there to provide services. Young and old Afghan women from these segments of the compact society at Mianwali would walk miles to receive jobs from our coordinators so that they could survive. The carpet-weaving center was near the entrance to the camp, next to the bazaar. Some camp residents set up shops and restaurants in this area to make extra money. The restaurants resembled those found in downtown Kabul, but with large *takht*. I usually held meetings with the tribal elders on top of those *takht*, where I could treat them to lunch and a view of the camp. Watching the refugees reminded me of Kabul with its dense traffic and street noises. The sound of the cars, mulls and karachis mingled with the voices of the retailers, waiters and shoppers creating a nostalgic atmosphere that made us forget the stress of life in the camp for an hour or two.

One afternoon, I had a meeting scheduled at one of these restaurants with several of the tribal leaders. Our office was initiating some new programs and it was my job to get the support of the tribes. Lunch started out great and the conversation flowed easily as we discussed camp life and our mutual interests. Khalid was a camp coordinator who, among the other coordinators, had the most experience at Mianwali having worked there for three years. Most of the elders knew him very well and because of this, Khalid and I often worked together when dealing with them. Khalid was with me that afternoon at lunch. We finished our meals and ordered tea. It was customary to begin the real conversation over tea cups and once these were in our hands, the conversation shifted to war and politics; religion was an inevitable topic, integral to any such discussion. At this point one of the elders mentioned the progress that the western block had made compared to the soviets when it came to weapons. In this vein, I continued the conversation by mentioning that future wars may well be held in space since both Russia and America were investing tremendous money in that sector.

"They've put up a flag on the moon!" I commented, "It's only a matter of time before they fight between them to claim it."

The conversation went still and then one of the elders, who belonged to the Hezbe Islami Gulbuddin, slammed his teacup down.

"No, no!" he cried, "That is the infidel's mentality!" He stood and rattled the table in doing so. I was shocked by his reaction, but he was quickly calmed by Khalid and the others. The rest of the lunch continued without incident, but I was left to ponder his anger for many days. As it turned out, this same elder came to the office the following day with his armed men and criticized me for spreading un-Islamic teachings among the Afghan refugees. He threatened to close our offices forever with brute force alone. I was able to calm him and draw him aside for a private conversation. According to his belief, the American's had never gone to the moon. In an attempt to make peace, I denied the human race their adventure to the moon as well and apologized to him and his men. It was more reasonable for me to do this than to deny the poor refugee families the goods and services provided by the Save the Children office every day.

In spite of these small differences, I built good relationships with most of the tribal leaders and I often helped their families sell their handmade goods. Many of the women in the camp made rugs to sell at the camp bazaar. In addition, each weekend I collected these handmade rugs from different families and distributed them to the retail stores in Islamabad where tourists readily bought them up. As the money that I brought back to the camp each week grew, so too did the share that the camp families gave me for helping them in their trade. This added to the money I made from my job at the Save the Children office. I soon began to see the benefit of this business to both myself and the shop owners in Islamabad who did not have to invest heavily in the goods, as well as to the refugee craftsmen who made the rugs and sold them at three times the rate in Islamabad than in the camp.

In the beginning of May, I received a letter from my parents that said they were finally able to secure their freedom from Afghanistan. After everything we had been through together, as a family, it brought tears to my eyes to hear the news and to think that we would all be together again in one place. When they arrived near the end of May, we met after our long estrangement with tears and hugs. I was able to visit them on the weekends when I went to Islamabad.

My manager, Mary Werntz worked in the main office in Islamabad and consistently praised me for the way I ran the office. These were my first experiences in business and I enjoyed them. Having been at Mianwali for two years, I was used to my routine. I continued to travel to Islamabad each weekend to sell rugs and while I was there I visited Baba Farid. My mail was still delivered to him and I had the opportunity to catch up on my correspondence each weekend. It was late in the month of May when I laid back on the thin mattress in the room we shared. I flipped through the mail and there in the middle of the stack was an envelope from the American Immigration office. I tore open the envelope, my heart pounding. The letter informed me that I had been accepted for immigration to the United States of America. My skin prickled and I jumped up, shaking the letter at Baba who was smoking hashish on the other bed.

"I'm going to America!" I shouted at him.

So I left Islamabad, much the same as I found her and parted from my family once again. Islamabad is transitory but her face remains the same. I could not help but think it was the beginning of a new life, a new story. I know better now. The craftsmen of the refugee village understood this; how the threads weave together to form a whole. History repeats itself and no age is separate from another, no stage in life complete without consideration for the past.

The city of Islamabad grew faster than ever at that time, mostly from money that was supposed to go toward helping the refugees in camps throughout the country. Still, many of the Afghan refugees starved in the camps, under their tents, or died as a result of illness and lack of health care. By the time the money made it to the refugee camps, a huge chunk had been distributed to the corrupt Pakistani government with its puppeteer warlords. This was an era when Afghan warlords were trained by the government of Pakistan. The motives were simple. By corrupting the government of Afghanistan, Pakistan could easily infiltrate it and control the government leaders. This plan was successfully executed a decade later with the installation of Karzai's government in Afghanistan.

Afghanistan now is the same buffer zone between the super powers that it was then in keeping the Russian's from crossing Pakistan's borders. Millions of Afghan lives were lost in the fight and in other parts of the world those involved in the cold war had no mercy for the innocent civilians who died every minute in Afghanistan. It happened before and it would happen again; Afghan blood has proven a high commodity in the world market.

We knew them then as Freedom Fighters, but have since come to know them as corrupt leaders, war criminals and terrorists. Little did we know that after the war, in which we sacrificed blood, sweat and tears, our nation would be transformed into a hotbed for religious warfare. Our history is long, our future uncertain. Afghanistan trembles in the wake of the great, moving tides of ambition and greed; a country at war without end.

*

22

~ ~ ~

THE BAY AREA, SAN FRANCISCO

I arrived at last in San Francisco airport on June 26, 1990 with twenty dollars in my pocket.

Friba and her husband were waiting for me when the plane emptied onto the tarmac. She ran to me and hugged me hard. We held each other and cried and it did not escape my notice that life for us had been a series of partings and reunions. This reunion was sweet, but it contained within it the sorrowful memory of other such events. I knew no differently and I could barely recall a time when my entire family had been whole and under the same roof. Those days belonged to childhood and left us long ago. My swatter's husband hung back. I had met him only once before, in Germany, and now I would be living with them indefinitely. I reached for him too, breaking the ice.

I stayed with Friba and her husband for a few months while I looked for work and tried to find other lodgings. I decided it would be easiest to stay in the area of San Leandro where they lived. Within the first week of my arrival in America, I got a job on the night shift at Burger King on East 14th Street in nearby San Leandro. I was eager to work after spending so much time in hiding and unable to make an honest living. The night manager was an Afghan like myself, but he was born and raised in the United States. While I felt that our common ancestry should make us friends, I don't think he felt the same. Immigrants like myself were a dime a dozen to him. At that time, the San Francisco Bay Area was home to the largest Afghan community in the United States. It surprised me to hear my native tongue when I was in a strange place, but it was comforting also and I felt at last I might come to know the place as a sort of home. I met many people quickly and begin to learn the way of life in my new country. Almost the first thing I noticed was the diversity around me. It went a long way toward making me feel that I belonged. More than that, the people I met in California asked me where I was from and when I replied that I was from Afghanistan, they smiled oddly. It was not long before I realize that they mean to know where in the United States I was from, so I began to answer that I was from the Bay Area and this was a more accepted answer.

Northern California was a more beautiful place than any other I had lived in and I accepted her quickly as my new home. I had been in many different cities and countries since I first left Kabul as a child and because of this I felt that it was easier for me to adapt to life in a new country. I was able to learn the language quickly, English being the fifth that I had tried to master. I was told by many of the Afghans around me that I would be wise to get involved in the flea market business as it has proved a lucrative business for many Afghans in the Area. I however, set my sights on a different venture. I saw the immense value of knowledge and so I chose to pursue my education. I enrolled myself and began to attend Chabot College, where over 200 other Afghans were also pursuing a higher education at the time.

I found a roommate and we moved into a small apartment near the school. My sister cried and begged me to stay with her until I finished school. At times I thought that others, including my sister, did not believe I would ever actually reach the end of my schooling. Moving out on my own was something that I needed to do, to feel as if the past had not been in vain. I could not explain this to Friba, who did not ask me much about the time between our last meeting because, I figure she was not prepared to hear the answers. Although we did not talk about it, the void hung between us. I had to get away from it and focus on my future.

It became evident at about that time that I was not working enough hours at the Burger King to support myself so I accepted a second job at Payless Shoe Source in the shopping mall that was within walking distance of where we lived. Since Friba taught me to drive and helped me obtain my driver's license—and with my increased income—I was able to purchase my first car. It was a 1978 Plymouth. Between two jobs and my studies, I had little time left over but I would soon find a way to fill even that. I learned of the Afghan Cultural Club at the college by talking with other members who encouraged me to join. I felt privileged to take part in a group that was dedicated to preserving the best parts of the homeland I remembered. But I would quickly learn that this was not always the case with the Afghan Cultural Club.

I was readily accepted into the club and made many friends. Because I was so newly immigrated, I spoke Dari better than most other Afghans at the school and the members sometimes invited me to be an announcer at the meetings, concerts and other events held by the club. In time, however, I began to question the validity of the Afghan Club's claim that they were sincerely promoting Afghan culture. Instead, it seemed that the Club was often used as a platform by different Afghan groups in the Area to advance their political agenda under the guise of promoting culture. Many of the students followed the political affiliation of their family without pursuing political discussions based on their own findings and conclusions. If the father was involved in Hezbe Islami, then the son would defend and argue his position without ever entertaining another viewpoint. I saw that in this microcosm of Afghan society, the problems that ran like fissures through the country itself were not muted, but magnified. I was shocked by the division among the students and the intensity of the various belief systems that they so voraciously cling to.

Many were not as newly emigrated as myself and there were those students whose entire families were living in the U.S. For some of them, I imagined the tragedies of their homeland were but a distant memory. For me, however, the betrayal of our motherland was fresh and I chose to believe that we might be enlightened rather than encumbered by the sins of our fathers. The Afghan Club's cultural events were more and more often transformed into a mouthpiece for the political agenda of one or another of the sponsoring groups or families behind the events.

One day, I was asked to announce a public event hosted by the Afghan Cultural Club and I initially accepted feeling honored. Then I learned that many of the speeches that were to be delivered by my fellow members had been written by their parents or other family members and when I listened to them, I heard the voice of political obstinacy ringing in those words that were not their own. I politely backed out and opted not to participate in the event at all. I joined the cultural club to embrace the best parts of our shared culture with my Afghan brothers and sisters, but instead I saw the worst parts of our shared history put on a stage for public consumption and I was ashamed.

I was not discouraged from finding common ground with those around me who were willing to open their minds, and I delighted in the friendships I made in the club. It was clear that I was not in the minority in thinking that things could be different. I watched as year by year, elections took place to instate the new leaders of the club and I listened as the speeches were given and the lines were drawn almost entirely among its members based on political affiliation. In short, I learned how I might do things differently if I were a candidate. Before long, I put together my own campaign and my friends rallied around me to bring a new perspective to the Afghan Club. In my final year at Chabot College, I became the president of the Afghan Cultural Club with over 173 votes out of 180. The other two candidates split the remaining votes between them.

By that time, I had been in the United States long enough to know that people are virtually the same everywhere. I adjusted to almost every aspect of life in the United States. The thing I had not grown accustomed to in all that time was silence. I lay down to sleep at night and sometimes it was so quiet I could get no rest. I think often about Kabul and my family. Though they had since fled to Pakistan, I still thought of them living in fear in a broken country. I spoke to them every chance I got. My youngest sisters now were nearly grown. For a long time I did not ask about the girl, and in truth I sometimes avoided speaking to Flora at all because I did not trust myself. But on the night of the election I was speaking to Flora on the phone, and I was in a mood that held me like an anchor to the past, so I asked her.

"Abdul, I would think you would be past it now," she said.

"I was only curious if you know what happened to her."

There was a long silence on her end.

"I have not seen or talked to her in years."

"But you know something of her. Something you are not telling me."

"I know that as soon as she was out of school, she was married. Her family married her to a man who was much older than her. I know nothing more than that."

"You cannot mean it. I know you are not telling me the truth, Flora."

"Abdul! Listen to yourself. She is gone, Abdul."

My mother was on the phone then and there was kindness in her voice, but the old remonstrance too, telling me to focus on my education and to make something of myself. She told me that they were fine, they were all fine and that I needed to stop worrying about them and let the world and everyone in it take care of themselves. It was an uncharacteristic message coming from my mother who had dedicated her life to helping others. I understood that she and Flora were trying to protect me, but it had the opposite effect. I hung up the phone feeling as if I had been cast adrift on a wide sea with nothing to tether me to any shore.

In spite of feeling lost, I did what they said and I moved on with my life. I focused on the things I had before me and dedicated myself with passion to both my education and to the Club. One of the main differences during the period of my presidency was that student's money went entirely to funding cultural activities instead of political and religious ones. The little money that was raised from the previous year was used to publish a student magazine in Dari and Pashtu which promoted Afghan culture. As any good investment will, that magazine opened up another door for me.

There were a few local TV stations in the Bay Area that provided news and other information on Afghanistan to the local community. Farida Anwary, who once worked as a director for Afghanistan Radio and Television before she immigrated to the U.S., started a new radio program that quickly captured the attention of the Afghan community. Her show was broadcast on a weekly basis and I, like so many others, was held captive by the voice with which she read her poems. Her fans included Afghans, Tajiks and Iranians who listened to her poems in Dari. Her programs were founded on culture and art and her poetry was music to the ears. So it was to my considerable surprise that Farida Anwary contacted me one day in my role as Afghan Club President. She said that she read one of the cultural magazines published by our members and asked if I would be interested in volunteering to work on a new radio program for youth called *Daritche Farda*, which means "little door to the future." I told her I would be honored, and so it was that I ended up working a few hours each week with Farida Anwary and the group of extremely talented women she had working for her. It truly was an honor to walk some distance in Ms. Anwary's progressive and enlightened path. I learned that she was a democrat who spoke out in favor of women's rights, and I believed she maintained a good balance between open-mindedness and adherence to her political beliefs. Under her tutelage, I also gained a new appreciation for Dari literature. I had loved reading since I was a boy and was first introduced to the novel by my old friend Hamed. But I learned from my work with Farida Anwary that literature has a transcendent power to unite people across any span of time; across any distance. I learned that words inspire, and inspiration is worth more than gold.

Radio and TV news were important to the Afghan community at that time, especially those who didn't have access to the internet. The Russians had left Afghanistan and the government of Kabul was changing hands every few months instead of years. More than forty-five mujahideen groups that were created with the assistance of Pakistan, Iran and the Arabs, now fought each other for control of the government in Afghanistan. The extremist group Hezbe Islami, along with its warlord affiliates, had brought the city of Kabul to its knees and left it a wasteland of debris. The residents of Kabul had witnessed some of the worst atrocities that Afghanistan had experienced in its 5000 years of history. Blood flowed in the streets of Kabul as Ahmad Shah Massoud and Gulbuddin Hekmatyar fought brutally for power. The city that gave birth to me was in tears and the world did nothing. The civil war in my homeland created an opportunity for the Arabs, Pakistanis and extremists to start a movement called Taliban which swept through the country from its breeding ground in Kandahar, and quickly took control of nearly 75% of the country.

To my surprise, Farida Anwary and many other Afghans initially defended the Taliban agenda over the reigning government of Kabul. Ahmad Shah Massoud was the army chief of the Kabul government. Farida Anwary and most other pro-

King Afghans were under the impression that the Taliban would restore power to King Zahir who shared an ethnic background with the Taliban, though this would not be the case. In time even the misguided supporters of the Taliban would be forced to change their tune.

During the three years I spent at Chabot College, I had the privilege of befriending Basir Yasini, who studied Computer Engineering with me and was a fellow member of the Afghan Club. Basir was only a few years older than me but married, with three children. He was smart, soft-spoken, well respected, and a lot of fun. In 1993, Basir and I both transferred to San Jose State University. I cut short my presidency in the Afghan Club and withdrew from my work with Farida Anwary, but I strived to maintain the many connections I made in both positions, and we parted on good terms.

When Basir came to my apartment to pick me up for our first day of school at San Jose State, he was laughing when I climbed in the car.

"That your trash?" he said, pointing to the can that I placed that morning alongside the curb.

"Yes."

"Abdul, you are a true American now, aren't you?"

He was still chuckling when I asked him what he meant. I knew Basir to be good-natured and I wondered what the joke was.

"No trash!" he said, "Your garbage can is only half-full! Have you ever known an Afghan to have less than an overflowing garbage bin?"

I thought about this and I began to laugh with him.

"It is true, no?" Basir went on, "Hospitality is not an American tradition. Americans have only their own trash. You will have to come to my house. I see I have neglected you for too long. I have people in my house always. Half the time I do not know them but somewhere in the past my great-uncle knew a man who lived in the same village as their great-grandfather. I love it! You will love it, too. It will be like growing up in your family, always with people around. You will see. My trash takes up two bins and still overflows!"

San Jose State University was a much larger world than that of Chabot College, and I was thrilled to feel that I would be learning from such a distinguished institution. Basir and I commuted to and from school nearly every day for almost five years. Basir did not speak Dari fluently so I helped him practice during our commute. When we weren't practicing, we were talking about politics or religion, or rehashing the brutality of our physics and calculus classes. True to his word, I was invited to his home often for tea and lunch. I met many people there, including his wife and children. It seemed to me that Basir must have known every Afghan in the Bay Area. Most of those who he entertained in his home shared his Pashtun background. Some were related to him and some were friends. I was introduced to his brothers and cousins, who were interested in hearing about my life. We shared our stories. One afternoon, I was telling his brother of my second escape from Afghanistan. He asked me detailed questions when I got to the part about my path through Gerde Ghauss and then he called Basir over. I had never told Basir my story in so much detail.

"Listen to this," his brother said, and I related to Basir that I had a friend, Dadmir, who helped me to escape through the Kuchi village at Gerde Ghauss.

When I looked at Basir, he had tears in his eyes.

"My village was called Kama," he said. "It was in Gerde Ghauss, only minutes from the Kuchi village you speak of. If I had known you, I could have helped you. To think that all this time and distance later, we should come to find that our paths crossed so closely."

Basir had been a young freedom-fighter at the time that I was in Gerde Ghauss. His father was a popular commander in the area and Basir both admired and fought honorably for the cause. Eventually, his family forced him to quit fighting for his country and to pursue instead his education. Basir was talented and intelligent and the decision served him well. He only attended a few years of school in Jalalabad, but in the United States he was succeeding in a challenging field of study at a reputable college and lamenting over one he might have helped in his past. I found it ironic that these gestures of brotherhood came more readily among almost strangers in an adopted country, than they came when I needed them most in my homeland.

It was with other friends in my group of acquaintances that I talked about girls in much the same way that Farhad and I used to talk about German girls back at Amani High School. In truth, I met many girls during my years at San Jose State, but not one of them came close to capturing the alluring originality of the one I left behind. Those other girls were mere copies, a dime a dozen. They were nice enough and I was friends with many of them but in time they each revealed a sort of falseness just before they flew away.

*

*

"My mother didn't give birth to me, that love did."
-Rumi

*

23

~ ~ ~

A MIRACLE OF SPARROWS

The young girl turned on her heel and ran. The sounds of fighting dogged her, long after she made her escape and crouched behind the hollow shell of a building that was once an appliance store. She huddled over her belly, feeling the sharp kicks of the baby. Pains in her side told her that she could not run much further. She would have to wait for the blasts to cease before she made her way home. She would be going home without the basket of produce she had purchased from the market. She dropped it as soon as the sounds of shooting erupted. She had little food left in bucket that she had sunk in the well at home, so the baby would be hungry tonight. In the morning she would try again.

She was married at sixteen and found herself pregnant almost immediately. Sometime in the third month, there was an explosion on the outskirts of Kabul. It happened that her husband was working in a building there. One corner of the building had been devastated in the blast. It happened that the office her husband was in at that time was precisely located in that section of the building that was now a gaping hole. When she heard that he was dead, she did not cry. She couldn't and she couldn't even bother to wonder why. She sat over her mug of tea as it grew cold, thinking how ironic it was that her entire family had fled the country only a month ago. She ran through lists of names in her mind, friends and relatives, and she came to the realization that she knew where none of them were. Her city was in turmoil. The civil war raged on and everyone had been uprooted. Something like a laugh escaped her mouth. It was not that she could not mourn her lost husband. It was not that she would not, in time, feel the pain deeply. It was just that there had been so *much* of it. So much loss and death and destruction. It was nearly impossible to separate one heartache from another. Impossible to distinguish between the discomfort of the baby in her belly and the discomfort of life in general.

She slept poorly and set out later the next morning. The sun was cresting over the jagged Hindu Kush, spilling shadows across the landscape and in other areas illuminating the patchy white snow. It was all that remained of the long winter. That and the devastation that touched nearly every part of Kabul. The city was wounded; crippled. The sunlight did little but accentuate the scars that were etched into the landscape. She was able to buy enough food to sustain herself for two days. As she was walking home, she felt the remaining money in her pocket. It was all that was left of the money she and her husband had saved. The morning was quiet and she found it was more unsettling to hear silence than the sounds of fighting.

By the time the next morning came, she had made a decision. She had to get to Jalalabad, and to do that she needed the remainder of her money. She had to leave quickly. She had paid little attention to her neighbors lately. There was no point in getting attached to any of them as they may not be there tomorrow. But now she watched. She observed and after a few hours she noticed that one of the mud houses in the same row as hers had its curtains drawn, but there was frequent movement of the curtains. Her heart quickened its beat. She knew she could not be wrong. She had seen this when her own family was preparing to escape. She and her husband had helped them pack what little they could into what they could carry on their backs. There had been a flurry of preparations in the little house. People left every day. No. She could not be wrong.

She knocked on the door. There were noises from inside the house and then the curtain beside the door twitched. A moment later the door cracked open and a face peered out from the space.

"I would like to come with you," the girl said and put a hand on her belly, as if in explanation.

The face stared at her a moment and then the door shut. She waited. It was several minutes before the door opened again and she was told to come inside.

"I am your neighbor," she said.

"We know who you are. You lost your husband. I have lost many people, too," said an old woman who approached her with her arms out.

They left that night and were in Jalalabad the following morning. The girl knew that the family had little to live on. When they asked her where she would go, she told them she had family in Jalalabad and she would go to them. Instead, when they parted ways, the girl walked through the streets. She was tired and hungry and needed a place to sleep. Eventually she came upon a clinic and she gratefully slipped inside. She explained that she had little money but she wanted to see the doctor about her baby.

When Momena met the young girl, she saw that the girl was scared. She took her into a vacant examination room and shut the door. She knew that the girl did not have money and she knew that she would not ask her to pay even what little she did have. Still, she examined the girl and checked the baby and when she was done, the girl began to yawn and Momena could tell that she was becoming comfortable. So Momena sat and her open demeanor suggested to the girl that it was safe to talk to this woman. She told the midwife her story and when she began to cry, Momena put out a hand to touch her on the knee.

"Please do something," the girl cried, "I cannot have this baby. I have nothing. I have to get back to my family and I will not survive; the baby will not survive, if we are on our own. I know there are ways…"

Momena explained to the girl that it was far too late and too dangerous to even consider an abortion. The girl put her palms against her face and cried.

"We will only worry about tonight," Momena said and patted the girl's knee, "Wait here one moment."

Momena spoke to the other two women who were working in the clinic at that time and one of them offered to have the girl stay with her. Momena returned and told the girl that she would have a place to sleep that night.

Many weeks went by and the girl came in to the clinic regularly for check-ups with Momena. The baby was growing healthy and strong inside his mother's womb, and the midwife could tell that the time to deliver was quickly approaching. The girl was staying with the clinic receptionist who had offered to house her the first night, with the promise that she could remain there until the baby was born. In exchange, the girl was proving herself both helpful and grateful for the kindness.

After each exam, Momena and the girl would talk. One day, the girl sat down on the exam table and she looked at Momena with eyes that were, for the first time since the midwife had known her, clear and unburdened.

"I have made a decision," the girl said, "I will leave the baby here. I want you to find him a home."

Momena was quiet and let the girl speak. She nodded her head when she finished, the girl let out a long sigh.

"These are not ordinary times," Momena said, "It reminds me of the story of the sparrow. When he was born into this world, it was in an empty nest. He knew no different, you see, because the nest had always been empty. He struggled to fly and fell more often than he flew, but he knew no different because he never had an example so he got up and tried again. The little sparrow grew and learned to fight for himself when necessary and also to live amongst the other birds in harmony. He knew no different because he never had anyone to either fight for him or help him. Forced to take on the world by himself, the world became his home; each sparrow his family. He struggled but he was strong, because he never knew different. There are some that say our sparrows carry the souls of the dead. There is death and there is life, one passes and another is born. The sparrow carries this memory of souls within them; the memory of those who came before. We call this instinct, or history or ancestry. Your sparrow will always have your memory with him."

When she finished her story, tears were streaming down the girl's cheeks. They were streaming down Momena's as well. She stood and left the girl alone in the room, where she finally shed the tears that she had been holding in.

Momena was right, those were not ordinary times. Most families were displaced. They had either fled or were waiting to flee and no one would spare the time, money or emotion to take on a motherless child in the midst of such strife. They had other things to contend with. There was the continuation of the civil war, the financial collapse during and after the People's Democratic Party departed from government and the brutal behavior of the warlords, religious extremists and the Taliban. The nation's people were forced to leave everything behind for yet another unknown destination. It was a time of survival and despite Momena's best efforts; no one came forward to accept a baby that did not belong to them.

The young girl kept her promise and when she delivered the baby, she stayed only long enough to recover under the care of Momena. The baby, a boy, was large and healthy and Momena cared for him and whispered to him that he would have every opportunity in life. But most of all, he would have love. She took it on as her duty to the child to secure these things for him, even when it looked hopeless that anyone would adopt him.

It was only a matter of days before the young Afghan girl, approaching her seventeenth birthday, bent over her infant son and closed her eyes. It was impossible to tell if her lips actually touched his skin or if it was only the breath of her words that caressed him as she whispered *my sparrow*. Then she was gone.

Since no family came forward to accept the child, Momena took the baby home to Peshawar where she lived with her two daughters. She was a recent widow and her daughters, age eighteen and twenty-one were her life. Momena was wise enough to know that life is elastic. It expands and contracts upon us all. Now her life was expanding, because the moment she took that baby across her threshold, she realized that it was meant to be. Her daughters met the baby boy and they fell in love with him. It was that night, as the three women bent over the makeshift bed they fashioned for the infant, that they tentatively discussed the idea of naming him.

"We cannot name him," says one.

"He cannot be nameless," says the other.

"He is a sparrow," says the third.

As the sun was rising on the next morning, the name seemed to suggest itself. All three women were tired from a long night of caring for the child. They named him Massie, the Dari name for Christian, one who believes in Jesus.

The world around them was changing and Momena and her daughters, and now Massie, were not exempt. They too saw the necessity of immigrating out of Pakistan. Momena had an older daughter who had been living in Canada for over a year and they had been making arrangements for almost that same amount of time to join her. Momena also had a relative who is living as a refugee in Islamabad who agreed to take care of Massie until Momena could complete his immigration documents in Canada. Between herself and her daughters, they were able to scrape together enough money to pay for Momena's relatives expenses during this time.

When the midwife and her daughters were in Canada, they cried for the little boy. No one understood at first the amount of affection they carried in their hearts for Massie. The rest of their family in Canada saw this, but they were also worried about the demands a child would make on a widow in her seventieth year. They were afraid that Momena did not realize the physical and financial demands of raising a baby, especially in a country where the cost of doing so was much higher. Some might have called Momena stubborn, but she preferred to consider herself devoted. At long last, the immigration process for Massie was complete. Daoud, one of the daughter's husbands, flew to Pakistan and brought Massie home to his waiting family Canada. By this time, Massie was almost two years old.

Years passed and Massie grew faster than anyone could believe. His extended family grew to love him as much as the woman who would raise him as her son. He had two loving sisters who lived with him and doted on him and no one thought of him as an adopted child. His siblings and his mother loved him more than he could possibly know.

There are years ahead of him still, but I can tell you what becomes of the sparrow. When he is seventeen he will be sat down by the only mother he has ever known. She will tell him the story of his birth. She will tell him that his history, his ancestry, his memory is what flows through his veins but it is also what is written on his heart. He will begin to cry, disbelieving. She will make the offer to help him find his biological mother. He will think only for a moment and then he will throw his arms around his elderly mother and say, "You are the only mom I know, and I don't want to know another."

Massie will grow to be taller and more handsome than much of his family. He will grow to be intelligent and compassionate, and yes, strong. He will become very knowledgeable about real estate and will work towards getting his real estate license in British Columbia. He will take computer courses and become an avid reader, looking for every opportunity to advance his interests so he can one day help his mother in

Vancouver, and his biological mother too if he should one day find her.

Massie has always known his older brother Abdul, and while they talk often with each other, there is much that Massie does not now about the generation his brother grew up in or the circumstances of Abdul's life.

But then, they each have their own stories. These long histories of connections made and lost; of life lived and love devoted, of moments in which we knew no different—or more importantly—moments in which we did know, but wouldn't change a thing.

*

24

~ ~ ~

THE GIRL WITH GREEN EYES

During one of our brief school breaks, just before the start of my final year of school, I arranged to take a week off of work from my job at Lockheed Martin to travel to Vancouver Canada to visit my mother, my sisters and Massie. She did not travel much anymore. Shortly after I left my family in Islamabad and travelled to the U.S., they moved on to Peshawar where my father passed away from heart trouble. Now she had a small child and it was necessary for her to stay home with Nazima, who was herself nearly of an age to go to college, and young Massie. I promised them long before that I would try to visit whenever I got the chance. Since Lockheed Martin picked me up during my last year at San Jose State, I was well-paid and able to do things I could not do before. On that particular occasion, I was able to fly to see her and bring her a new computer that I would teach her to use so she might keep in touch easier with family and friends. And after all of this I would still have money left to pay my rent. For so many years I worked multiple jobs and still had a hard time scraping together a $300 rent payment. Now I was breathing easier and the promise of better days was all around me.

I rented a car to drive to my mother's home. I had not been in this part of Vancouver city before, but I could have recognized it without any help. Having taken none of her possessions with her when she fled from Afghanistan years ago, she managed to somehow make her new home in Canada look and smell exactly like each home we ever lived in. There were little modern touches here and there that acknowledged the influence of Mariam and Nazima and my young brother, Massie. There was, however, virtually nothing by which to remember my father who never made it to that place. My father died in Pakistan just after I arrived in San Francisco. My mother told me at the time that he waited for news of my safety before he would depart from this world. His heart condition overwhelmed him in the end.

My mother and I had a quiet lunch while Massie was napping and we sat talking late into the afternoon. I could see that she was tiring. Raising a child after her own were mostly grown must have been exhausting. While she was retrieving fresh linens to make up a bed for me, I scanned the contents of a bookshelf in a dusty corner. On the bottom were two photo albums. I picked them up, hoping to find pictures of my younger sisters who I had not seen in years. I did not have a chance to look through them as my mother came back into the room then and I help her make up the bed. As we were finishing up, there was a knock at the door. She went to answer it and when I followed her into the kitchen, she introduced me to her friend Khadija.

"Khadija is my neighbor here," my mother explained and the woman put her arms around me and kissed me, laughing and holding me at arm's length as if I was known to her.

"She was my neighbor too, when I was a young girl in Shor Bazaar," my mother said.

"I knew your mother when we were girls," Khadija said, "I knew your grandmother, too. And your grandfather. Don't you look just like him! But then, I also knew your father. I knew him before your mother even did. His family and mine were old friends."

The three of us sat down at the table and my mother poured tea into tiny fragile cups as cracked and chipped as if they'd been in the family for years. I thought of the money I had sent to my mother. I thought perhaps I would buy her a new set of china to serve tea on. Then I watch her pick up her cup and worry the flower pattern with her thumbs as had been her habit in all the time I'd known her and I understand that she did not yearn for a new set of china. She yearned for the old. Her face lit up as her friend chattered on about those days.

"I do remember," Khadija said, "That there was a story they told in your father's family and I was telling your mother only the last time I was here visiting that I would try and remember what it was, and do you know that I had remembered? It was his great-grandfather, I believe, that the story was about. Abdul, that would make him your great-great-grandfather. He was a *Kuchi*, they say. Born to the nomadic people who were passing through the village. The midwife tended to the mother, but it was no use and she was lost in childbirth. As was often the case, the father could not care for the child on his own and as it was he had lingered behind too long while his wife labored. His people had moved on and he felt that the child would be safer with the people who helped bring him into the world. He left his infant son in the care of the midwife. I recall the story went that she had a large family of her own to care for and would not be able to add another mouth to their number. She turned the baby over to her young, newly married sister and her husband. The infant was nursed by the young girl's sister and was cared for and raised as the newlywed couple's child. That child was your great-grandfather. I recall the story because it was told in your father's family with pride and I recall thinking as a child how romantic it was to be descendant from the nomadic people. I was more adventurous than your father was as a boy, and I daresay your mother was as well," the two women shared a private laugh at this, "What of her son?" she said, looking at me with sudden interest, "Could it be that he has the Kuchi spirit in him? You did not know you were born a nomad, did you Abdul?"

I shook my head. This was news to me. The old woman laughed at my reaction. My mother looked at me with tears in her eyes.

"I am in need of rest. I will leave you two to talk."

I went into the next room and sat on the bed. The photograph album still lay on the table beside the bed. I picked it up and began to flip through it. The pictures were all recent. A hodgepodge of photographs sent from friends and family, all pieced together to form some semblance of a life. I recognized my mother's efforts for what they were; an attempt to replace old memories with new hope. I went through the album slowly, examining each face to see who I recalled from my own past. I made sense of who many of the subjects were; distant cousins and family and friends now living all over the United States, Canada, Germany, and some still in Pakistan. I thought of these shattered lives all scattered across the world. How very unusual that we should be the ones to inherit the entire globe. How ordinary it seemed to call each place home that had a small claim on our hearts. And then I turned the page and found that the heart resides where it will. One cannot account for what the heart calls home.

The photograph was a glossy print, one among many obviously taken of the same wedding party at the same event. The picture that caught my attention was a candid photo of the bridesmaids, leaning together and smiling over the bride, who I did not recognize. I recognized my sister Flora, smiling brightly. And next to her I recognized the green-eyes and ivory skin of one who would insist, after so many years, on taking her rightful place in my heart. I knew suddenly that I had never forgotten, and likewise I would never move on. I made a promise to her, long ago in a High School concert-hall and she promised me, too, that she would find me. There she was, smiling in a picture, and making good on that promise. Her arm was around my sister's shoulder; her hand was without a ring. I dared not hope. Or so I told myself. Because I did dare to hope. It was nearly all I could do.

I removed the single photograph, proof of my longing, from under its filmy cover. I put the albums away on the dusty shelf where I knew—as my mother knew—that gathering dust was a privilege. I did not sleep that night, but lay awake trying to decipher that photograph like a code. Who was the bride? Where was the picture taken? How could I get to her? How could I be sure that the absence of a ring meant what I thought it meant?

My younger sisters, Mariam and Nazima, came in late from their respective jobs. My mother had gone to bed early. I hugged my sisters tightly and they were excited to sit with me and catch up on where the years had taken each of us. They were both young women now. Mariam was engaged to be married and Nazima was months away from her community college graduation. After some time, I removed the picture from my suitcase and put it on the table. When they recognized what it was, I saw them exchange a look.

"It's just as I thought," I said, "You all know about her. What can you tell me?"

Nazima looked at Mariam who appeared as though she was trying to decide something.

"It was not Flora's fault," Mariam said, "We all decided it was best."

"What was best?"

"That you move on with your life. Mama was so afraid you would come back to Kabul again, like you did when they sent you to Germany. They were always so worried for you, for your future. We all worried."

"What about *her*?"

"Flora told you she was married. It was not the truth. We only wanted what was best for you. We wanted you to forget her and to have a good life."

I felt tears stinging my eyes. How could I explain that *she* was my life? She had seen me through the difficult times without ever being present. She inhabited my dreams and could not let her go. I did not know what I would have done if she had been married. I never was prepared to lose her.

Mariam spoke up then, "She was nearly married, to an older man. Her parents arranged the marriage, but she refused to marry him. She threatened them that she would run away. Eventually she did. She ran away so she wouldn't have to marry him."

"She's a strong girl," Nazima said and she and Mariam exchanged a look of wonder over the bravery of one of their acquaintances. It was clear that they found the idea of it romantic.

"Where is she?"

"The picture was taken in Pakistan. Three years ago. I don't know if she's still there. Flora would know."

I nodded, the realization sinking in that even though I felt as if I had found her, I was still so far away. I waited until I had returned to my home in Fremont and I called Flora on the phone. We talked often at that time, though rarely about the past. I believe it surprised her when I brought up her young friend again.

"I found a picture, in mother's photograph album, of you and your friends at a wedding," I said and Flora was quiet. In a moment I could hear her sniffing and knew that she was crying.

"I did not want to lie to you, Abdul. We all thought it was best for you to think that she was lost to you. I assumed she would be married eventually and it would not matter anyway. I assumed you would meet someone else and move on with your life. We only wanted you to become successful as we knew you would."

"Is she married now? It has been five years since the picture was taken."

"She is not. I talk to her often. Abdul, there is more. She was supposed to be married, years ago. To an older man who her family chose for her. She fought with them and she ran to one of her relatives. When the civil war broke, she joined her family to escape to Pakistan. She lives there with her family."

I felt my heart hurting for the girl I did not know, who had been so strong in the intervening years while I was unable to protect her.

"Abdul? I have something to send you. I will put it in the mail. You must forgive me, Abdul. I have always loved you, brother. You were the only son in our family. You must understand what it has meant to all of us to protect you. Your choices were never entirely yours, because you were never entirely safe."

I was not sure anymore what she was saying. I told her I forgave her. I told her I love her and I understand. I told her I was tired and I must sleep. I opened the window as I did each night before I slept. The weather in Northern California reminded me of that in Afghanistan during the spring and summer, when the nights were mild and sweet. Just before I fell asleep I heard the sounds of doves cooing nearby and I was unsure if the sounds belonged to the present or the past. I was caught in the arms of sleep and suddenly I was among the birds, warm in the nest as their feathers close over me. The cooing in their chest vibrated through my own body and I forget to remember that theirs was a secret, primal world. Their cooing was a code, a history of the world, a bittersweet symphony of love and lies.

I waited for the letter that Flora promised to send and when it arrived, I tore it open. I knew that the world would change for me as soon as I read the words on the page, but I welcomed it. I felt that I could not live without the world changing, in fact.

My Friend,

Abdullah Nasser, son of Qabela Momena of Micro Rayan, my letter will find you if I cannot. All these years I had been left with the memory of those words you spoke to me that day in the concert hall. Do you remember? I cannot know if you meant it, but I like to think you did. Sometimes it was all I had; that memory of a boy forcing me to make a promise. You anchored me and I was forever in your debt. I had seen you so many times in so many years. Sometimes I cannot remember which of those times were dreams and which were real, but I think it does not matter. I had known you all my life. It only seems right that I should know you again, but I was afraid I will not. The world seems so small when I know that you were somewhere in it. I talk to your sister often and she tells me little of you, but as long as she does not give me bad news, I know the news was good. I had never told her that you spoke to me. I had never told her of the promise I made to you. Until today. I wrote it in a letter and I left the letter for her, along with this one, to be given to you, Abdul. I am leaving this place. It is no longer my home. I am being forced to marry a man I do not love and I will do all that is within my power to never let it happen. I will do what I have to do to keep my promise to you. Whatever happens, you must know that you have saved me.

I hope you are happy. I hope you have made your every dream come true,
Zeba

There was, included with the letter, another slip of paper. This one was written in my sisters own hand and it contained only a phone number. I did not wait. I only took a moment to wipe the tears from my eyes before I picked up the phone and dialed the number. Then it was her voice on the other end of the line and I was saying,

"Yes, Zeba, now I have made them all come true."

*

25

~ ~ ~

A NEW BEGINNING

When I first heard her voice on the phone after so many years, it took my breath away. I looked at her picture and lost myself in her amazing, innocent eyes. She was still in Pakistan, but after the first conversation she agreed to speak with me again over the phone. Before long I was falling in love with her words. She was a world of contradictions I had yet to explore. After two months I decided to go to Pakistan to meet her in person. When I saw her at last, she was more beautiful than in her picture; more refined and mature than her younger self. Still with those green eyes that seemed to promise so much. I took this to heart and in exchange for her smile; I solicited from her the greatest promise of all. I asked her to marry me.

"Abdul," she said with tears in her eyes, "You have broken the rules. *I* was supposed to find *you*."

"I couldn't wait."

"And I cannot wait to be your wife," she said, laughing and crying as her arms went around me.

For the remaining days of my visit, we made plans. When we finally had to say good-bye it was with both sadness and hope. We talked every day for the next six months and she keeps me informed of the status of her immigration papers. Then the time came when she received her approval. On a fiancé visa, Zeba moved to the United States where I had been waiting for her and we were married almost immediately in Reno, Nevada. Suddenly she was my wife and I was baffled that life had delivered this most impossible dream right into my arms. I never thought I would marry someone without knowing them for years.

"So you see, it is you who break the rules," I said to her by way of explanation.

She laughed, "But we have known each other for years and years."

"Not long enough, by far."

I wrote this to her the night before our wedding:

You are candlelight on a dark night. My life as it was before you fades away. Bittersweet dreams of yesterday transform themselves into your poetic words; into every graceful movement. The more we learn the more we appreciate this life we are fortunate enough to share.

Zeba had dreams of her own. I encouraged her, as I had encouraged my sisters and friends, to pursue an education. It was the surest way to success in any country. She enrolled herself in community college where her intelligence shined. She easily grasped technology but her passion was to become a nurse. I saw the ambition in her eyes. I loved her for her dreams and for every attempt she made to reach for them.

Time went by quickly. Basir and I were about to graduate from the Computer Engineering Department when a new program, Software and Information Engineering, was introduced. We both changed our majors and spent a few extra semesters in our new field of study. During my last semester at San Jose State University, I joined Clarent Corporation, a startup Voice over IP Company in Redwood City. In 1999, Basir Yasini—who finally spoke Dari as fluently as if he had grown up on the streets of Kabul—and I both graduated from San Jose State University. Along with three other students, we held the Universities first degrees awarded in Software and Information Engineering.

Once again I was at a crossroads in my life. Each moment was a culmination of everything that came before and all that was yet to come. In that transitory time of life, I felt peaceful. I felt that I now had the tools with which to build a successful life. Some family members who had emigrated over the years and settled nearby came to my graduation with balloons and flowers and I was proud as I walked forward to accept my degree. My wife beamed at me proudly and I basked in her smile. I felt as if everything in my life had a purpose and meaning beyond its momentary relevance. After the ceremony, Basir's brother and children walked to where we stood after the ceremony. Basir's brother shook my hand and invited me and Zeba to join them for dinner as I had on a few occasions in the past. He invited our family members as well and we enjoyed that night a traditional dinner like those great familial feasts we had when I was a child.

It is similar wherever you were. The unpredictability of life seems to rise up to announce itself just when you are most comfortable with the status quo. When Clarent's stock went public and reached its zenith at over two hundred dollars a share, the market crashed. The money we made in a virtual second was gone. Zeba was with me through it all.

We were married almost a year when Zeba discovered that she was pregnant. It was something we would never forget, the birth of our first child. It was like venturing into a new world. I could hardly grasp the amount of love and fear that came with the experience. When Omar was born I saw that he got the light in his eyes from his mother. From the first moment, he ruled our hearts.

Although we were newly married and had to make our way in the world as three rather than two, we did not live on anything other than what came home in my paycheck. When the dotcom bubble burst and so many others were instantly destitute, we suffered the pangs of disappointment, but were otherwise unharmed. My workplace became a second home for me; the people I worked with a second family. One of the founders of Clarent, Mike Vargo, remembered that I had a young son and asked me about my family each time we passed in the halls. I made many friends and in both my work and home life I felt that I had achieved great success. Zeba and I talked in great detail about our options and ambitions for our lives. I began to notice new businesses were cropping up and using Clarent equipment without associating themselves with Clarent services. Many of them became successful in a short amount of time. For myself, I decided to apply for other jobs and soon accepted a position with GlobeSpan Virata. While all of this was going on, Basir and I united our perspectives once again and put together a plan to establish a Voice Over IP service company. It would prove to be an ever-evolving project for both of us over the next several years. Based on the models I had seen that used Clarent products, we instead partnered with one of Clarent's major clients to offer affordable VOIP services.

We gradually formed the business while maintaining our day jobs. At this point in our lives, Zeba and I were busy beyond belief, but we had the energy to make everything happen for us. She truly desired to stay home with Omar and any future children that we were to be blessed with. I felt pride at being able to give her this. I promised her that any time in the future when she wanted to return to school and further her education, I would support her. Even while she was home with our child, Zeba did not stop learning. She became focused on perfecting her English skills. She read often and continued to learn about technology from me and from books and practice. I admired her resolve and dedication to attaining knowledge. We shared that passion, too. Zeba quickly established herself as a necessary component of the VOIP business by handling many of the daily financial and technological demands of the business.

I looked ahead to the future. I believed that we could learn the most about ourselves and about the world through an understanding of the past. Only by understanding the past and the present can we bring any level of creativity and innovation to the world. This was how progress was made, and I was determined to put life's measured disappointments behind me and move on. I began, at that time, an MBA program for Global Business Management.

I mentioned the unpredictability of life; its tendency toward chaos just when everything appears to be going smoothly. No living being is exempt from these laws of nature. It soon became evident to the majority of Afghans living in the States that the previously underestimated Taliban was a blight on Afghanistan and her people. By 2001, the Taliban was advancing towards the northern part of the country and were in control of almost 90% of Afghanistan. Young Afghans across the U.S. planned protests against the extremist group and its affiliates. The internet was used to mobilize efforts such as these and to educate people and the popular media about the Taliban's brutal actions against women, culture and the country at large.

I had friends in the Bay Area where we lived who never missed any of the protests against the Taliban no matter where the events were held. In 2001, I began to hear about Farhad Ahad. Several of my friends spoke of his efforts in organizing anti-Taliban protests and uniting Afghan-American's against the Taliban agenda. I looked at his website and saw a picture of him. I read his views and I heard the call to action that so many Afghans were responding to at that time. I was eventually introduced to Farhad on a conference call. He lived on the east coast and wrote numerous articles that excited young Afghans to organize and raise their voices against injustice in their homeland. I liked the idea and gather from his confident and articulate speaking voice that he was an intelligent man with similar political values as my own. Soon after this call, I joined his organization and became a member of his online group, Afghan Solidarity. Over the next few months, several protests were organized with Farhad's guidance on both the east and west coast. Hundreds of Afghans were in attendance at each gathering. Word began to spread and the reports that we got of events in Afghanistan become more disturbing with each passing month. Eventually even older generations of Afghans were being swayed to the cause of the younger generation. Afghan Solidarity was leading the anti-Taliban movement in the US.

One September morning, as the sun was rising over the far coast I slept peacefully and woke with a sense of calm and renewal, as on any other day. How often do we do this? How often do we sleep and wake and move through life, taking for granted the gift of the moment; failing to acknowledge that we are fortunate enough not to be suffering in this moment when so many in the world are?

I slipped from the bed quietly since Zeba was still sleeping. I peeked in Omar's room, with its door opened to his call if he should needs us in the night. He too slept peacefully. As on every other day since I had arrived in the U.S., I made a cup of tea and turned on CNN. It was 6:30 in the morning on September 11, 2001. The smoke from the first tower billowed over Manhattan, obscuring the building and painting the morning an ugly gray. Even the announcer at the CNN news desk was unsure what was going on. Reports continued to arrive in his earpiece and he paused, before relaying the information. Suddenly I was one of thousands, glued to a television set. I woke Zeba and left for work almost immediately as she stood with her hand to her mouth in disbelief as the second plane crashed into the second tower. We had seen such things before. Such atrocities. It did not change the impact of our commiseration with human suffering. In spite of the sympathy I felt, there was a small amount of fear. I learned that these things had repercussions. As I listened to the radio on my way in to work, I heard the suggestions of terrorism and I began to understand. I had lived long enough to know that terror was a quickly spreading disease; it leaves no one unscathed.

I usually left for work early to beat the heavy traffic on I880 towards San Jose. That morning I arrived long before most others. The parking lot was sparsely populated and I imagined most of my co-workers had been detained in front of their TV's. There were several employees already in the building and they had turned on the television sets in one of the labs that GlobeSpan used for video compression. I opened the door of the lab and eased in to sit among the others and watch, appalled, as the tragedy unfolded. My instinct about the terrorist attack was that the Taliban camps in Afghanistan were behind it. I followed the news regularly and many of the terrorist attacks around the globe had originated from these camps in recent years. Only a year earlier, I watched as President Clinton fired missiles at those same groups after the USS Cole attack in Yemen on October 12, 2000. Sure enough, before the morning passed, information coming in to the newsroom began to pin the source of the attack on Al-Qaeda, who were harbored by the extremist Taliban in Afghanistan. Before much longer we all learned the name Osama Bin Laden, and we were able to put a face to the fury that laid waste to so many lives.

In the video lab, no one spoke to each other for a long while. Everyone seemed to be in shock, concerned only with absorbing the information that we were getting. Slowly some small, private conversations started but it was clear that none of them had any focus on work. In the coming days I noticed how many of these private conversations stopped when I came near. It was within a week of the tragic events in New York that I noticed I had not received any e-mail in the past few days. I approached the IT manager and told him of the situation. His face changed a little and he did not answer immediately, so I knew that something happened that I was not aware of.

"Yeah," he said, rubbing his neck. "We had had some issues with our email server. I think it should be fixed today."

He did not meet my eyes as he spoke; only gestured with his open hand at the equipment around him. The next day, I still had no new emails in my inbox. I went back to the IT department. The manager was not there and so I approached another man. I asked him if the email situation would soon be resolved. He looked at me, perplexed.

"We haven't had any problem with the email server, lately."

"Oh, I haven't been receiving emails for the past three days."

"Well, I can check that out for you,"

A few moments later, he said, "Well that's strange. It seems like there's been a block put on your email. Do you know anything about that?"

I told him I didn't. He continued to work away on his side of the desk and looked up at me occasionally. I could tell that he was trying to decide what he should say, or if he had already said too much.

"Mr. Nasser, I'm going to have to talk to the manager about resolving this issue. I will call you in your office as soon as I've had a chance to speak with him."

Just before it was time to leave for the day, the phone in my office rang and I answered. The IT manager apologized for the inconvenience. He said that they would be providing me with a new email address and that the problem would not happen again.

I was frustrated by having to deal with notifying all of my contacts of the new email address, but I thanked him and hung up the phone. Sometime later that week, in the company newsletter there was an article requesting that all employees refrain from sending hate mail and e-mails and cautioning us all to exercise tolerance in these difficult times. As I read this I understand that the block on my email was a precautionary step. I understood that hatred bred of ignorance was not to be taken personally.

More than ever before, I felt the necessity of educating those who cared to learn who I was, where I came from, what I believed. There were those who avoided the subject in my presence, but there were yet many more who asked questions. I took the opportunity to explain the differences between the Northern Alliance and the Taliban and I clarified that while I *was* an Afghan, Osama Bin Laden was *not*. I saw by many blank stares that the fact of his being an Arab and not an Afghan did little to establish much of a distinction, in their limited view, between those like him and those like myself. Many, however, were interested in learning of the differences between our cultures and asked my further opinions on the U.S. plans for invading Afghanistan. I spent every day explaining to friends, co-workers and neighbors that Taliban was a creation of Arabs, Pakistani Intelligence and some extreme Afghan mujahideen groups that remained after the fight with Russia. I tried to explain that most Afghans were rigidly opposed to the Taliban and other extremist factions long before the events of September 11. I told them about groups like Farhad's that had long tried to educate people in the U.S. about the horrors committed by the Taliban.

The IT manager who originally blocked my email after the events of 9/11 became one of my greatest supporters, and one of the most eager to seek my opinion as he learned about unfolding events. After a long discussion one afternoon, he asked, "Do you think the U.S. will be able to defeat the Taliban quickly if we go to war?"

"It doesn't take a million dollar missile to destroy a mud building," I laughed, "We are fighting an extreme ideology and to defeat that ideology we need to focus on the root of the issue. All we need to do is shut down their *Maddrassas*, religious schools, in Pakistan and block the border so that terrorists don't cross into Afghanistan to fight us."

Suddenly Afghanistan was in the public eye. Journalists from all around the globe traveled to the United States—many to Fremont, California in particular—to meet Afghan-Americans and interview them about these current events. How had recent events affected our lives in the United States? How did we feel about President Bush's declaration of war against terrorism? One local news channel approached me and asked how I would feel if the US began bombing Afghanistan.

"I will support the decision to punish and bring justice to those that committed such atrocity against humanity. But I will hope that Afghan civilians will be protected at all costs if U.S. does begin bombing," I responded.

This, in fact, got me thinking about our involvement in Afghanistan. Since the beginning, I had seen the benefit of declaring war on terrorism. I longed for Afghanistan to be free from Pakistani influence; free from the long manipulation of powerful and greedy governments who cared nothing for the advancement of the country, but only for their own gain. I thought perhaps this country that I now called home might step in and create positive changes in my motherland. I thought perhaps I might make a change myself.

I spoke at length with Basir about the advantages of taking our technology business to Afghanistan. We agreed that information technologies would advance the interests of the Afghan people as their country was freed from tyranny. We were not alone in rejoicing in this opportunity for our people. Young Afghans around the world organized and prepared themselves to help rebuild their homeland once it was free. I spoke more and more often with Farhad Ahad and we began to forge a friendship. We talked for hours at a time on the phone, considering the various opportunities that might open up once the Taliban, Arabs and Pakistani agents were forced to leave Afghanistan. I shared with him my passion for telecommunications and next generation technologies and told him of mine and Basir's decision to take our business to Kabul. He was interested in the possibilities of this venture and within a few weeks, he accepted my offer to join our company as one of the directors. Basir had family living in Pakistan and Afghanistan, so while the U.S. prepared to go to war in Afghanistan, Basir agreed to manage the project full-time in Afghanistan while I took responsibility in the states.

When the U.S. began bombing the mountains of Tora Bora in search of Osama Bin Laden, Basir and I were on a plane heading into Afghanistan. It was the first time I had flown since the terrorist attacks on the Twin Towers and I tried as much as I could to make others feel comfortable about my presence in the plane. I was unnerved when the airline personnel at the gate called my name loudly. I would rather have remained inconspicuous. It was a lot to ask for, I knew. I sensed that my appearance made others uncomfortable around me. I found that I could not blame their lack of education or information. The media was an imperfect machine that sometimes provided the public with information that was neither fair nor balanced. Although I was sitting in the second row of the plane, I used the restroom at the back of the plane and kept a friendly look on my face so that I did not cause suspicion in the other passengers.

I tried to start conversations with the people next to me in the plane as I did in bars, restaurants, shops and elsewhere. I wanted to assure them that I spoke English well, that I was a software engineer and not one of the faceless, nameless 'bad guys.' If I was asked about my origin, I tried to respond quietly so as not to alert anyone who may overhear. How different it was from those earlier years when people considered me an American and nothing more. Now when they asked me where I came from, they did not mean where in the States, but wanted to know what my country of origin was. I missed the easy times I spent in the Bay Area, when I felt a sense of belonging with every community that I intersected with. I was a proud American. I was a proud Afghan. But now I had to learn to censor each word and gesture to protect myself and those around me. We were all afraid, for different reasons.

I did not worry so much for Zeba, with her lighter skin and green eyes, and almost complete mastery of the English language. Most people didn't even believe she was an Afghan when she told them. The thought of her made me smile.

Basir and I initially flew to Pakistan, and then took the UN plane to Kabul as there weren't any regular flights into Kabul. During our stay, we secured our license to provide Internet and other telecom services in Afghanistan. Once we had analyzed the situation in the country, I returned home to Fremont and started acquiring satellite equipment, voice over IP and network equipment. Zeba and I decided to fund the project initially by refinancing our home. After a few weeks of testing, trials and frequently working between two time-zones— Afghanistan and the U.S.—Basir and I were able to establish the first voice over IP service in Afghanistan. I immediately connected DialGlobe's network to our Voice switch in Kabul and allowed Afghans in the U.S. to make extremely low cost phone calls to their loved ones in Afghanistan. In the same way, Basir was able to make calls around the globe from our office in Karte 3, Kabul.

During that time, I was interviewed in Fortune Magazine Online and by NPR for my efforts to take my company to Afghanistan in the midst of political and social upheaval. Likewise, Farhad was interviewed by MSNBC and quickly landed a job with Enron. These were times of tragedy and loss, but also of hope and renewal. All across America, Afghanistan and the world, people like you and me dared to expect more from the future. It was just one of those beautiful, heartbreaking things about the human condition.

*

*

What strikes the oyster shell does not damage the pearl."
                    -Rumi

*

26

THE LIGHT THAT SHINES THROUGH THE UNIVERSE

The roots of religion can be traced as far back as you wish. Most Muslims in Afghanistan are aware of and celebrate the knowledge of their Buddhist history. The Taliban, of course, is the exception. There was, in the year 647 C.E. a Chinese Buddhist named Xuanzang who had long been immersed in Buddhist teachings but who saw that these teachings were divergent in many ways.

As religion so fundamentally encourages the follower to travel to the ground source for Truth, Xuanzang devised a plan wherein he would travel to India along the Silk Road, which was then one of the main trade routes in the world, let alone in Asia. The Emperor of the Tang Dynasty forbade travel into the dangerous eastern regions, so Xuanzang fled under the cover of darkness with a horse and a guide, passed through the gates of his world and into another. Like any journey, Xuanzang's travels were fraught with danger and discovery. One can hardly fathom the things he saw.

The moonlight over the Gobi desert that seemed to illuminate nothing but undulating dunes of sand for miles on end, until the dunes suddenly gave way to the scent of roses and jasmine and there could be seen a wild garden with waves of scent rising off of it, visible in the pastel dark. Through the garden a gate, and through the gate a Kingdom. He must have believed he was dead or dreaming. Perhaps it was Nirvana, but it did not matter as beauty enfolded him. He met with Kings and shepherds, travelers like himself. He preached and observed, prayed and learned and moved on endlessly from one oasis to another; each one different than the last because along the Silk

Road, treasures and sundries were not the only things that passed from place to place. Ideas were traded, histories were relived, and art was shared. These things have a way of changing the hearts and minds of men, so that as time wore on, each trade stop along the Silk Road became a stunning jewel in and of itself, bearing the imprint of time and the luster of amalgamated ideas.

As a traveler through these lands, Xuanzang saw the progression of ideas from one place to the next. He saw the influence of Buddhism, the implementation of various art forms, and heard the evolving legends of people's and places that he could hardly have imagined existed. It was, I presume, like travelling through a dream, where consciousness was a stream and everything was linked in some way but there was a great, overarching uniqueness to every image, every thought, taste, smell, sound and texture.

When he reached the valley of Bamiyan in the ancient capital of Balkh, he was still miles from his destination of India and less than halfway to the completion of his journey. By that time he traversed the some of the most treacherous mountain ranges in the world and there were more to come. But the bare fact of the matter is that at one point in his journey he descended into the valley of Bamiyan. From the valley floor rose enormous sandstone cliffs and into these cliffs, caves and tunnels had been dug in which thousands of monks resided.

As he descended into the valley, likely in the company of other pilgrims he had met along the way and with horses and camels long overdue for a rest, he turned onto the lower road and his eyes met with a sight unlike any he had seen before. Carved into the sandstone fascia's of the cliffs were two enormous statues of Buddha, towering above him. He must have stopped enthralled by the sight. The smaller of the two forms wore indigo robes and the larger wore crimson. Each figure was encrusted with untold numbers of jewels that glittered in the rising sun and sent prismatic colors sparking into the desert.

Here too, in Balkh had the capitals location on the Silk Road brought about a convergence of artistic styles that were evident in the great statuary Buddhas. From the villagers, Xuanzang learned that the largest of the figures was constructed after the first. As soon as the first figure had been constructed, the builders saw that they were capable of so much more. It was only fitting that they should pay homage to their faith by executing another statue that would tower higher, radiate brighter, and more completely integrate the elements of their craft.

The largest figure was known as Salsal, the "light that shines through the universe." Beside these figures, and somewhat less prominent was the statue of a reclining Buddha. Balkh was then, a living breathing hove for religion and philosophy and art. It was but one stop along his path but Xuangzang knew that like a jewel in his path, it was both an ending and a beginning in itself.

March 1, 2001

Across the valley of Bamiyan, the sunlight slid over the dirt, changing it from brown to orange. The sky was mottled gray and shades of pink hovered over the mountains as the destruction began. There is rage in the world, clear and undisputed. There is power too. When the two are drawn together and thrust at the perceived enemy like a sword, conflict will never cease.

In Buddhism, there are ideas about impermanence so there was a quiet humility in the statues as they endured the repeated blasts. Imagine the contradiction between their solid repose and the angry thrusting and firing of the men below, bent on annihilation. There was not much left of Afghanistan as it was, but in the valley on a morning that promised to be a beautiful day, the Taliban began to bring down the Buddhas of Bamiyan. It was not an entirely unforeseen event. Four years ago, just before taking control of the area, the Taliban had expressed their intentions to obliterate what they viewed as false idols. Mullah Mohammed Omar spoke out against the destruction of these landmarks. But in 2001, the very man who condemned these actions gave the decree that the Buddhas were to be destroyed.

They began firing at dawn, using anti-aircraft guns but the sandstone would not break. The Taliban leaders re-convened to devise a new plan and it was decided that mines would be placed at the base of the statues so that falling debris would set off a chain reaction of damaging blasts. In the end, destruction of the Buddhas took over eight days and was completed by putting dynamite into holes carved into the sandstone figures. The blast that was ignited left an enormous scar across the face of history.

Mullah Muhammed Omar stated that, "Muslims should be proud of smashing idols. It has given praise to God that we have destroyed them."

It is hard to dispute religion as a cause, but it is equally hard to stomach the sacrifice of religion on the great and all-consuming altar of political propaganda. What's more, it seems the intentions of one bent on destruction can never be fully realized. The blasted cliffs revealed caves that had been previously undiscoverable in which some of the earliest examples of oil paintings were found, painted there by ancient travelers on the Silk Road. In addition, a new statue of Buddha reclining was uncovered. The last record of the reclining Buddha had been made by the pilgrim Xuanzang when he traveled through Bamiyan and recorded the splendor of the place thousands of years ago. The human spirit is evident after adversity and can be seen to resurrect itself. In times like those it is hope that shines like a light across the universe, touching each and every thing in its path regardless of time. We bear the imprint of our history and we live by hope and hope alone. The builders who erected the statues of the Buddhas in Bamiyan revered the Buddhas transcendence above earthly law and the absence of the idolatrous Buddha's only promotes the tenets of these beliefs. There is no right or wrong of it to those who care to learn what they must in order to forgive.

*

27

~ ~ ~

THE LOSS OF FRIENDS

There are moments we look back on and say that everything changed then. I had countless such moments in my own life. As a culture—as the people of one world—we collectively share such moments as well. 9/11 was one of these moments that we, as a nation, will never forget. The collective memory of the human race is complex. There are so many overlapping tragedies and triumphs. The life of an individual is similar, and all too often cut short, leaving only the memories of others to fill in the blanks of what was. I will teach my sons this someday. I am hopefully teaching them already; that life is not to be taken for granted. Freedom and justice too, are rare and fragile gifts. We learn from such acts of terror as those of 9/11 that we were not immune to the pain and suffering of the world. More than that, we learn that through pain and suffering we were all connected. Reality can be terrible; the human spirit, conquering.

In 2002, with Afghanistan in the forefront of global news, the Afghan plight drew many more people than ever before. People across the world were suddenly interested in what was happening in that distant part of the world. While most settled for the limited information attained through local media, still many more actively pursued an understanding of the Afghan culture and history.

I knew Farhad at that point for over four months since we were introduced on the conference call. He left his job at Enron after their fall and was dedicating himself entirely to helping his native country. He was offered a job at the foreign ministry in Afghanistan. He told me in one of our frequent phone conversations, with much excitement, what the opportunity meant to him. I felt sometimes, in talking with Farhad, the idealism of youth returning. It was not impossible to change the status quo, or to live life with purpose. It was not impossible to fix Afghanistan and to remind her people of their shared history and triumphs. Many would call such idealism hopeless. I would say hope is the breath of life.

I was speaking to Farhad one evening on the phone. Omid had gone to bed and Zeba was in a plush chair in the corner of the living room, reading a magazine under a lamp. The door to the small room we used as an office was open and I sat at the desk inside. I could just see her through the opening of the door. It was such a scene of peacefulness. I did not want to alter the moment or my view of it. I was reminded of past dreams and began to share with Farhad some of my memories of Kabul. Full of nostalgia for the land of his birth, he joined me in reminiscing and mentioned that he was excited to return to his country in his new position.

"I have not been to Kabul in almost sixteen years, Abdul," he said, and I can hear the disbelief in his voice that so much time has passed.

"The years go by quickly. I am making my second trip back next month," I say, alluding to the business that Basir and I would conducting there, "I was surprised last time by how little and how much she has changed. I dream of Kabul, but I have nightmares just the same."

In her chair, with her feet tucked beneath her, Zeba yawns.

"Do you think I will find it so different? In my mind I imagine meeting faces from the past. I will try to find my friend while I am there. I have not had much luck here. I have a picture of us from the time we were in high school together."

I was suddenly tired, too. I thought of all the friends we had lost as a culture. Every emigrated Afghan I knew was looking for lost friends or relatives. We were all displaced.

"You've spent a lot of time with Afghans on the west coast. I should send you the picture. Maybe you will recognize my friend."

"Do that. I would be happy to help. I look for my old friends when I return to Kabul as well. I spent many years and passed through many countries hoping to find a face I knew. I had succeeded once or twice."

Zeba looked up at me from across the room with a smile.

"Well, I just sent the picture over. It brings back many memories."

I opened up my e-mail while we talked. We discussed some of the business decisions that he would have a say in as a board-member. He told me more of his position for the foreign ministry and the goals he hoped to accomplish now that he would have a larger platform from which to launch his efforts to unite Afghans across the globe. Meanwhile, the picture he sent downloaded slowly.

"Did you get the picture?"

"It's downloading now. Where was this taken?" I asked. Something about the rooflines in the background looked familiar.

"It was at my school. Amani High School."

His answer sent a chill through me as this was the same school I attended.

"What year was it taken?"

"1985."

The same year I was there. By this time, the picture revealed its faces and I saw myself at sixteen. It didn't make sense immediately. I had seen pictures of Farhad before, through his website, but I did not recognize him as someone I had known, let alone the beloved friend from my past. There in the picture,

Farhad and I smiled into the camera. The walls of our old classroom were a familiar backdrop.

"Farhad? This has to be a joke."

"What do you mean? Do you know him?"

Tears stung at my eyes and in this Farhad's voice I could suddenly hear my old friend. This was the same friend that sat next to me when we were in class together at Amani, sixteen years ago. I could not believe that I had been talking to him for months without realizing that he was the same person I had known and looked for in so many strangers' faces.

"It's *me*, Farhad. *I* am the person in the picture."

"Abdul," he said, disbelieving, confirming the name in his own mind, "You're kidding me."

"Yes! I mean, no. Abdul...Abdullah. You are Farhadak! I came from Germany and you sat next to me. I brought the camera to school and Wali took our picture."

"I can't believe it."

I wished I could see his face as he reacted to this. We were both in disbelief. We spoke a while longer, reliving the past. We talked about the things that had happened to us in the past sixteen years. We remembered the day we wiped our tears and said good-bye in front of the foreign ministry in Kabul. Before we got off the phone, I promised him that on my next trip to Kabul, I would visit him at the foreign ministry.

When I hung up the phone, I stared at the picture while my eyes blurred with tears. Then I shut my computer down for the night. I turned off the lights as I moved from the office into the living room where Zeba had fallen asleep in the chair. The light cast her in a warm glow and I watched her for a moment, in a mood that turned my thoughts upon the past. She was frozen there, preserved as if she were a photograph herself; a distant memory. I nudged her awake and she stirred. We walked together to bed.

"I was having a dream," she said.

"So was I," I kissed her on the forehead and she leaned against me, warm and real.

Basir and I worked tirelessly toward making our business a success. He established himself almost permanently in Kabul. I traveled there every few months to join our efforts and make changes to the business structure to allow it to run more efficiently. Most of this time was spent in meetings with investors and wholesale partners and in trying to expand our distribution of services.

The next time I planned to visit, I notified Farhad so that we might meet. Things were hectic and between his meetings and mine, we had difficulty scheduling time to visit. The time came for me to leave and we finally arranged to meet, on the day my flight was set to depart from Kabul. We decided that I would go to the foreign ministry at 7:30 a.m. so that I could drive from there to the airport without delay to catch my 10:30 flight. Basir and his driver picked me up from Khair Khana at 7:00 and we drove through the already busy streets of Kabul. The golden glint of the sun on the surrounding hills and the city itself remind me of childhood and I was swept away on waves of nostalgia.

I hoped to spend at least a half hour in meeting with Farhad after so many years, but a dozen obstacles delayed our efforts to arrive on time. I called him on his cell phone to tell him that we were running late. Farhad agreed to meet me at the gate of the ministry so that I didn't miss my flight. Our car slowly made our way past two accidents on the road and was stuck in traffic only a few blocks from the ministry for almost twenty minutes. By 8:20, we finally pull up in front of the ministry and the driver parked at the curb. A few minutes later, Farhad stepped out of the building and walked toward us. I recognized him as I had not in the photographs I had seen of him. He was as much my old friend as he ever was.

"Abdullah," he said in a voice choked with emotion.

We hugged each other, laughing and crying as we did so many years ago in our boyhood as we said our good-byes in the very same spot. I dried my tears and introduced Farhad to Basir. Farhad's face may have changed to that of a man, but his smile was the same. We made a promise to meet each other for lunch when he came next to the U.S. or I to Kabul. I apologized for having to rush to catch my flight, but I was on my way to Frankfurt Germany.

"I always return to the U.S. by way of Germany," I explained, "It has been another home to me."

"I heard years ago that Wali was in Germany. He had a shop there, in Frankfurt. I always did want to visit Germany. Do you remember? Maybe I will meet you there next time, instead," Farhad laughed.

"I found him years ago, by letter. Just after I escaped to Islamabad. We lost touch after that. My journey was not yet finished."

I thought life was more different than we ever imagined it would be, and I shared this sentiment with Farhad.

"I don't know that we ever looked so far ahead. So much of my life in the past was spent trying to figure out the next step. I had little thought for what my life would be like past tomorrow."

"Now, then," he said, "Now we will plan our future and the future of Kabul!"

We smiled and hugged, parting ways almost exactly as we did in the past: with a promise to meet again and every intention of guiding our own destinies so that it would be so.

In Frankfurt, I met Herr Krause and many of my old friends as I had on several occasions since immigrating to the U.S. The first time I returned to Germany, the local newspaper printed an article entitled 'Local Boy Returns Home,' and everyone I remembered from our small town showed up to welcome me back. My friends from the soccer team gathered at the same soccer field where we used to play to welcome my return. I found out that some had traveled hours just to meet me again. Later that evening I met many of my old school teachers and friends, including Fatih, Wahid, Reinhard and Thomas in a nice downtown restaurant to celebrate my visit and to share my story. I had never been so moved in my life by a showing of love and support. Having left the country and its people once, I did not want to leave again. I made a promise to them and to myself that I would return as often as possible. Hospitality was a distant memory of my childhood. It was a deep-rooted concept in the Afghan culture that had been slowly whittled away. There in Germany, it was alive and well. It refreshed me to go to one place—like going home—and find that everything was exactly as I remember it. All of the familiar faces were there, ready to greet me and take me in as if I never left.

November, 2002

I returned home to the Bay Area and continued with the running of the business. I negotiated other deals and Basir and I continued to try to turn a profit. We had been set back, but not defeated. I needed to make another trip to Kabul to setup wireless devices and to train the team on the new product. I was on the voice over IP via satellite with Basir and we were trying to work out our schedules. I was looking at flights when he said he wanted to take a break and visit his family in Pakistan for a few days. I agreed to book the trip so that I arrived after he returned to Kabul from his visit. It was around 9:30 at night that we said good-bye to each other. I felt strangely unsettled that night after our conversation.

The next morning, I flew to Vancouver, BC to demonstrate a VoIP system integration with mobile infrastructure to a telecommunications company that promised great things for Afghanistan if we were able to close the deal. As on the previous night, the strange foreboding did not leave me. I understood later that these odd feelings of premonition are not unlike the eerie calm just before a massive storm. On my first day of meeting with the vendor, I had only been there for a few hours before I received a phone call from Shirsha, one of our employees in Kabul. His voice was sad as he told me that Basir had been in an auto accident on the way to Jalalabad and died in the hospital.

I was unable to continue my demonstration with the mobile company as I mourned for my friend and business partner. When I returned to Kabul, it was for a funeral. On the airplane I thought ceaselessly of Basir's wife and young children, whose lives would never be the same. Throughout the twenty-two hours that I spent travelling, I had time to consider that my life too had changed forever with Basir's death. I never anticipated his loss. It seemed ironic now that I should have been so excited to find one friend, Farhad, just as I lost another.

Kabul was not the same as on my previous visit. I had been used to having Basir by my side. On previous visits we would spend every day together meeting with government officials, partners and investors from the start of the day to curfew, which was around 10:00 p.m. This time I realized the business could not continue without a trusted person in Kabul. I had run the other end of the business from the states, but I could not manage both sides remotely. I stayed in Kabul for two weeks in which I buried my friend and tried to determine the future of the business we had run together. I decided then that I needed some time and a place away from Kabul where I could come up with a plan for the continuation of the business.

I was at the airport waiting to catch the usual flight home by way of Germany. In the rush of the crowd I did not pay much attention to who was around me. While I waited for my flight I stood so that others might sit in the few chairs that were available near the terminal. As I looked up I saw a man sitting alone nearby. His head was turned to the side, but something in the profile stirred a sense of recognition within me.

"Wali?" I said, certain that I was mistaken; that the man would not turn at the sound of a name that was not his own.

Then the man looked at me and after a moment of shock, a slow smile spread across his face. We hugged and Wali suggested that we have drinks while we waited for our flights. I could not believe my luck at finding two of the friends I had sought for so long, on paths not so far diverged from my own.

We lingered only briefly over our drinks, talking about what we had been doing in recent years. I found that Wali was reluctant to talk about the past. I told him that I met with Farhad briefly and he brushed aside my comments, more interested in what I was doing in Kabul and why I was travelling to Frankfurt.

Wali told me that he had several retail businesses in Kabul and frequently travelled there. In Frankfurt, he owned two billiards clubs with full bars and restaurants which he converted to night clubs in the evenings by rearranging the tables and chairs. Although the U.S. recession had hurt international economies, Wali was still doing well with these. From his talk, I gathered that he still maintained as many connections as he ever had. I enjoyed our conversation but as we parted to board our flights, I could not help but think that Wali had changed. He was guarded now. Against what, I could not guess.

In spite of these observations, Wali and I promised to meet once we arrived in Germany. He was interested in discussing the business opportunity further, it seemed. I was grateful for his long discussions of business. They reminded me that he was the same street-smart businessman I knew in my youth. I remembered our conversations when we were boys, in which we discussed the future like it was ours for the taking. Wali always had such dreams of wealth.

Our conversation gave me much hope for the future. Wali was single at the time and I stayed with him at his apartment in Frankfurt for a few days before flying home to San Francisco. He spent much of his time convincing me that he was not after my business. He simply wanted to help and support me through the difficulties I found myself in. A few weeks after I returned home, Wali flew to the states to meet with me and discuss the business in more detail. I offered him three percent of the company and promised that if he proved successful in his responsibilities I would increase his share of ownership to five percent.

Once these details were arranged, I gave Wali all of my trust in running the business from Kabul. He returned to Frankfurt after a few weeks in the Bay Area and I asked him to pay for some equipment while he was there since my vendor was based in Germany. Once this was done, Wali and his IT friend, Saboor flew to Kabul to set up the equipment. Before long, Wali called and told me that Saboor was having some difficulty with the particular configuration on the new equipment we were using. In response, I flew to Kabul to train the local team there as well as Saboor in the setup of the satellite equipment.

While I was there, Wali introduced me to some of his friends in Kabul. I immediately felt a sensation of dread creep into my body. I recognized their names immediately from news reports. They were all high-profile warlords in Kabul. I met Haji Atta and had lunch with his entire close circle of trusted friends. Throughout the meeting they asked me many questions about my background and my business. All the while they dodged any question I put before them. At the end of lunch, Haji Atta promised to support our business in Northern Afghanistan.

A few days later, Wali introduced me to the former Army General Dostum and his speaker Zaki. During subsequent meetings I learned that Haji Atta and Dostum did not get along well, at least at that time. Wali also wanted me to meet the defense minister, Fahim Qassim, but I thought it was not necessary since his nephew; Haji Rateb was already signed on as one of our partners. Basir had already talked to Haji Rateb to secure our license for twenty percent of our company shares a few months ago. At that time Fahim Qassim's family were twenty to fifty percent shareholders in every business that was started in Kabul. I only realized that Haji Rateb was the Vice-President of my company when I saw his picture next to mine on our business license.

All of the warlords we met with were excited to sell our equipment in the territories that they controlled. Knowing that I had no other choice but to trust Wali and his friends, I left Kabul feeling anything but excitement over what the future might hold. I spent the following weeks communicating with the Kabul team from San Francisco and trying to organize the company by setting up work processes and quality control standards.

One weekend I was playing with Omar in his room when I received a call from Wali. He told me that the three to five percent share we had originally agreed to was not enough. He did not say what he wanted but told me explicitly that he had made the decision that he would take a higher cut, perhaps even all of my shares.

February, 2003

It was at that time, however, that I learned of another death. They were on their way to Pakistan to observe mining operations there so that they might bring back knowledge to aid in the reconstruction of Afghanistan. Farhad had a background in engineering and he volunteered his time to these reconstruction efforts. He was determined to set an example and to contribute to the growth of the country that had been torn apart by war. The plane crashed just outside of Afghanistan and Farhad was one of three Afghan-Americans who were killed in the crash. Farhad dedicated his life to his homeland. To him, it was the inescapable truth of his existence. He died a role-model and a hero to the many Afghans who heard his message of solidarity and took it to heart. He was mourned by many, but I was devastated by his loss. It was a loss of goodness, a loss of innocence that his death represented. I mourned the young boy with the light of the future in his eyes and I mourned the man who—despite struggle and adversity—never lost faith in the redemptive powers of human nature.

What was perhaps most disturbing about his death was a comment he made in a Newsweek article upon taking the position of economic advisor with the department of foreign ministry. Shortly before Farhad's arrival in Kabul, the minister of public works, Haji Qadir was assassinated. He had been unpopular with many factions and Farhad felt the repercussions of this.

"I realize I'm a target as well," he stated, "But if I'm destined to die in Afghanistan, let it be."

I waited and waited, as many of his followers did, for news of the investigation into his death. As far as I am aware, no concrete evidence as to what caused the crash has ever been released. The waste of life that land has been a travesty. I felt at times that hatred and corruption were spreading like a disease; none of us could escape it.

While I mourned the death of our mutual friend, I continued negotiations with Wali. He continued to reject my offers after his initial change of heart and there seemed to be nothing I could do to persuade him. In the last conversation I had with Wali, he told me that if I wanted to resolve the issue I would have to come to Kabul to do so. I knew then what it all meant. There are no negotiations in Kabul. The warlords always get what they want. From that moment on, I no longer received replies from any of my employees and I understood that my business had been effectively overrun by those whom I had no option but to put my trust in.

In speaking later with some of the employees who were ousted from their positions, I learned that these men were among the contacts that Wali boasted of in Kabul and whom I had later met. I was not sure what level of involvement Wali himself had in the taking over of my business, but it did little good to me to question his motives. I tried to contact him but he would not return my calls. The business we had worked for was no longer mine to worry about. Because of my own contacts, I was able to secure a position with a company I had done work with before and I took the opportunity to consider my next steps.

I believe that Wali was manipulated by the people around him. Many of those with our background found themselves distrusting of anyone. That was what war had done. It had corrupted the people. Our culture as a whole was once prideful and loyal. Since then, demonstrations of power and greed had bred the same behaviors in society. There was little integrity left and men would use whatever means necessary to gain the advantage. They would create obstacles and threaten. This was the product of war. Just when I thought I had found my friend in the rubble, I feared he might have been claimed by it after all. Only time would tell if our friendship could be repaired.

In this way, I went on: taking strength where it was offered. I found I was able to bear with loss and sadness and still be grateful. My family was a blessing and I was thankful for my home and my job. I missed the friends I had lost and I was honored to be counted a friend to those who remained. As life goes on, I have born with countless disappointments. But most importantly, I have found that I am not satisfied with endings. I determined then not relinquish my losses and let them harden into regret. I may have been beaten for the moment, but I kept close my dream of bringing business to Kabul. I kept close the memory of my friends.

*

28

~ ~ ~

MOVING TO LAS VEGAS

The feeling of sadness stayed with me, but I continued to dream of rising above it. I was hurt by the tragic loss of my friends and felt that I was no longer ready to pursue by business in Kabul. I came home from work on a Tuesday, exhausted but full of hope and excitement for the future after a conversation with another friend from the past. Zeba greeted me with a kiss. My son was in the yard playing soccer and seeing him reminded me of how far I had come since my own days of playing soccer in the fading light of day. I sometimes think the years are like fabric. They stretch and fold over on themselves. They spread tight to reveal the gaps in the material of what might had been. What fine or sturdy stuff our lives were made of does not matter; it is how it is all knitted together that makes it a story.

"This has been the only home we have known together," I said to my wife, "Have you ever thought there might be something else out there…some other opportunity…that might be just as right for us? There is so much we might do in this life. I sometimes think about what we are missing out on."

"You are restless," Zeba said, but she smiled as she spoke.

"Not restless, I think. Just curious."

"And what are you curious about?"

"I've been thinking about Las Vegas."

"Ah. I might have guessed," seeing my surprise she smiled a little, "You aren't so secretive as you might think. As for me, I'm sure I would like it very much. As for you…I know you've been suffering from what you have lost. It would be good for you to start again, someplace new and fresh."

284

Zeba rested her hands on her round stomach, holding close the promise of the child that stirred within her; a brother for Omar. Was it too much to ask? To uproot her, to change the life we shared and that of our son and our unborn child? Zeba soothed me and her eyes were laughing.

"I know you get this way," she said, "You worry about doing what's right. I've seen this on your face for months. What does it matter if we're right? Instead of doing what's right, let us worry about doing what we *can* and see what happens."

"I should have talked with you about this weeks ago," I said, smiling at her and putting my hands over hers, small and white on the black cotton stretched over her belly. Underneath it all I felt the movement of the baby inside. It was a small thing, with jutting elbows and knees, rolling in its viscous world like a bird in a shell. We are none of us so different. We were all creatures of the same mother. Because of this I felt we could do anything, Zeba and I.

She said what I had always felt, "We are here when we could be there. We have opportunities that others don't have. What good would it all have been for if we didn't treat each day as a gift—full of possibility? We owe it to those who don't have the opportunity, for whatever reason."

I put a hand up to her cheek and gently brushed the scar there with my thumb. Before Omar was born, Zeba and I had visited Las Vegas. We met my mother and Freba and her family there. We spent four days visiting the hotels and indulging in the lifestyle that no place but Vegas can offer. I did not realize it then, but the trip had settled a seed of thought in me that time and circumstance would nourish. There is something strange about memory. About the indefinite aspect of it; the way we generalize experiences. After that trip, whenever I heard about or thought about Las Vegas it brought to mind an image of the sun over the desert; the way the hills and mountains sloped into a bowl that seemed to catch the sunlight like so much glittering gold. It reminded me of books I read so many lifetimes ago in my childhood, on a hillside with my friend Hamed. In those stories there were lost lands, treasures and all manner of riches in the world for those with an open heart and an adventurous mind. Every time I thought about Las Vegas I felt like a boy again and life was an open book before me. Every time I thought of Vegas, I was reminded of Kabul. I did not know this though. I hardly knew my own mind until the phone call came that afternoon. But Zeba had seen it in me; the wandering spirit that always sought to grow in a different soil.

During the time we were living in the Bay Area, I was working as a consultant for a telecommunications firm. We lived comfortably and life at any given moment was better than many in my shoes could have expected. I had always felt I owed a debt because of this, a sort of obligation to do more and be more. It had been one of my greatest joys over the years to meet people and to form connections, always looking for ways to repay the generous hand of fate. These efforts had come back to me in many ways and I was grateful for each.

On that particular afternoon, I had been sitting at my desk when a phone call came through for me. The line was silent for a moment and then a voice came on the other end and I recognized it though it was several years since I heard it last.

"Andrei," I said feeling warmth come into my voice at the memory of this old friend.

"Abdul," he said, "I am so glad I've found you. What has it been…five years at least?"

We spent several moments catching up before he mentioned the reason for his call. "I can see you remembered the conversations we had, back in college," he said, obviously pleased. "I was glad to hear you have done well for yourself. You were one of those rare people I've met in my life who has shown me true friendship. I never knew how to express my gratitude for what you did."

In truth I did not know what he was talking about. I had benefitted as much from his friendship as he had from mine, I was sure. When I was in college, an Afghan friend of mine introduced me to Andrei. At the time he was newly emigrated from his native Russia. He spent all of his money on airfare and had no place to live and no means of doing so. Andrei was my height and age, but had the look of a boy in his teens. Upon meeting him, I was instantly put in mind of how it felt to be alone and without money in a new land, at the mercy of anyone who might offer to help.

I was splitting the rent of a condo at that time with four other young Afghans who attended school with me at Chabot College. None of my roommates were home at the time that Andrei arrived on our doorstep, so I brought him inside and we talked for a long while. He had travelled most of Eastern Europe since he left his home nearly two years before and had spent a year in Paris where he washed windows on the high-rises to earn the money that would eventually get him to the U.S. Like many young immigrants, he was in search of an education in a place that promised safety and freedom. If I did not understand that at least, I would have been no better than a tyrant. I learned in the course of our conversation that Andrei's father had been in the Russian Army and had served in Afghanistan during their long occupation there. Andrei looked shame-faced at this, sitting nervously on the worn couch in the condo I lived in, as if I might throw him out over his admission. Instead, I shook his hand and told him I would do all I could to recommend him to my roommates. I as much as told him that he had a place to live. I told him I would pay his expenses if the others would not agree to chip in while he got on his feet.

Andrei was grateful and there were tears in his eyes as he thanked me. My own emotions rose as I felt again the influence of good fortune and opportunity in my own life.

"Do not think of it, brother," I told him. "I was where you were and soon you will be where I am. Past that, life is whatever you dream it can be."

When I spoke to my roommates about Andrei, they refused to entertain the idea of housing him. The Russian Government had only recently pulled its forces out of Afghanistan and feelings were still high among Afghan communities against the Russians.

One of my roommates, Jamil said, "Why should we help a Russian? We never got help from them."

"Maybe not, but each of us got help from *someone* when we arrived here. Andrei is no different from you or me in that he tried to escape the oppression in his homeland and does not have the means to live now that he is here."

"Well, I sure as hell didn't get help from any *Russian* when I got here."

"No. That was because the Afghan community was here to embrace you. That was because our culture knows the meaning of hospitality. Andrei is not so fortunate. Shouldn't we teach him the kindness we are capable of? It was our strength, after all," I said, ribbing Jamil, "that was the reason his government could not last against our people."

Jamil let go of some of his hostility at this. The others were skeptical too, but when I said I would consider looking for a room elsewhere so that I could help Andrei and others like him on my own, they told me not to go doing anything stupid. The thought of losing the income of one, and possibly two tenants, had the desired effect and they agreed to meet Andrei to settle the details.

All but Jamil were quick to warm to Andrei and his optimism and enthusiasm for what life might hold in our adopted country. It was impossible not to be reminded of how that felt. We had all been there. I often thought that if I lost that enthusiasm I would be worthless. I vowed to remember, in any way I could, the promise of the future and the truth of the past.

Andrei was ambitious, determined to make money. He studied finance and the connections he eventually established with other Russian's in the same field taught him much about real estate. Because I was the only one in the house who made any real effort at friendship with him, Andrei shared all of his bright hopes and burgeoning ideas with me. I asked many questions and considered the advice he gave and in the end I learned much from him. I weighed my own thoughts and ideas against his and though we eventually went separate ways and lost contact, I carried the spark of his enthusiasm and knowledge with me throughout my future forays into real estate purchasing and investing.

When Andrei called that afternoon, six years after the last time we had spoken, I was reminded of our long conversations and of the promise I made to myself back then. It was due to this that when he told me about the real estate opportunities developing at that time in Las Vegas, I realized the connotations that place held for me. I realized the deeper feelings that I harbored for the place.

"He said the whole face of Las Vegas is changing," I said to Zeba when Omar was in bed, "The real estate market is ideal and between that and the new concept for putting a new face on the city, the opportunities to get in on the ground floor and make money are endless."

She nodded, but was quick to point out that there were bound to be things we must consider before jumping into anything. She tempered me and it was often what I required.

Throughout the following days I researched the real estate market and the prospects for growth in Las Vegas. I found that the city was trying to reach a more sophisticated, exclusive clientele. Las Vegas could cater to any segment of the population and they would come. Only years ago the swing was towards attracting families to the notorious "Sin City." Now, however, the shift was toward the elite and there was talk of bringing high-rise living to the Strip. I went home each day after work and shared everything I learned with Zeba, who evaluated and offers counter-points and ultimately conceded that we had examined the opportunity enough and that whatever we decided would be in our best interests.

We put our house in Fremont up for sale in preparation for the move. I would have to commute during the week to my job in San Francisco until I was able to find an equally stable and profitable job in Las Vegas. The baby was due at any moment so we awaited his arrival before we made final preparations for the move.

It was only when Omid was finally born that I looked around us at what we had in Northern California and felt some sorrow at leaving it. The Bay Area had been such a part of my life for so many years. It offered salvation in times of need and familiarity in times of change. It was the only home my Omar had known. But I thought too about what I could offer my sons if I only work hard enough and if I remember that inside I was still that young boy who stood on the precipice in a dream, staring out at the world that lay at my feet. If I held onto the dream then it would be the dream of my sons as well.

When Zeba and I talked about it now it was with excitement. We packed our things in boxes and realized that the most important things go with us wherever we might travel. We talked of settling down in Las Vegas. Each of us felt that it was the right place for us. We planned on building our security and our future there and on raising our boys so they would know only one home and not many different ones as both Zeba and I did. I remembered as a boy that even in the most precarious situations I found myself in; there was always the accompanying sense of adventure. Even when there was dread there was hope.

Las Vegas was a hub of creativity. It offered that which modern Afghanistan could not. Even as I flew in over the city I was reminded of the times I flew over Kabul and I wondered what my birthplace might have become if her lands had not been tied up for decades in the throes of war. The plane landed and as soon as I stepped into the terminal I was surrounded by the lights and sounds of slot machines and bustle and promise. Or maybe I only saw it as promise and profitability because I was sure that would be the place in which our fortunes were made.

I met with a real estate agent during the week and I was shown through several properties. The cost of living was so much less in Las Vegas than in Fremont's developed and highly concentrated market. The homes we were able to afford in Las Vegas were twice the size of the home we were selling. I found a house right away that view of the strip. As the agent walked me through, I pause for a moment on the balcony of the master bedroom and looked out over the city. The desert landscape was so familiar it almost felt that I was back in Afghanistan. The warm breeze stirred up the scents of the desert that I left behind, the sky was a dome of blue and the hills that surround the valley that Las Vegas sits in were reminiscent of those that surrounded the valley of Kabul. I told the agent that I would like to buy this house and she was chatty and cheerful as we drove to her office. It seemed that she was meeting with nothing but success in the quickly growing market and I recognize instantly that this place was on the brink of something great. It was just as Andrei said. A man can live like a king here while he multiplied his fortune. I was going to be in on it. I thought of the friends and family who were worried about our decision to move. Many thought it was a gamble because they had heard that Vegas had the ability to chew men up and spit them out. I couldn't wait to bring Zeba here and to show her that this was something even better than we expected.

When Zeba saw the city for the first time she had tears in her eyes. "It reminds me," she said with a far off look in her eyes. "It reminds me of being home."

"We are home," I said.

The first night in our new house we spent in front of the fireplace in the master bedroom. The electricity was not yet on and it was the middle of winter. It gets cold in the desert but we were warm and Omar was excited, running through the many empty rooms. He fell asleep quickly on his mattress on the floor. It took time for Zeba to settle Omid but he too fell asleep and we looked at the boys in their peaceful slumber. It was pride that I felt then, knowing that we had consistently given them warm beds in which to sleep and a place to call their own where they would never know what it was like to run in fear.

Kabul was once the hub for all kinds of trade. Merchants travelled through it on the Silk Road from the Far East and Central Asia to the Middle East and Europe. She once maintained a history untarnished by defeat. Kabul once cherished its cultural traditions of hospitality and honor. She had since fallen into despair following three decades of strife. Now Kabul had become the center of the largest opium production in the world and warlords and drug lords controlled the city and the government. Kabul had followed an inverse path of Las Vegas, whose origins began under the rule of the criminal class rather than ended there, and whose growth had multiplied into a world-class industry based on trade and hospitality. These things were distant memories for native Kabulis. But in Las Vegas it seemed the legends and pride of our forebears could be reclaimed and we once more had a stake in a budding empire, though it was located in a different country. I was sure that things were meant to come full circle in my life. Otherwise I was sure I would not have lived through the danger and defeat and made it so far.

I lead Zeba onto the balcony and she gasped at the view we had of the glowing center of Las Vegas; the beating heart.

She put a hand up to her mouth and leaned into me. I folded my arm around her and that was peace. In our homeland, the residential area at the center of Kabul was raised on the hill that divided the city. The kerosene lights burning in the homes there could be seen from every corner of the city. It was always a reminder of life, a confirmation that war could not destroy the human spirit. It was a flicker of life amid destruction. Here, the twinkling lights in the distance were a symbol of opportunity. Here there was nothing to hold us down.

August, 2004

The evidence was all around us: Las Vegas was going vertical. In every vacant plot of land city-wide, developers were breaking ground on new projects. The sky was the limit. During the previous decade, Las Vegas experienced a major revival when the first major resort to be built on the strip in 16 years kicked off a period of growth and development that brought tourists to the city in droves. Add to that the increasing willingness of banks to write creative loans for eager homeowners and the once luxurious valley, named for the meadows that thrived there in prehistoric times, once again flourished as a symbol of American decadence. Not only tourists, but residents and investors flocked to the paradise in the desert. Caught up in the glitter and gold, it was hard for many people to remember that history always repeats itself. The springs that once made the valley a lush oasis dried up and so too would the bounty of the great city of Las Vegas. But shimmering gold was blinding. Success was a fickle mistress. At the dawn of the new decade, we were all courting her.

I realized immediately that the purchase we made on our house was a wise one. In the nine months since we bought the home, we built over $80,000 in equity. I talked to Andrei often about my prospects.

"I feel I am missing out on the opportunities that are out there. I feel like I am biding my time when I could be doubling my money on a monthly basis," I said.

Andrei had been successfully involved in the mortgage business and told me he competes regularly with Afghan-Americans who had read the writing on the wall and submerged themselves in the real estate industry. Across the country the real estate industry was booming, but unlike so many other places, there was nothing but room to grow in Las Vegas, and grow it would.

On Andrei's advice, I watched the market closely. I read real estate news and saw the property values rising practically overnight. I read about the creative options that mortgage companies were using to get people into homes and I learned about the best options for purchasing investment properties. At that time, legislation hedged against the possibility of falling prices by preventing investors from buying up the inventories of available homes. High-rise properties afford an exception to this rule for investors. I followed the development of these properties in particular.

Years ago, when I had my first taste of success and with Andrei's advice in my ear, I purchased real estate and experienced the satisfaction of watching my investment grow. While it had been on a smaller scale than the current growth we witnessed, I was able to increase my buying power dramatically over the years that followed. Now, in Las Vegas, I continued to work at my lucrative job in San Francisco and Zeba and I agreed to use the disposable income from these properties to speculate on high-rise real estate. The plans I saw for these towering residences seemed to represent the pinnacle of opulence and success and I began to dream that they would make me a rich man.

On a Saturday afternoon, with the sun beating down on the desert, I sought refuge in the sales office of Krystal Sands, one of the high-rise projects on the Las Vegas strip. The interior was cool and decorated in brushed metal and sleek mahogany. The woman behind the reception desk looked up at me with a smile. Her eyes ran over my suit, and my attire was apparently sharp enough to warrant her continued attention for she stood and came to shake my hand. There were other people in the office, men and women of professional stature whose aims were in line with my own. They perused the artist's renderings of the proposed buildings and various sketches of interiors and spoke in exuberant tones with the agents who circulated among them. A tall woman with blonde hair and a pretty face approached me. She was in her late forties and her eyes were a soft shade of blue that made her seem easily approachable.

"I'm so sorry I didn't see you come in," she said and puts her hand out for me to shake.

"Rachel," the receptionist said, "this is Abdul Nasser. Abdul, this is Rachel Gabriella, one of the managing brokers for the property. She can help you with anything you need."

"Thank you, Sara," Rachel said and turns back to me.

"We're quite busy today. Forgive me for not helping you sooner. I'd love to get all of your questions answered but first tell me what brought you in to see us."

I told her of my interest in purchasing a unit on spec because I continued to hear that buyers were gaining equity on properties that had not even been built. Across the skyline one could see the towering shapes of cranes at each new building site. It made me feel prosperous to be part of a growing urban metropolis, but I could not sit still because I was afraid the opportunities it afforded would pass me by. For so long I watched my native Kabul wither and die. Las Vegas was a reminder of redemption; the city had reinvented itself and it reminded me that anything was possible. Since the beginning, this hub in the middle of the desert had been built on big dreams. It was nothing more than a financial fantasy, an empire in the dirt then, but entrepreneurs and visionaries built it from the ground up and continued to do so. In some way or another I realized I had said all of this to Rachel because she responded, "I like your spirit. Optimism is the root of progress." I did not think it then, but later I would wonder if what she said was true at all, or if progress generates optimism instead of the other way around.

Rachel went on to explain the purchasing requirements to me and showed me the available inventory. About half of the units were already sold and it was only the second week they had been on the market so she cautioned me that time was of the essence. Her attention was frequently demanded by other interested parties in the room, so at her suggestion I made an appointment to meet at her offsite office, which was in one of the most successful RE/MAX offices in town, to discuss the opportunity without interruption.

I went home and told Zeba about the detour I took that afternoon. I told her what Rachel said and together we sat down and examined our finances. We could see that we would have to move around some of our money and assets, but overall the thing was possible. I began to dream about the wealth that we would accumulate on this property alone and to fantasize about what life would be like on the tide of such success. Zeba smiled at me indulgently.

"I love to see you get something you want," she said.

"Then you must love a lot. I have everything I want right here."

She laughed as she batted me away with her hand and got up to put Omid in his bath.

"Tomorrow you can go out and buy up all of Las Vegas," she said, "But tonight you can help me with the dishes."

"You see?" I teased her, "Everything I want and more."

"Troublesome man!" she called from the next room. I smiled to myself and went back to calculating growth rates in my head while I filled the sink with hot water.

29

~ ~ ~

THE REAL ESTATE BOOM

When I entered her office, Rachel stood and greeted me with a friendly handshake.

"It's good to see you again, Abdul. I'm so glad we'll have a chance to talk in private. The sales office can get a bit out of control. You saw, though, how much interest these properties are generating did you not? We sold three more units after you left. I'm hoping we can count you in among those fortunate enough to take advantage of this opportunity."

We sat down on either side of her desk, and for the next 45 minutes Rachel went over the pricing structure and availability of the units. It did not take her telling me that the property values were expected to nearly double within 1 year for me to be fully committed to the idea that this was something I needed to jump at. The only problem was that to secure the property and to reap the benefits of the increasing property values, I would have to act immediately to lock in the price. The values were steadily increasing as buyers snatched up the remaining units. To do this, Rachel required an earnest money deposit and a 20% down payment so I could go to contract.

"Can I reserve a unit to lock in the price and then try to refinance my home to pay the earnest money deposit at a later date?"

"Well, it's not typically done but I really do want to help you out. Let me talk to James Randall. He's our broker and owner. Give me just a moment to run this by him."

She left the office and returned a few moments later saying, "Well, good news Mr. Nasser. We can get this going for you. I will be happy to work with you to reserve your unit today and you can do what you need to do to get the earnest money to me as soon as possible."

I thanked her enthusiastically and we proceed to handle the details. I asked Rachel a bit about the market in Las Vegas and since she had worked there for several years, she had a deep understanding of recent trends. She expressed to me what an exciting time it was for both buyers and sellers, and especially for agents who were not only getting phenomenal commissions but also had an abundance of clients. She said she couldn't blame anyone for wanting to get in on any part of it. My interest in the business aspects of real estate prompted me to question her about the profession and about licensing. She was extremely helpful and said if I was considering getting a real estate license now I was almost guaranteed to make a fortune. Over the years I had helped other friends to purchase new homes and referred them to agents or brokers I had dealt with myself. Since I moved to Vegas, many old friends and acquaintances had come out of the woodwork with questions about the low cost of living and the housing availability they had heard of through others. I told them it was true, better than they imagined even, and many of them had followed up through the avenues I suggested. What if I were able to handle all of those sales myself? I would have made money already, just on the contacts I already had. Over the years I amassed a great number of connections with people all over the country. It would be relatively easy for me to do just as Andrei had done with me; to call up those people that I had met over the years and tell them of the amazing opportunity that awaited them in the desert.

"You can even get a 3% discount on this property if you pass the real estate exam within 6 months," Rachel said.

I thanked her for all of her time and asked if I might meet James Randall to thank him for his willingness to work with my particular situation. She led me back to his office and opened the door to let me in. Mr. Randall was sitting behind his desk, a large man in his fifties with red, mottled skin and gray hair.

"I want to thank you, Sir, for your willingness to negotiate in my case," I said shaking his hand. He looked surprised at first, then stood and shook my hand saying it was a pleasure to work with buyers who were as serious as me.

"You do not know how serious, Mr. Randall. I was only just speaking with Ms. Gabriella about the process for becoming licensed as an agent. I believe I might pursue the option so that I can participate in these ventures with professionals like yourselves."

"Well, I certainly hope you'll come back to us when you get that license. There's much to learn out there."

"Yes, sir."

The following day I purchased the Nevada Real Estate Self-Study Training Kit and spent the day at Barnes & Noble studying the requisite books. I scheduled and took the Nevada Real Estate Exam the following day and passed it on the first go. I was given a printout of the results and took them with me to visit Rachel at her office when we met to sign paperwork. I slid them across the desk to her. She read them and looks up at me, startled.

"You did it? I had no idea you were serious! How on earth did you manage to do it so quickly?"

"I told you I was serious. I valued our conversation."

"Most people are just talk. I can't even tell you how many people say they are considering getting into real estate, but next to none of them do anything about it. You are the exception, Mr. Nasser."

"I'll take that as a compliment. I thought I might as well get that 3% commission taken off now rather than later."

She laughed, "Come with me," she said.

I followed Rachel down the hall to James Randall's office. She rapped on it gently and he called for her to come in.

"You won't believe this, James. You remember Mr. Nasser. He was in last week and reserved a condo. He expressed an interest in becoming an agent and here he is again. He passed the exam within 48 hours of our conversation. Can you believe that?"

James looked up at me like he was seeing me for the first time. He walked over to me and clapped me on the shoulder, congratulating me.

"This is remarkable, Mr. Nasser. I value a man who has ambition and drive. I have to confess, I didn't think I'd see you again. I told you to come back when you got that license, didn't I? Do you know how many times I've said that to eager young up-and-comers? Dozens and I've never been in this position. Well—Abdul, is it?—I'm nothing if not impressed and it takes a lot to impress me in this field. When you get that license in hand, you come see me. We're always interested in employing truly motivated and exceptional agents."

I thanked him and Rachel and I completed our business. She was still laughing when we parted ways and said she couldn't wait to tell her husband and her daughter, both agents in the same office, about my accomplishment.

It was several weeks before my license was processed and delivered and when it was I contacted James Randall immediately. I returned from my job in San Francisco earlier in the week than usual and met with James for a formal interview. We discussed my resume and he observed that I had the entrepreneurial spirit that made me a promising candidate for success in the real estate business. I spoke of my skills in networking and generating contacts and he laughed and said, "Well, that's self-evident Abdul. You got yourself into my office for this interview within a matter of what? Days? I'll tell you, that is not an easy feat. I am the number one real estate broker for RE/MAX worldwide and I own several offices here in town and enjoy an unsurpassed reputation for success. My leadership translates into success for my agents and brokers as well and I guarantee you that as a member of my team you are among the elite. I told you that there is much to learn in this business. You have the foundations you need to be involved in this industry and if you follow me I'll show you the ropes. You'll be earning stellar commissions in no time."

I was able to quit my consulting job in San Francisco and Zeba was overjoyed that I would no longer have to commute during the week to Northern California for work. Our life in Las Vegas was quickly getting off the ground. We were the owners of a high-priced condominium in one of the preeminent high-rise developments on the Las Vegas strip, I was an employed real estate agent, and we lived in a luxurious house in the hills overlooking the city. Life was full of promise.

Omar adjusted well and quickly to his new school. He had my dark eyes and his hair was as silky as his mothers, but he had a character all his own. He was often serious and I could not tell at times what he was thinking although I was sure his mind was constantly working and interpreting the ways of the world. He liked to play soccer so we put him on a team and watching him was like reliving my own childhood, only better. Zeba and Omid sat on a blanket at the soccer field, Omid just able to push himself up off of his stomach. I walked across the field toward them, carrying Omar's equipment and Zeba waved. There was a breeze stretching across the field and a flock of birds took flight from a nearby tree. My memory took me back to Kabul so often most days it was almost as if the past has been resurrected, only this time it was the way it should be. This time I was playing soccer as a boy with the same careless enthusiasm Omar had when he played. This time there were no explosions, no missing friends, no hiding in the shadows or running in the dark. I almost forgot that it had not always been that way. Almost!

November, 2004

Each week I found myself at the airport picking up investors and others who were interested in buying properties in Las Vegas. I called everyone I knew and told them about my involvement in real estate. Some of them were friends, investors, acquaintances. It didn't matter who they were, I welcomed them. Like everything else in Las Vegas, it was a game. I had the luxury at that time of working for the house and the house always wins. But the odds were great and this was my sales pitch; there was money to be made and property was a sure thing. As sure as the sun.

I could not help but notice that they came for a good time and they came for a vacation or they came for business. It did not matter what they come for, they all ended up convinced that what I was selling was worth buying. Each week I was entertaining friends and acquaintances, I was showing them the dream. I was showing them how impossible it was to resist grabbing at it when it is right in front of you. Las Vegas was the focus of real estate investors worldwide, but when they arrived; their eyes always grew a little wider. King Midas had been there and everything in the valley turned to gold at his touch.

While many other agents and brokers were still busy with resale properties, I focused on new properties, particularly high-rises. There were many new construction projects in the works and by selling these I was able to spend more time marketing and generating leads than in showing homes. Almost 70% of the investors buying at that time were from California which worked in my favor because I was familiar with the people and the housing market there. What did not work in my favor was that in Las Vegas there were an abundance of beautiful women selling real estate. I was no fool to think I could compete with them. They represented the very lifestyle they sold by maintaining the image of accessible luxury. I immersed myself in the business at hand, focusing all of my attentions on new marketing strategies. I learned about construction and kept myself apprised of every new building project on the horizon. I attended conventions and spent every available moment in casinos, restaurants and bars where I might meet a prospective client or generate a new lead. I spent hours on the phone and on the internet, contacting various persons or creating websites to draw people in and market my services.

With the amount of people I entertained and their unrepressed enthusiasm for the Las Vegas experience and the real estate opportunities I put in their way, I began to wonder if some of them were merely there for the party. While they were on my turf I was able to keep them dangling from the end of the line, but the second they were no longer immersed in the surroundings, their resolve began to falter. All but the most serious of prospects actually generated a sale. I saw little return on the money I spent showing potential clients a good time.

"Of course not," Zeba said, as if she had it figured out long ago, "You are more than willing to entertain them. They don't need to buy anything when they're already getting a free vacation out of you."

"The interest is there, it just doesn't translate into sales."

"Abdul, I think you are mistaking opportunity for interest. They see the opportunity, that is true. But not the opportunity of investing in property. They see the opportunity afforded by your wallet. You keep telling them how successful real estate has made you, how they can do the same but all they hear is that you have money and you're willing to spend it to get their business."

I could tell that she was bothered by my business strategies. She had not expressed her opinions on the subject before that.

"What is it you do not agree with?"

"For one thing I am surprised you bring this up. With all the time you spend in the casinos and bars I would have thought you were having too much fun to stop and remember that money can be spent twice as fast as it can be made. It seems to me you enjoy your 'marketing' as much as your friends do."

"Zeba, I am trying to make a business work. We are in Las Vegas. I cannot very well sell real estate on the Las Vegas strip without ever setting foot on it."

"Well then, perhaps you should sell one of your properties to me so that I might at least see you once in a while."

"You saw me less when I was flying back and forth to work in San Francisco! What is this really about?"

She looked at me, hurt, and I could tell that I had touched on something.

"Before we left, remember our families saying that we would get caught up in the lifestyle of Las Vegas? And we said we wouldn't. We talked about it, you and I, and we agreed that it would be fun but that we would never lose our perspective. I don't know who these people are that you meet at the bars and restaurants, but in my mind they are all one thing. They are all those people that our families were afraid we would become. And I am watching you get drawn in by it."

I was upset by this. Her irritation was evident but, to my mind, unfounded. We argued about it for some time and while I was insulted that she felt my intentions were not entirely motivated by business, I began to concede the point to her. I realized that we were in a new place where she knew no one. We were away from friends and family and she spent all of her time caring for Omar and Omid. I had the luxury of being out in the world, enjoying the lifestyle that it was my business to promote. And the truth was I did enjoy it. I had always enjoyed meeting people. In Las Vegas and Kabul both, I never know who may be sitting next to me. There were such extremes of wealth and poverty in both cities. I enjoyed the conversations and stories of strangers and the adventures of life that every personal experience attests to.

I pulled Zeba close to me and told her gently that she had nothing to worry about. I told her that my intentions were good even if they were not the most appropriate. I told her that I had been second-guessing my approach anyways. I handed out my business cards at any given opportunity but as of yet, hardly any responses had been gained from those contacts. We agreed that I would step back and reassess my marketing strategy and I told her I knew just the thing she needed.

"What was it?"

"If I tell you, it won't be a surprise."

*

*

"Blood will have blood."
-Afghan Proverb

*

30

~ ~ ~

THE DIVORCE FROM LOVE

Imagine Afghanistan as a marriage between the different factions, ethnic groups, religious associations and languages that have existed there for the past five thousand years in which there has always been hate, but there has been also love.

I was once told a joke by a U.S. military man who had been involved in Afghan affairs for over a decade: "A young boy walks with his new friend from the same tribe in a remote village. During their conversation, the boy learns that his new friend's great grandfather killed his own great grandfather in a family dispute almost a century before. The boy pulls his gun out and shoots his new friend on the spot to take his revenge for the crime his friend's great grandfather had committed. The boy then goes home and tells his father that he was finally able to get revenge for his great grandfather and fulfill one of the familial honors that he bore as a son of the family. The boy's father turns to him and pats his son on the shoulder as a sign of appreciation of his courage and keeping of the tribal tradition of revenge, but then the father shakes his head and says, 'My son, you took revenge too soon!'

Afghanistan has long been home to many different ethnic groups, religious groups, political parties, languages, and foreign soldiers who have made Afghanistan their home. These various identities have combined in unique ways in the villages of Afghanistan so that when travelling from one village to another and from one province to another, you experience completely different cultures, traditions, foods, languages and people. Travelling through Afghanistan is like browsing through a living history of human civilization in this region of the planet.

Many people still live in the simplest of ways—in caves in the farthest corners of the country. Not far away, you might encounter a small region full of people who still believe in the religion that served the area thousands of years ago, while they have no knowledge that any other religion has surfaced within the last centuries to be practiced by over 99% of the population. This is the essence of Afghanistan and it is beautiful to me and to the family I was brought up in. Unfortunately many groups find ways to make something ugly of this uniqueness.

In Afghanistan, those factions with the upper-hand have consistently failed to exercise fairness with the less powerful members of society. The powerful are concerned with keeping power and passing it down as the legacy of their dynasty. They will take advantage of differences in a culture and use it to rule the land. This has consistently occurred within the broken country of Afghanistan so that there has always been a division between the oppressors and the oppressed. Likewise, each subordinate group has a story of unfair treatment that they pass down from one generation to the next. This has resulted in an age-old history of revenge taking a center stage in the cultural identity of most Afghans. Revenge has been taught from infancy to Afghans as a component of a sacred code of ethics by which we must live our lives. This stream of thought—passed down through the centuries—runs deeply in the blood of the Afghan people and to take revenge is to be honored in the society and revered in the family. There have always been and will continue to be internal disputes and revenge among the various tribal groups and factions in Afghanistan as long as this way of thinking persists. Revenge has become the way by which government entities come to power as well as the way by which two boys might start and end a friendship.

Unfortunately, this mentality is not easily forgotten, regardless of where a particular Afghan community may reside on the map. After Pakistan invaded Afghanistan through their militia group, most commonly known as the Taliban, and corresponding events made their way to the forefront of news in the world community, the Afghan community in the Bay Area of California came together to make plans for the future. I was given the opportunity at that time to give a short speech at an event where several U.S. national news channels were gathered. The conclusion of my speech in front of at least 500 Afghans and media highlighted the idea that if we want to bring peace to Afghanistan, we must find a way to unite peacefully in a country where we have the benefits of democracy, freedom and the protection of human rights.

"If we, as Afghans," I stated, "cannot get along in the Bay Area where the largest Afghan-American community resides, how can we go back to Afghanistan where ninety percent of the population are illiterate and thirsting for knowledge and productive information, and spread a message of peace, democracy, human rights and freedom?"

I continued by making a call to all Afghans in our community to come together to throw off the negative effects of a long history of irrational teachings to embrace common truths and positive aspects of our cultural history.

More than a decade later, we are still tearing each other down through social and other forms of media, streaming hatred through whatever lines of communication are available to us at a faster and deadlier pace than ever before. Afghans do not need another TV producer that promotes hatred or another technology professional that designs hateful websites demeaning particular ethnic groups or backgrounds. Afghans do not need another government to tear us farther apart with hatred and division. Afghans do not need another leader who associates him or herself with a tribe, religion, empire or political party or who will allow themselves to be a puppet for any of these groups.

What Afghans need is a leader who promotes love and forgiveness instead of hate and revenge. Afghans need foreign friends that encourage reconciliation instead of unrest and war. Afghans need the world community to put aside the popular media accounts and learn for themselves; to support them with infrastructures for education, health-care, security and a better life instead of with military camps, military airports, military transportation routes and concrete defensive buildings that protect the instated leaders while the Afghan people are left homeless and in misery. Afghans need the world community to stand for their women's rights instead of their own self-interest. Afghans need writers and journalists who understand their pain as human beings, not simply as a story that will promote them in their career.

On the home front, Afghans need to change their hearts in order to forgive and love each other for the sake of their children, and future generations of our ancient region. Afghans must embrace the art, history, culture and beauty of their mother country and teach others to embrace it as well. There will be no rest in Afghanistan until this is achieved; until humanity is put above all else.

Afghanistan is the birthplace of early philosophers, poets and scholars. It is home to the silk road of ancient civilizations and the center for many religions including Hinduism, Buddhism and Zoroastrianism. In the villages of Afghanistan, family is a long, unbroken chain of children and grand-children. Family is deeply integrated into the culture of the village and vice versa. For this reason, while marriage disputes inevitably occur, divorce is never deemed a reasonable or logical solution. The structure of family, in this case, is too strong to be broken. We must begin teaching our children and future generations now that revenge is not the answer. If we follow this path we are on, we will be divorcing ourselves from thousands of years of marriage and love for the sake of hatred, whose roots may be as deep but never as strong.

*

31

~ ~ ~

THE HIGH-RISE HIGH-ROLLER

December 31, 2004

A new year was before us.

In Afghanistan, Hamad Karzai along with his war lord circle and his corrupt brothers have officially robbed the presidency of the country in the first so-called election. The United Nations met to contemplate the rising drug problem in Kabul and to orchestrate a solution. One problem appeared to be solved as another grew. The media has a way of making things seem so cut and dry, but I knew differently. I remembered a time when the United States supported the cause of the mujahideen because it seemed obvious to do so to thwart the Russian enemy. But they were thousands of miles away. They were not sneaking through the pitch black mountains, trying to get away with their lives; enemies on both sides no more than a breath away. I watched the news, I heard the facts as they were presented, but I did not take it at face value. The world did not try to be fair, once again, to Afghanistan. It was a time in which the world should have focused on making Afghanistan a model for the rest of the world; it should have been a lesson to the world community that, unlike those previous empires who only looked at their own self-interest, we could truly give the Afghans freedom, democracy, infrastructure, and—most importantly—peace. Contrary to the opportunity before them, the United Nations, NATO, the U.S., Europe and many others formed a new Afghan government that consisted mostly of former warlords, criminals, and those with their hands covered in the blood of the innocent. They selected

Karzai, a warlord, as the head of the intermediary government, opening the door for yet another decade of war.

There was no single country at fault. The fault lay in the lack of creative thinking that had become the human condition. We believed what we were told and we were willing to die for it. I thought often of the pilgrim travelers who crossed vast expanses of land, never in the same place but gathering, gathering as they moved along. *These* were the enlightened people; the free.

The surprise I promised Zeba was that I had arranged for her sister Sweda to fly in from Montreal. We had been invited to James Randall's home for a New Year's Eve party and I want to take Zeba out and put her concerns to rest. Sweda agreed to watch the boys. Neither one of us was comfortable leaving our young boys with a babysitter we did not know well, and I was sure the added benefit of having time to visit with her sister, and having a hand in the housework would help eliminate some of the stress that our change in lifestyle was generating. In a sleek black dress with her dark hair falling over her shoulders in waves, Zeba's green eyes stood out like emeralds. She was stunning.

We kissed the boys and her sister I drove her down to Las Vegas Boulevard. I wanted to show her some of the places that I spent time in when I was meeting with clients. We had appetizers at Maggiano's Little Italy and walked through the new shops at the Bellagio. Zeba stopped and admired the luxurious items in the windows of upscale stores and I promised her that when my sales were more consistent I would bring her back and she could buy whatever she wanted. We watched the fountain show in front of the resort and then we drove to James's house. The home was in an upscale, guard-gated community on a golf course. The yard was immaculate and lit in a way that showed off the meticulous landscaping. The sound of music drifted to us across the deep lawn. The front door was open and I held Zeba's hand as we passed through it into an interior courtyard where a fire burned and people mingled. Inside we found James in the crowd and I introduced him to my wife. There were tables laden with different foods and a tended bar serving cocktails. Glass walls had been retracted to open nearly the entire back side of the house to the yard, where a live band was playing Jazz. The opulence of it was breathtaking and the magic of the lifestyle it represented was as intoxicating as the drinks we were quickly served. James and his wife moved through the house and the yard, spending time talking with each of their guests. I had met his wife, Lena, at the office before and she approached us now. She took to Zeba immediately and drew her away. I was left to use the opportunity to speak with the other guests. The party was a great opportunity for me to meet other agents and brokers who worked from other offices in other parts of the city. The next hours flew by as I talked with one person and another, all professional and knowledgeable about the industry we shared in common. I spotted Zeba across the room from time to time, sipping champagne and laughing with the other women. I knew she never liked champagne before, but she seems to be enjoying herself and—not for the first time in our marriage—I admired that ability she possessed to transform so seamlessly from mother to wife; from simply beautiful to stunningly elegant. I was reminded of the first time I saw her in a crowd, so many years ago. I thought of the great distance we had come since then.

I realized during a break in the constant chatter that every conversation I had so far that night had revolved around either real estate or golf. At times the subject shifted from residential to commercial real estate or real estate development but the general subject was the same. When that subject grew tired it was, "Where do you play?" or "You look like you'd make a fine golfer," after which the conversation was steered back to real estate since I had never played golf a day in my life and was determined to avoid the subject. Finding me alone for the moment by the refreshments, James guided me with a hand on my shoulder to a man who stood nearby.

"Abdul, I want you to meet Mike. He's one of my oldest friends in the business. Mike, I want you to teach Abdul everything you know about real estate in the next five minutes. Abdul's a go-getter and with the right advice I know he's going to make it big." James clapped me on the back and left us alone to talk.

"How'd you get past me, Abdul? I've been in this business 20 years and I pride myself on getting to all the talented new professionals before James does."

"I happened to be in the right place at the right time," I laughed.

''Well, I imagine there was something more to it than that. James didn't get to where he is in this business without knowing how to recognize an opportunity to make money. Well, I'll tell you the secret and it won't even take five minutes. Look around you," he said. "Surround yourself with success and it'll rub off on you. It takes years to learn the business, but it takes seconds to earn money. It's all about who you know. Do that and I bet the next time I see you it will be in the newspaper under a glowing headline."

I was enjoying Mike's candid conversation and I recognized that he had valuable connections. I told him that I was interested in getting into golf since I had learned tonight that it may be one of the requirements for success in this business. He asked me how it was that I had never played golf, as if it should have been a requirement for citizenship. I told him that where I come from, soccer is the sport of choice. I did not mention to him how truly American golf was. Many countries would not be able to fathom the amount of time and money that American's put into the leisure activity.

"And where is it that you were from? Your name is Arabic, right?" I could see that he wanted to impress me with his world view and I was delighted at the change of subject.

"I'm from Kabul, the capital of Afghanistan."

"Oh, you mean Pakistan?"

"No, Afghanistan. The country was used as the base to launch the attack on 9/11 and helped the U.S. defeat the Russians during the Cold War. It's a long history."

Mike still looked confused and I like to think the two glasses of scotch he knocked back since we began our conversation were affecting his memory.

"Well, Abdul, I do wish you luck in your career. I think you made the right decision and I hope to meet you again," he said and moved to join a nearby conversation. I made a mental note to stick to the subject if I wanted to make the evening a success.

A few months later I was invited to a grand opening party for another real estate project; a new high-rise project on the strip. In the few months since kicking off my career, I had registered dozens of buyers for each new development project I had been a part of. In doing so, I captured the attention of many developers and I was granted the opportunity to register my clients at pre-public offerings which allowed my clients to build equity even before public investors could get involved. This was an allowance made almost exclusively for high profile agents and brokers and I felt the honor of this keenly.

The grand opening was an elaborate affair and the elite agents and brokers were in attendance. It was the same routine of mingling with various guests and I was introduced by a mutual acquaintance to Diane Moon. She was a middle-aged woman who made a success of her career along with being the single-mother of a teenaged boy. I recognized immediately that her professionalism and ambition were the cause of her success and I was eager to talk with her more. My guess was correct and I learned quickly that Diane's career had followed a path similar to my own. She too focused her efforts mostly on high-rise projects and had numerous contacts in her native country. She was South Korean and made great efforts to draw investors from the contacts she had there. I found Diane to be a smart lady with a good sense of business who was able to visualize future opportunities. Likewise, she was impressed with the number of sales I closed in my fledgling career and expressed an interest in exchanging ideas. As the party was underway and there was not time for lengthy discussion, we exchanged our business cards so that we might talk again.

The following week, I received a phone call from Ms. Moon. She said, "Abdul, I was looking at your business card here. Do you mind me asking if you generate many leads from giving your cards out?"

I confessed to her that this has been an area of concern and she told me she had some ideas. After we talked I visited the printer and had new business cards made up, this time on glossy paper and my name printed as "Abe Nasser" rather than "Abdul." In a few months, I began to get phone calls from people who had kept my business card and were interested in learning more about an opportunity to invest.

The more I learned about Las Vegas real estate and the more the investment opportunities here became popular nationwide, the more competitive the real estate sales game became. However, I already had my next marketing plan in place. Instead of waiting for investors to find me and before they even arrived in Las Vegas, I needed to have the opportunity of speaking with them first. I started setting up events in the Bay Area where I had already spent fourteen years of my life and where most of my contacts resided. I spent large sums of money on these events where I drew in not only investors, but also out of state agents and brokers. By doing this I was able to give referral fees and become their contact in the fastest growing city in the nation. Similarly, I invited finance companies, high-rise developers, condo-conversion developers, title companies and other entities involved in real estate to introduce their Las Vegas projects at these events. After a few months, most of the events were sponsored by the invited entities rather than myself and I no longer had to act as host.

Within the first year of my new career, I was a Platinum award winner within RE/MAX and after a year and a half; I was number two in sales volume in the State of Nevada. In one day I registered over thirty-five potential investors when the Hard Rock Casino and Resort launched its Condo-Hotel project, with the promise of making over a half-million dollars in commission in a single day. But these were mere promises and I knew better than most that there was no guarantee.

I was at the height of my career in real estate. A newspaper article was written which called me the "High Rise High-Roller of Las Vegas," and in it I was standing with my arms folded in front of the towering condominium complex that had made me a rich man. My dreams grew bigger but the past was always with me. I missed the kinship of my fellow Afghans, the embrace of my mother country. I thought of their eyes, always reflecting the hardship of the past and hope for the future. We shared that. I looked around me at the eyes of my acquaintances now and I wondered if they knew the kind of hardship my people had suffered. If they knew that they were lucky to be in this place, enjoying the kind of success that America sells. I thought of the steady burning lights of Kabul's hillside residences. The mud houses that stuck to the dirt, and I looked at the neon lights of Las Vegas and the buildings rising into the sky. We were all the same; sometimes down-trodden, sometimes limitless.

In the warm embrace of success I dreamed of uniting the two. I dreamed of bringing a bit of Afghanistan to Las Vegas. I planned to use my new wealth to open the Bamiyan Hotel and Resort, a dream that I whispered to Zeba in the night. The dream had grown until I could visualize every aspect of the reality. Each time I flew in to McCarran airport, I saw that blank spot in the desert at the south end of Las Vegas Boulevard where I wished to build my empire and I saw it filled with the cave-like structure of my Bamiyan Hotel. I would introduce a past civilization to the modern world. The real Bamiyan welcomed visitors to her valley for thousands of years. It was an oasis on the Silk Road, beckoning to weary travelers just as my representative hotel would do to thousands of visitors entering Las Vegas. I had the image of a building in the shape of a cave into which was built the tallest statue of Buddha exactly as it appeared over 2,000 years ago and before it was destroyed by the Taliban. There would be a constant flame burning at the top of the cave to represent the light of Zoroastrianism. I wanted each visitor to Las Vegas to see the flame, regardless of whether they drove or flew to the city it would be the first experience they realized there, just as fire has been a symbol to the followers of Zoroaster of guidance and connection with God. Just as the lights of the Luxor hotel captured the eye from any corner of the city, I wanted the flame of the Buddha statue to catch the eye of every visitor; to symbolize the connection we all share in eternal strength and the hearth we gather before. Here, in this stage of my career, I was sure the dream was about to become a reality.

And then I started to see signs of trouble.

The economy was on the brink of faltering and there were changes in the way the banks were handling loans. I met with Diane Moon and she echoed many of the thoughts I had been afraid to entertain.

"Have you been following the legislation changes?" She asked and I told her I had.

"They're tightening up on the loans. It's part of a broader trend and I'm afraid of what it means for us. So much of the industry is turning a blind eye to the reasons *why* the price of homes is decreasing. I have to be honest with you though, Abe, I'm not betting on this ride lasting much longer. I know there are people out there in the same position as us who disagree with me, but they're fools to think this bubble we've been in won't pop. I won't tell most people this, but I know your history and I know you have ambitions for your own business in Afghanistan, but I have been focusing much of my attention lately on other endeavors. I'm trying to focus on the South Korean market. I have contacts there and I can carry on after Las Vegas collapses."

It was when I get home that Zeba told me of her suspicions that she was expecting. I was thrilled of course, but there was the part of me that was desperate to never let my family want for anything and that part of me was afraid of what was on the horizon. I began to look for clues in every real estate market report and in the rumors that were circulating. I gathered all of my resources around me. I prepared myself so that when the time came I would be ready to sell my investment properties in California and Las Vegas.

When it happened, it happened quickly. The downfall was much larger in proportion than even I imagined, but then the success was much larger than I imagined too. No one realized how heavily the banks and builders were leveraged. We were caught in the downward spiral of a recession and there was no recovering from it. I began to sell my California properties early on and I finally told Zeba the details of the crumbling economy and what they meant for my career and for our livelihood. The money I had counted on getting for the sale of condos in the projected high-rise developments would never be realized. The development companies went bust and bankrupted, leaving either skeletal structures or nothing at all where the promised buildings should had been. The equity that had seemed such a real and tangible asset only a year ago vanished in the air. It became harder and harder to move resale properties and even the house we lived in, which had been such an affordable luxury when we first arrived in Las Vegas, was now a hefty burden whose value diminished steadily.

All through the year, Zeba and I were caught up in financial matters and all the while, the birth of our third child approached. When he was born we forgot entirely what difficulty was. I sat with Zeba on the hospital bed, holding Sahel and we recount the reasons we were thankful. Omar and Omid, growing every day, were excited to have a little brother and we delighted in watching the three of them together for the first time.

"What is money," Zeba said, "What is money when we have this? We're still young, our boys are young. We can start from nothing again if we have to. I think of those who weren't fortunate enough to come here, to America; who can only wish they had an opportunity to make and lose the kind of money we have seen in past years. Just to be here is good enough."

The truth was we had been through it before. Sometimes I wondered if my life was destined to be like this, a constant rising and falling of fortunes. I learned one thing well in the years since I was a young boy. I no longer yearned for that which I had left behind. I learned to turn my mind to the future, to banish regret, to move on. That time in my life was one of the best I can recall. Even with the economy crumbling around us, I felt that I had all I needed. Our family was complete; we did not have the money to attend various events or to entertain visitors any longer so we relied entirely on each other. My grief over losing my Basir and Farhad was blunted by time and my sadness over my falling out with Wali and the loss of my business was dulled too. I once again felt up to the challenge of creating the business that had long been my vision. I began to spend more time on the business that had always been my passion, and less on real estate. The business promised to give back to Kabul what had been taken for so long. The business did not promise untold wealth, but something more than that: it promised redemption.

Diane Moon and I consulted with each other regularly because our interests in pursuing other avenues had taken a similar turn. She was starting an internet real estate company for the Korean market. I had already begun setting up a data center in the Bay Area that would stream video and IPTV services for ethnic communities in the U.S. Diane said that many of her investor friends in Korea would be enthusiastic about an opportunity that would allow Korean-Americans to watch their ethnic television channels. When discussing our paths forward we were surprised to find that our ideas were so complimentary and we decided to combine our efforts. I had the technology background and she could turn Korean investors onto my business.

In January of 2008, I travelled with Diane to South Korea to meet with several investors among her contacts, who might be interested in investing in my business. It was a very successful trip in which I received great feedback from several investors. I returned home excited, feeling that I would soon be securing the funds necessary to launch IPTV services in full-scale to the ethnic communities in the U.S., including Afghans and Koreans. I received the initial seed money from Diane Moon's investor friends and launched our pilot project with some ethnic TV channels to showcase our service for the next phase of funding. Our IPTV service took off without a hitch, proving that immigrants to the U.S. are generally hungry for news and information from their homelands. It was rewarding to see such global outreach first-hand and in doing so, I hoped that the project would give me further credentials for future business endeavors.

While it was rewarding to bring ethnic groups in touch with their cultures of origin, I recognized, not for the first time, an overall disregard by the general population of foreign affairs. Much as I did not understand Mike, who had illuminated his ignorance of current events at a party not so long ago, I did not understand the complete disinterest of so many people in global politics. It seemed to me we were fortunate to live in a country where freedom was a right, but it didn't mean that we were free of culpability as members of the human race. In observing the news surrounding events in Afghanistan, I became of aware of a

Senator from Illinois named Barack Obama. When his candidacy for President was announced, I dug a little deeper. I followed the speeches he gave and found that he had a global perspective that I agreed with. The nature of politics and politicians in Afghanistan and elsewhere was that they were so often out of touch. They lost sight of the complex, globalized view of the world, in which everything was interconnected. In reading about Obama, I got the impression that he was an exception. I visited his website and got in contact with his campaign manager, expressing an interest in working for the campaign as a blogger for the website. I offered my background and my support for Obama's platform, as well as my commitment to keeping abreast of the political situation in Afghanistan and elsewhere in the world. I received a response requesting that I submit a sample blog article. I did so, and was invited to continue writing the blog that appeared on the campaign website for the duration of Obama's candidacy.

In retrospect, I think perhaps it was a blessing in disguise that I did not grow too full on real estate successes. I was thankful for a life where every bend in the road offered a new adventure. As my prospects in Las Vegas dwindled, my commitment to the IPTV business increased. The business had been in some stage of progression since 1997 and now I was determined to bring it to the forefront. I put all of my resources into hosting Live Event broadcasting online and the response I got was as expected. Those who utilized the service were enthusiastic in praising it. I began to contact investors and garnered some interest for my efforts. In the interest of creating a new entity that provided broadband internet service to other countries where it was unavailable, I attended every telecommunications conference and trade show in Las Vegas trying to find a satellite hub provider that served Afghanistan at a lower cost than the extremely expensive internet services available at the time. There were none as yet, but I talked extensively with Astra Satellite who was planning to launch a satellite that would exactly serve my purposes. Now it was a waiting game.

Our home value continued to diminish while Zeba and I avoided talking about the possibility that we may have to let the property go. When we arrived in Las Vegas, I had such hopes that my sons would grow up there, among the same group of friends and with memories of their childhood entirely spent in one place. Now we watched as the neighborhood slowly emptied of families. Homes foreclosed at a steady rate. One moment they were occupied and the next they were not. History repeats itself. I wanted to spare my children from ever losing their friends. I wanted to spare them that, at least. It brought tears to my eyes to remember saying good-bye to Hamed and Baraymal; to Herr Krause who I left with a smile because I thought life and opportunity were synonymous; to Petra and to my dream girl; to my father and my sisters; to so many more, later in life. There were those I never got a chance to say good-bye to. And for them I held myself above the tide of life and would not give up. For them I was unafraid. For all the uncertainty of the future, I knew we would persevere. I knew we would be successful, no matter the situation or the ways of the world.

*

*

"Now the two primal Spirits, who reveal themselves in vision as Twins, were the Better and the Bad, in thought and word and action. Between these two the wise ones chose aright; the foolish not so."
-Zoroaster

*

32

~ ~ ~

YOU GO ON LIVING

Frankfurt, Germany Present Day

Wali, standing in the shop in Frankfurt, was a smaller man than I recalled. As if the years since I saw him last had whittled away the largeness of his personality. He shook his head slowly as I told him that we were the only two left of our friends. He, too, had heard about Farhad.

"Let us go for a walk," he said.

Outside, the air was sharp to inhale. Watching the cloud of my breath was a reprieve from the concerns of life. Children were running in the square. We walked away from them. A motorcycle sped past us and snow fell on us in a shower from the tall trees that lined the street. After a long while of walking in silence, Wali spoke.

"I try but I cannot forget. I cannot go on as if nothing happened. The past is too real. Too present."

"It is different for all of us."

He nodded, shoving his hands deeper in his pockets and shrugging his shoulders against the cold.

"It has been years since I went back there yet it feels like days. I will not be returning."

"In that regard we are the same, my friend. I cannot go back without fearing for my life. It is hard to go a lifetime being afraid of the very thing that you love."

Wali looked at me, as if he wanted to question what had transpired to put an end to the idealism that kept me going back to Afghanistan. But asking would mean he might have to reveal something of himself and that would be too much. Wali had fallen for the same trap that continued to plague development in Afghanistan. For as long as I'd known him, Wali always had to walk the fine line between business smarts and street smarts. In our interactions of the past, his business sense and his sense of friendship had been in conflict with each other. I felt for him and his difficult decisions. He was an innocent who tried to be too strong too soon and his strength was born in a different time. He hadn't cultivated it over the years, but neither, I felt, had he been fully overtaken by the evils of power and greed.

"We have all made the same mistakes," I said. "I made it only recently. I tried to get the business going again but we are struggling in the same ways. It makes me wonder if things ever change. But I am sure they do."

Wali looked at me then, assessing the man he saw before him. "How do you do that? How do you remain so optimistic about Afghanistan? I'm sure that nothing ever changes there."

"I can't forget that there was a time when things were better. It will be that way again. We have to trust in our leaders. We have to do what we can."

"Maybe you're right. You at least are the same as you ever were."

"I still see in you the young boy who was my friend."

Wali nodded, "I always meant well."

Before I knew it we had walked the block and we were standing at the door of his shop. I knew better than to ask him what had happened to the old nightclub he owned the last time we met.

"I have to go close up."

"Let me catch a cab, I will drop you and Nargess by your house on my way to the airport."

He looked around like he's trying to remember something. "I don't think that's a good idea."

"Can we part as friends at least?" I ask, extending my hand.

He shook it, but he did not look at me as he turned and went inside. The bells on the door seemed to set the bells in the square chiming and I stood there for a moment, watching his daughter stand as he entered and then I walked toward the sound in the square. The trees were lit and all around strings of light hung from the shops. Carolers were singing around the German pyramid at the center of the square. There were hundreds of people gathered around. Out of so many people, so many lives, it felt strange to stand alone. Even with so many years spent lost to each other, it felt strange to think that I might not see Wali again.

December 31, 2011

I worried for days about Zarghona and Freshta because I had not spoken to them since we met in the *hotal* in secret. It was two weeks before I received an e-mail from Zarghona.

Abdullah,

It has been difficult finding time to contact you. I am sorry to cause you worry when I did not respond. I am sorry for this and for everything that I must tell you.

After we met, I went back to the office to speak with the police, but when we arrived, Osman and Jamshaid were waiting with them. Freshta was with me and she tried to get me to leave, but they had seen us and I knew that either way we were not safe. They had set up the whole thing, of course. Osman had bribed the police to overlook the raid and to arrest any employees they found on the premises. He kept saying that they knew you were there. They had seen you on the street and so they expected we were hiding you somewhere and demanded to know where it was. I thought at first they were only threatening us, but when they could not find you they became angry. The police arrested most of the employees. They kept them in jail for three days. Osman and his gang have put men outside of our house at all hours. They follow us and the members of our family whenever we go out.

Abdullah, I am sorry but they called my father. I did not want for this to happen. As a military man he swears they cannot do this to him, but he does not understand. He never understood. He went to the warlords to pay them off to stop Osman and Jamshaid, but I have not seen him since. Freshta was told that he was in the jail. I hope that they will release him quickly as they did us but I am afraid. I never wanted to disappoint my family. They rely so much on their integrity and their old-fashioned values.

This time I pray you will let it go. Just let it go. I am begging you. Another man came asking for you and twice I saw him passing by my house. They are watching to see where I go. I am not afraid for myself, only for Father and Freshta and the others. Osman met me this morning on the street. He said if I do not get you to abandon the business, he will burn our house. God help me but that I have to ask this of you. Please. Let it go.

With respect,
Zarghona

It was with this letter that I realized what I needed to do. The option had been present for some time without my seeing it or taking advantage of it. I arranged to meet privately with Senator Rasheed, who I had spoken to months earlier about Baktaj. The Senator was hesitant at first to meet on such short notice until I explained to him that it was urgent. I flew from our home in Fremont, California to Dubai and met him there. His plane arrived several hours before mine and he arranged to occupy a meeting room at the airport. It was evident that both of us had gotten little sleep and I did not want to take much of his time.

I told him what had transpired in the past weeks with the business. The sabotage and the threats. The lack of ability to do anything about it. I then showed him the e-mail from Zarghona. Watching his face while he read it, I realized he had known all along that this would be the outcome. He warned me about Qassem, but I did not heed his warnings. I was desperate then and I was desperate now. And he was constant. I had come to know the Senator to be a smart man, but over and above that I did not know much about him. He was smart enough to know that I could not dream of running this business without the backing of someone such as himself. He had waited in the wings.

It occurred to me that he may have been behind the whole thing. He may have owned the warlords and marked me out from the start as a target he wanted to break; organizing the downfall of my business for his own gain. Or he may have only seen that I would have need for him. He may have been a refuge of honesty in a sea of corruption. I had no way of knowing. I had no choice but to trust him. In the end we shook hands, the Senator and myself, and he walked away with the majority share of the company I started. I was relieved. This was the difference. This was what I could not tell Wali: that with all the evidence directing us to despair, the only hope for us is to maintain faith in humanity.

I was waiting in the airport terminal in Dubai for my return flight to San Francisco. It was late at night on the last day of the year. Around me, travelers slept with their heads resting on luggage. A couple talked quietly nearby. Most of the stations around us were dark, but at one a woman stood, typing at her computer. Outside, I watched the plane land, coasting down the runway and out of sight. In a few moments it would be led to the terminal at which I sat and I would board it and fly home. I thought of Zeba and what I would tell her. I watched the clock on the wall and when it touched midnight there was not a sign anywhere that this was a new year. The waiting passengers went on sleeping. The couple went on whispering. The woman at the desk went on typing. *You go on living*, I remind myself, *we all do*. It never escaped me, the fact that we live two lives. The one behind us and the one ahead. I did not know what I had yet to overcome. I was a descendant of the *Kuchi* people and I have lived my life in much the same way as them. I owe my perseverance to my wife and sons. I owe it to the friends I lost along the way.

*

*

"Change will not come if we wait for some other person or some other time. We are the ones we've been waiting for. We are the change that we seek."
-Barack Obama

*

EPILOGUE

ANCIENT VISIONS IN A MODERN WORLD

The heart of this ancient region has been captured by many names in the past five thousand years. She has been called *Ariana*, *Bakhtria* and *Khorassan* and now goes by the name of *Afghanistan*. Throughout history this land has served as a battlefield for the major empires of the world to spill blood over simply because of its strategic geographic location. There were different reasons for the wars, different beliefs as to who was right and why. The fact remains that throughout history, the seed of war has been furrowed in her soil and brought misery and suffering to her residents. Over this wide vista of time, nothing has changed.

At various points in history, many approaches have been taken to resolve the issues of unrest in this region only to be successful for short periods of time and come at an extremely high cost. I have come to the conclusion that to free Afghanistan's residents from further suffering, only the Afghan people—especially the younger generation—can save themselves. They cannot do it with the help of any foreign government, or with the promise of any religion or any social system. Only by seeking the truth through our own hearts, in our own homes, through the words of our own philosophers and scholars can we ever hope to be free. So many of the figures of the past understood, thousands of years ago, the plight of this region better than we understand it today. Many of them still have the power to enlighten the hearts and minds of millions, from East to West and from North to South, in this twenty-first century.

The Arab invasion centuries ago did not change the life of the people for good in the region; Great Britain acted as any other super power—in their complete self-interest—as did Russia and

Pakistan in the 80's and 90's. The recent hope offered by NATO and the U.S. has been just as quickly drowned in disappointment. Afghanistan is yet again the playground for the super powers to install corrupt individuals to serve their own interests in a foreign land and at the cost of millions of lives. It is not that the Afghans no longer know the game and how it is played; it is the world community that falls again and again for the same old government tricks delivered through the media. The information takes different shapes and forms in different eras; but the promises are given as before and including the promise of freedom, women rights, democracy, health-care, education, and a better life. Unfortunately, the cost is not negotiable and in most instances the cost is unknown not only to the Afghans but also to the people of the invading countries. How is it possible that the geographic location of Afghanistan serves the national-interests of so many countries in such a way that they cannot resist having a hand in her? The goal has never been to bring a system that serves the interests of Afghanistan or her people, but to create a corrupt system that can be easily manipulated to serve the interests of those who only play by their own rules.

Afghans of recent years have broken away from their tradition-centric ideologies and thoughts surrounding their tribal, linguistic, religious, and other associations. This is a difficult thing for elder members of society to bear. Almost sixty percent of the population of Afghanistan today is comprised of a younger generation of Afghans. It is time for this generation to stand up and realize that their lives, their children's lives and their grandchildren's lives will continue in misery if Afghan society continues on the path it is on. This realization can only be come to by revisiting the ideas of the past and by tying themselves once again to the ideas that have kept the country whole throughout its long history as the world's never-ending war zone.

The solution starts by not blaming any other nation for our troubles, but by bringing the world community to our cause—by becoming part of the world community as our ancestors did.

As Rumi wrote:

O Pilgrims, where are you? Come here!
The Beloved is much close to here.
The Beloved is your next neighbor,
you are lost in the desert, with no border.
See the faceless face of Beloved once,
you become Pilgrim and Kaaba with sense.
You tried hundreds homes for proof
yet you have not looked once at own roof.
If desire to see the home of soul,
polishing that mirror first shall be goal.
Where is the bunch if you saw the garden,
or the pearl of soul if you were in ocean?
With all the efforts still you suffer
you are the veil to your treasure.
Hidden in soil is that magic treasure
Watch how moon deals with dark cloud pressure.
O Pilgrims, where are you? Come here!
The Beloved is much close to here.

Rumi so aptly acknowledged that we are trapped in our prison, lost in our own home, and do not know where we come from and where we go. Decade after decade and century after century we have been offered the seeds of hope and the seeds themselves have proved infertile.

Rumi says we have tried—hundreds of times different homes and different options, but we have not once tried to look at our own rooftop for the solution. We have not looked in our own hearts. We have associated ourselves with a tribe, a religion, a specific linguistic community, or with a system (socialism or capitalism) which has not in itself brought us the happiness we seek; therefore, let ourselves fly free and for once look beyond those options and find the truth in our own hearts. Rumi says that Truth is hidden under the dirt; we must courageously remove the dark cloud as does the full moon in the sky. Courage is required by this generation as much—or more than—as in any generation before us. As Rumi tried in the 13th century to answer the hard questions of cultural identity and came to his own conclusion that being free means *not* being in the trap of a religion, ethnicity, language, border, theology or ethereal and political systems; so too must we come to an individual conclusion about our place in the world. This is only possible when we look beyond all of the above trappings and remove the veils that separate our hearts.

The solution may not ever come from super powers and foreign governments intent on serving only their national interests. It is up to us to recognize the seed of a new hope for our future or to see it as yet another trap that binds us to our own prison. Afghans don't need to search for their peace in the desert of Saudi Arabia. They don't need to search for their peace in the system of socialism or capitalism. They don't need to shed blood for their neighbor's border protection to bring peace to their homes. They don't need to search for their peace outside of themselves. Comfort, peace, stability can be found only in their own home, in their own hearts. No invader will ever be able to divide us when the people of Afghanistan are one in their hearts.

The ancient land of Afghanistan is the birthplace of Zoroaster whose thoughts and philosophy, *Zoroastrianism*, have been identified as one of the key early events in the development of philosophy—the mother of knowledge—that has in essence interpreted the meaning of our lives and the way we live. The ancient land of Afghanistan is the birthplace of Rumi whose thoughts from the thirteenth century have enlightened the path for millions throughout human evolution and still continues to do so in our modern time. The ancient land of Afghanistan has kindled the fire of enlightenment, revolutionary thought and transformative knowledge throughout her 5,000 years of history. While the rest of the world removes the dusts from those ancient books that have the potential to change generations of lives through philosophy, literature and spirituality, and turns those pages in order to transform their words into modern solutions for sharing and finding truth, peace, and prosperity in life, we Afghans are sinking in a sea of ignorance and grasping at straws to hold ourselves above the water.

It is time for the world community to come together with one heart and take the conscious, ethical risk to save a nation that has suffered not for a decade or a century, but for millennia. What would Zoroaster and Rumi say if they were alive today to see their homeland and her children under constant fire from both internal and external sources?

Perhaps Rumi would once again call to mind this ancient verse, and perhaps we would listen at last:

Not Christian or Jew or Muslim, not Hindu
Buddhist, sufi, or zen. Not any religion
or cultural system. I am not from the East
or the West, not out of the ocean or up
from the ground, not natural or ethereal, not
composed of elements at all. I do not exist,
am not an entity in this world or in the next,
did not descend from Adam and Eve or any
origin story. My place is placeless, a trace
of the traceless. Neither body or soul.
I belong to the beloved, have seen the two
worlds as one and that one call to and know,
first, last, outer, inner, only that
breath breathing human being.

*

Made in the USA
Charleston, SC
14 January 2013